Hegel's Theory of Intelligibility

Hegel's Theory of Intelligibility

Rocío Zambrana

The University of Chicago Press CHICAGO AND LONDON

Rocío Zambrana is assistant professor of philosophy at the University of Oregon.

The University of Chicago Press, Chicago 60637
The University of Chicago Press, Ltd., London

Printed in the United States of America

24 23 22 21 20 19 18 17 16 15 1 2 3 4 5

ISBN-13: 978-0-226-28011-0 (cloth)
ISBN-13: 978-0-226-28025-7 (e-book)
DOI: 10.7208/chicago/9780226280257.001.0001

Library of Congress Cataloging-in-Publication Data
Zambrana, Rocío, author.
Hegel's theory of intelligibility / Rocío Zambrana.
pages ; cm
Includes index.
ISBN 978-0-226-28011-0 (cloth : alk. paper) — ISBN 978-0-226-28025-7 (ebook)
1. Hegel, Georg Wilhelm Friedrich, 1770–1831. Wissenschaft der Logik. 2. Normativity (Ethics). 3. Philosophy, German—19th century. I. Title.
B2942.Z7Z36 2015
193—dc23
2014048486

♾ This paper meets the requirements of ANSI/NISO Z39.48-1992 (Permanence of Paper).

CONTENTS

For Nadya Marie García

ACKNOWLEDGMENTS

My gratitude extends above all to Jay Bernstein. Jay's lectures on Hegel's *Phenomenology of Spirit* at the New School for Social Research were formative for my thinking at every level. His support, guidance, and intellectual energy have been vital during and beyond my time at the New School. Richard J. Bernstein's philosophical pluralism and Socratic spirit continue to inspire me, and his encouragement continues to support me. I am also deeply grateful.

If Jay's lectures opened up a philosophical universe for me, the late Gillian Rose, Angelica Nuzzo, Karin de Boer, and Rebecca Comay's work made me dream of writing this book. Angelica, Karin, and Rebecca offered incisive comments on my work. A philosophical friendship with Martin Hägglund around Hegel and Derrida was decisive for my views about Hegel's *Logic*. Conversations about Hegel with Karen Ng and María del Rosario Acosta have been seminal. Discussions about Kant, Fichte, and Hegel with Robert Pippin and Clinton Tolley in the context of the Master Class on Post-Kantian Idealism generously funded by the *Journal of the History of Philosophy* were important for the argument I offer in part 1. Dean Moyar's insightful comments were also important for the book as a whole. To all, I am profoundly indebted.

My colleagues in the Philosophy Department at the University of Oregon provide a rich intellectual environment and have offered encouragement without fail. Colin Koopman's intellectual friendship is invaluable. Conversations with Alejandro Vallega about decolonial thought always expand my thinking. Bonnie Mann and Scott Pratt's support, as well as Beata Starwaska's, have been vital. Matt Jacobs and Brock Baines became important interlocutors as

I wrote this book. Brock's comments on the manuscript and work on its final version were extremely helpful. I am also grateful.

Without Fanny Söderbäck, Anita Chari, Matt Condgon, Michael Allan, and Michael Salter's love, care, and brilliance this book would not have been written. I owe a special debt to Fanny, who has been my unfailing sister in a journey that began in but extends way beyond philosophy. As an undergraduate student at the University of Puerto Rico, Anayra Santory Jorge taught me the power and value of philosophy. Her philosophical-political insight continues to inspire me. Katie Terezakis offered support and encouragement upon my arrival in New York City. She paved the way within and beyond the New School. I am also deeply indebted.

Words cannot capture my gratitude to my family: Gabriela Mercado, Giancarlo Burgos, Elimari Zambrana, and Nadya Marie García. I traded sharing life with them on our island of contradictions for philosophy, and they supported me throughout the long stretches of silence that writing a book entail. Their patience, love, and presence have been remarkable. I am especially indebted to my mother, Nadya, whose strength is extraordinary, love unending, and friendship irreplaceable. This book is dedicated to her.

I am grateful for T. David Brent's interest in the project and support of the manuscript, and to Ellen Kladky, Richard Allen, Renaldo Migaldi, and Ryo Yamaguchi for their work on the manuscript. Two readers for the University of Chicago Press provided insightful comments and suggestions. It was my great fortune to have readers who grasped the intentions of the book so deeply. The book is stronger as a result of their careful attention. Early versions of parts of chapters 7, 4, and 3 appeared as "Hegel's Hyperbolic Formalism," *Bulletin of the Hegel Society of Great Britain* 61 (2010); "Hegel's Logic of Finitude," *Continental Philosophy Review* 45, no. 2 (2012); and "Hegel's Legacy," in *Continental Philosophy: What and Where Will It Be?,* ed. Ted Toadvine, *Southern Journal of Philosophy* 50, no. 2 (2012). I thank the journals for permission to reprint the substantially revised parts that appear in this book. I also thank the University of Oregon's College of Arts and Sciences for various Junior Professorship Development Awards that helped support research for this book.

ABBREVIATIONS

WORKS BY G. W. F. HEGEL

Hegel's texts are cited by volume and page number from *Werke in zwanzig Bänden*, ed. Eva Moldenhauer and Karl Markus Michel (Frankfurt am Main: Suhrkamp Verlag, 1969–70). The English translation of the *Phenomenology of Spirit* is cited by paragraph number. References to the *Encylopaedia of Philosophical Sciences* and the *Philosophy of Right* are cited by section number. Wherever translations have been modified, I have made a note in the text.

EG: *Hegel's Philosophy of Mind, Part Three of the Encyclopedia of the Philosophical Sciences (1830)*. Trans. W. Wallace and A. V. Miller. Oxford: Oxford University Press, 1971. *Die Philosophie des Geistes. Dritter Teil, Enzyklopädie der philosophischen Wissenschaften im Grundrisse (1830). Werke in zwanzig Bänden*, vol. 10.

EL: *Hegel's Logic, Part One of the Encyclopedia of the Philosophical Sciences (1830)*. Trans. William Wallace. Oxford: Clarendon Press, 1975. *Wissenschaft der Logik. Erste Teil, Enzyklopädie der philosophischen Wissenschaften im Grundrisse (1830). Werke in zwanzig Bänden*, vol. 8.

FK: *Faith and Knowledge*. Trans. Walter Cerf and H. S. Harris. Albany: State University of New York Press 1977.

GW: *Glauben und Wissen. Werke in zwanzig Bänden*, vol. 2.

LA: *Lectures on Fine Art*. Trans. T. M. Knox. Oxford: Clarendon Press, 1975. 2 vols.

PG: *Phänomenologie des Geistes. Werke in zwanzig Bänden*, vol. 3.

PN: *Philosophy of Nature: Part Two of the Encyclopaedia of the Philosophical Sciences* (1830). Trans. A. V. Miller. Oxford: Oxford University Press, 1970. *Die Naturphilosophie. Zweiter Teil, Enzyklopädie der philosophischen Wissenschaften im Grundrisse (1830). Werke in zwanzig Bänden*, vol. 9.

PR: *Elements of the Philosophy of Right.* Trans. H. B. Nisbet, ed. Allen W. Wood (Cambridge: Cambridge University Press, 1991). *Grundlinien der Philosophie des Rechts. Werke in zwanzig Bänden*, vol. 7.

PS: *Phenomenology of Spirit.* Trans. Terry Pinkard. Draft available at http://terrypinkard.weebly.com/phenomenology-of-spirit-page.html.

SL: *The Science of Logic.* Trans. and ed. George di Giovanni. Cambridge: Cambridge University Press, 2010.

WL: *Wissenschaft der Logik. Werke in zwanzig Bänden*, vols. 5 and 6.

WORKS BY IMMANUEL KANT

References to Kant are cited by volume and page number of *Werke in zwölf Bänden*, ed. Wilhelm Weischedel (Frankfurt: Suhrkamp Verlag, 1968). The *Critique of Pure Reason* is cited by the pagination of the first (A) and second (B) editions in the standard manner.

CJ: *Critique of Judgment.* Trans. Werner S. Pluhar. Indianapolis: Hackett, 1987.

CPR: *Critique of Pure Reason.* Trans. and ed. Paul Guyer and Allen Wood. Cambridge: Cambridge University Press, 1999.

CPrR: *Critique of Practical Reason*, in *Practical Philosophy*. Trans. Mary Gregor. Cambridge: Cambridge University Press, 1997.

G: *Groundwork for Metaphysics of Morals.* Trans. Mary Gregor, in *Practical Philosophy*. Cambridge: Cambridge University Press, 1999.

INTRODUCTION

Hegel's Modernism

Throughout his intellectual life, Hegel thought intensely about three historical developments that complicated modernity's promise of freedom.[1] The development of the market economy, the effects of the French Revolution, and the legacy of the Reformation are the concrete conditions that actualized the distinctively modern understanding of freedom. Distinctive of a modern conception of freedom is a promise of freedom from all external authority.[2] Religious, social, and economic institutions that purport to guide a way of life independently of concrete conditions specific to the society at hand are deemed to lack authority. The modern conception of freedom is accordingly a commitment to "self-governance."[3] To be free is to be able to "lead one's own life," to "have a life of one's own," to be subject only to norms and institutions that have been authorized by the individual.[4] The rise of capitalism, French Republicanism, and the Reformation actualized the promise of freedom in highly ambivalent ways, however. On the one hand, these historical developments express the actualization of the commitment to autonomy, since they represent the concrete articulation of the ideal of self-governance. On the other hand, Hegel notes, these developments degraded the bodily and social existence of economic subjects, fragmented social bonds, and distorted individual authority.

For example, in the 1802 *The German Constitution*, Hegel argues that the fact that the freedom of the individual is "sacrosanct" is the effect as well as the cause of a market economy which, based on free labor, "has seen the gradual emancipation of the individual, giving him through his labor a sense of his own worth and a sense of himself as a center of subjective freedom."[5] And yet, Hegel notes in both the 1805–6 *Philosophy of Spirit* and the 1820 *Philosophy of*

Right, internal to a *functioning* market economy are forms of exploitation and misrecognition that compromise the very possibility of freedom made possible by it.[6] In 1805–6, Hegel observes that "a vast number of people are condemned to labor that is totally stupefying, unhealthy and unsafe—in workshops, factories, and mines—shrinking their skills. . . . [T]his inequality between wealth and poverty, this need and necessity, leads to the utmost dismemberment of the will, to inner indignation and hatred."[7] And in 1820, Hegel argues that, given the humiliation experienced by those subjected to poverty, "the individual's freedom has no existence."[8] Therefore, he concludes, "the recognition of universal freedom disappears."

Similarly, in the 1825–26 lectures on the history of philosophy, Hegel argues that the Lutheran emphasis on conscience and the Protestant commitment to individual responsibility is crucial for the modern articulation of autonomy.[9] Luther's "here I stand and can do no other" is central to a commitment to self-governance. The truth of the Reformation accordingly resides in the fact that, because "inwardness . . . is now set forth and firmly grasped, the dead externality of authority is set aside and regarded as out of place."[10] The principle of the Reformation "is simply this," Hegel thus maintains, "that it led man back to himself."[11] Hegel elaborates this thought in the lectures on the philosophy of history delivered in 1822–23, 1824–25, 1826–27, 1828–29, and 1830–31 by arguing that with the Reformation "there lived in the German world an entirely new *Geist*, through which the world was to be regenerated—namely, free *Geist* which rests on its own self, the absolute self-will of subjectivity."[12] And yet, as he shows in his discussions of morality and the Terror in the 1807 *Phenomenology of Spirit* and of an ethics of conscience in the 1820 *Philosophy of Right*, the Lutheran emphasis on individual authority turns into hypocrisy, subjectivism, irony, or sheer violence if the intersubjective and institutional ground of autonomy is denied.

Hegel's assessment of the ambivalence of the economic, political, and religious development of modernity extends beyond his social theory, however. His account of the ambivalence of the actualization of freedom moves from an analysis of social disintegration to an analysis of what in this book I will call *normative precariousness* and *normative ambivalence*. It moves to an account of intelligibility that responds to the truth of modernity revealed by its concrete development. This book focuses on Hegel's theoretical philosophy in order to show that what Hegel calls a "logic" and also "proper metaphysics" is a theory of intelligibility that responds to the ambivalent development of modernity.[13] It takes seriously Hegel's insistence on the continuity of his system of science, which develops the relation between logic (metaphysics), a philosophy of nature, and a philosophy of subjective and objective *Geist* (self, society, history). It offers a reading of Hegel's logic as the philosophical justification of the necessary historicity of intelligibility. It also shows that Hegel's logic provides the philosophical justification for the necessary precariousness and ambivalence of forms of intelligibility.

To be is to be intelligible, according to Hegel. Hegel gives the commitment to intelligibility a distinctively post-Kantian twist. He moves away from Kant's insistence on the first-person perspective for an account of knowledge, truth, and moral worth. Intelligibility is the result of historically specific practices of rendering intelligible—what Hegel calls *Geist* (spirit).[14] *Geist*, an elusive notion that I will discuss in part 1, privileges history for understanding the nature of intelligibility. To be, then, is to be always already historically mediated. Historically specific practices, discourses, and institutions articulate concrete forms of understanding nature, self, and society. They articulate what is true in a given society at a given moment in time. Modern science, for example, articulates the nature of nature on mechanistic rather than teleological terms. A market economy and an ethics of conscience articulate the nature of social and moral worth in terms of individual freedom. Concrete forms of intelligibility are the result of ongoing articulation by and within practices and institutions given that they depend on the authority or currency of central normative commitments. Specific normative commitments articulate what is true, not merely what is taken to be true, given their currency within a form of life. They comprise a specific form of life, a specific shape of *Geist*.

Hegel's idealism should thus be understood as a post-Kantian philosophy of *Geist*. In the first and last instance, Hegel's idealism is a philosophy of *Geist*. Hegel's system of science begins and ends with *Geist*. It begins with logic, which gives a theoretical account of intelligibility, and ends with philosophy, which Hegel understands as a form of absolute *Geist*.[15] Art, religion, and philosophy—all forms of what Hegel calls absolute *Geist*—are historically specific practices and institutions of articulating truth. As a work of philosophy, a logic develops a view of intelligibility that expresses not only the commitment to autonomy germane to a modern understanding of truth. It also develops a theory of intelligibility that expresses the truth of modernity revealed by its concrete unfolding. A logic thereby accounts for ambivalence as a feature of intelligibility, as this book will show. This book focuses on the *Science of Logic* and clarifies Hegel's view of intelligibility implicit in the relation between logic and *Geist* that pervades not only the *Logic* but also the system laid out in the

Encyclopedia of Philosophical Sciences.[16] It aims to take stock of the consequences of that view and suggests an alternative understanding of the relation between logic and *Geist* central to Hegel's idealism.

Robert Pippin has described Hegel's philosophy as a form of philosophical modernism—a characterization that I find helpful, but one that I will take in a different direction in this book.[17] Hegel's modernism, according to Pippin, resides in Hegel's affirmation of autonomy specifically elaborated through a rewriting of Kant's critical philosophy. Autonomy is arguably the centerpiece of Kant's practical *and* theoretical philosophy. Rational agency, for Kant, is a matter of self-legislation (*Selbstgesetzgebung*). Kant glosses autonomy as a matter of authorship when he argues that self-legislation is a matter of the will's own giving universal law.[18] Distinctive of autonomous willing is being governed by a norm that one is coextensively instituting, authoring, albeit as equally binding for any rational creature. Hegel's engagement with Kant in his theoretical philosophy inherits the implicit role that autonomy plays in Kant's critical epistemology. Kant elaborates an account of discursivity in order to establish the very possibility of experience. The spontaneity of concepts and the capacity to judge central to Kant's discursive model of the mind is the epistemic version of what becomes autonomy in his practical philosophy. The sensible given, as I will discuss in part 1 below, is only taken as a determinate object of experience thanks to the capacity for concept application by a self-conscious subject. The human standpoint legislates the lawfulness of nature, not just the strictures of bindingness to the moral law.[19]

Hegel radicalizes Kant's critical philosophy, Pippin argues, by rejecting what he sees as Kant's slip into dogmatism—the appeal to any source of justification other than reason itself. For Kant, the sensible given and the postulates of practical reason (freedom, God, the immortality of the soul) are touchstones of knowledge, morality, faith. For Hegel, the only legitimate touchstone of a thoroughgoing critical philosophy is reason itself—the justifiability of a way of life and its specific way of understanding nature, self, and society. In order to be critical, then, philosophy must insist on what Pippin calls the "autonomy of reason"—only reasons are sufficient for articulating the ways in which nature, self, and society are understood.[20] A thoroughgoing critical philosophy therefore ought to examine the history of the development of concrete forms of rationality. It should, in other words, examine the development of norms that articulate historically specific ways of understanding nature, self, and society. Such a history is the only source for assessing the justifiability of a way of life in a way that does not appeal to a given.[21] Hegel's modernism, according to Pippin, thus resides in his insistence on giving a philosophical justification for the necessity of historical difference in what counts as an authoritative justification.

This book argues that Hegel's modernism is stronger than Pippin suggests. Pippin understands modernism as a commitment to autonomy and autonomy as a matter of the authority of reason. In contrast, I argue that Hegel's modernism turns on understanding the idea of philosophical modernism as the "self-consciousness of modernity."[22] Rather than expressed by the autonomy of reason, Hegel's modernism resides in his assessment of the truth of modernity revealed by its concrete development. Hegel's modernism is accordingly expressed by his assessment of the ambivalent development of modernity not only *all the way down* to his account of the economic, political, and religious articulation of modernity but also *all the way up* to his account of intelligibility. This book thus makes an admittedly counterintuitive case. It argues that the *Logic* is the highest point of Hegel's philosophical modernism. Hegel's analysis of the ways in which the modern commitment to autonomy at the same time sustains practices of self-legislation and economic degradation is not only consistent with his account of intelligibility. It can only be properly understood in light of a normative precariousness and normative ambivalence clarified by the account of intelligibility given in the *Logic*. Hegel's modernism, then, runs deeper than an attempt at a completion of Kant's critical project and its commitment to autonomy. It resides in Hegel's insistence on tracing the paradoxes of autonomy from an assessment of social diremption *all the way up* to a philosophical exposition of intelligibility.

NORMATIVE PRECARIOUSNESS, NORMATIVE AMBIVALENCE

Above I stated that this book clarifies the relation between logic and *Geist* that runs throughout Hegel's system by considering the theory of intelligibility developed in the *Logic*. Intelligibility according to Hegel is the result of distinctions drawn and redrawn by and within specific shapes of *Geist*. The *Logic* thus provides the ground for understanding the necessary historicity of intelligibility. Under the banner of the idea (*die Idee*), Hegel discusses strictures that establish that intelligibility is a matter of *Geist*. Through a critique of Kant's notion of cognition that culminates in a discussion of what he calls the absolute idea (*die absolute Idee*), Hegel establishes that intelligibility is a matter of *normative authority*. In what is perhaps the most puzzling passage of the *Logic*, Hegel describes the absolute idea as personality (*Persönlichkeit*). While puzzling, this passage is not mystifying. It is in fact key. It helps us specify the status of the absolute idea as the concept that elaborates the view that intelligibility is a matter of normative authority. It indicates that *binding* is the structure of intelligibility, as we will see in great detail. That this odd characterization of the idea follows Hegel's critique of Kantian theoretical and practical reason is no small detail. As the unity of theoretical and the practical, the absolute idea shifts the structure of binding distinctive of Kantian autonomy and central to Kant's critical idealism from the first-person standpoint of an epistemic or moral individual to the determinacy of *die Sache Selbst*—the thing itself, the matter at hand, matters themselves.[23]

Now, it is important to distinguish between the theory of intelligibility and the theory of determinacy developed in the *Logic*. Although they are closely related, they should not be run together. Determinacy is a question of form, while intelligibility is ultimately a matter of practices of form-giving—of rendering intelligible—that depend on historically specific content. In the *Logic*, Hegel pursues an immanent critique of classical ontology, philosophies of reflection, and transcendental idealism that allows him to elaborate his distinctive view of determinacy as a matter of the dialectical relation between ideality and reality. For Hegel, these accounts of the relation between ideality and reality fall into a variety of problems that I will consider in this book. The crucial point is that they fail to see the inseparability of form and content implicit in any account of the relation between reality and ideality. Throughout the *Logic* and especially in the very last move of the *Logic*, in the account of the absolute idea as method, Hegel argues that form is nothing but negation or, more precisely, negativity (*Negativität*).[24] Negation is necessarily a negation of something—whether a logical category, a philosophical position, a historically specific identity or institution. Form thus requires content in order to be negation. The central claim of Hegel's theory of determinacy, then, concerns the negativity of form and the necessity of content. Negation is not a function imposed externally by an epistemic subject, however. It is the work of articulation of things themselves. Form should be understood as the inner negativity of content, and content as the conditions that establish concretely the work of negativity. That form is inseparable albeit distinguishable from content and vice versa allows Hegel to argue that the ideality of things, events, institutions is based on the articulation of concrete conditions that produce them in the first place.

This book draws attention to the way in which Hegel's signature emphasis on negativity transforms the theory of normative authority developed under the banner of the idea. It shows how the theory of determinacy places constraints on the theory of intelligibility that have important implications for how we understand Hegel's transformation of Kant's critical idealism. The theory of determinacy developed in the *Logic* articulates the one ahistorical principle that establishes the necessary historicity of intelligibility as well as the necessary precariousness and ambivalence of historically specific forms of intelligibility. The one ahistorical principle expresses the negativity of form and the necessity of content. When considered from the perspective of the necessity of content, negativity follows the logic of historically specific practices and institutions. Negativity is the inner determination of the way in which intelligibility is articulated within practices and institutions. When considered from the perspective of the necessity of form, negativity calls into question the assumption that the content of any normative commitment retains authority or stability within a historically specific form of life. Concrete forms of intelligibility are precarious, then, since they are based on commitments whose currency depends on their bindingness within a given shape of *Geist*. They are also ambivalent, given that they accommodate opposite meanings and valences even when enjoying normative authority. They are subject not only to reversals of meanings and effects but also to coextensive positive and negative meanings and effects. For these reasons, no determination can be understood as final or fully stable. Specific conceptions of nature, self, and society should be understood as positive developments of a history retrospectively and provisionally. A thoroughgoing critical philosophy accordingly takes stock of the necessary historicity of intelligibility together with its irreducible precariousness and ambivalence.

A PLURALIST STRATEGY

My two key terms—normative precariousness and normative ambivalence—are the product of a pluralist strategy that does justice to strengths in contemporary analytic and continental readings of Hegel.[25] To be clear, my pluralist strategy is not meant to enter into the debate about the status of analytic versus continental philosophy, but to move past such a divide by culling what I find helpful in both traditions. Indeed, this book does justice to Hegel's own texts with interpretive tools from what are seen as competing approaches.

Specifically, this book mines insights from a deconstructive understanding of Hegelian negativity in order to transform the Kantian interpretation of Hegel's idealism as a theory of normative authority. Robert Pippin and Robert Brandom have situated Hegel within Kant's critical project by arguing that Hegel's idealism is best understood as a theory of normativity.[26] Their work is thereby often understood as a contribution to an analytically inclined engagement with Hegel's corpus. Deconstructive readings of Hegel, in contrast, have elaborated the power of Hegelian negativity.[27] Karin de Boer, for example, has developed important implications of negativity for understanding Hegel's corpus, namely, a logic of entanglement that indicates normative undecidability. While I will develop further their insights, both interpretive traditions have limits that this book seeks to correct. They share a classical reconciliationist view of Hegel's idealism that weakens the power of their own accounts.[28] Pippin and Brandom's stress on the stability of institutional rationality suppresses the power of their accounts of negativity and determinate negation. Deconstructive readings of Hegel fail to consider the *status* of "absolute knowing," "absolute idea," "*Aufhebung*," and "absolute negativity," thereby failing to see that they are consistent with and in fact necessary for understanding Hegel's "almost absolute proximity" to deconstruction, to quote Jacques Derrida.[29]

Pippin's 1989 *Hegel's Idealism: The Satisfactions of Self-Consciousness* undermined readings of Hegel as the most extravagant post-Kantian proponent of a precritical metaphysics.[30] Citing a passage from the *Science of Logic* where Hegel states that "[i]t is one of the profoundest and truest insights to be found in the *Critique of Pure Reason* that the *unity* which constitutes the nature of the *Concept* is recognized as the *original synthetic* unity of *apperception*, as unity of the *I think*, or self-consciousness," Pippin showed that Hegel's philosophy seeks to inherit the "apperception theme" in Kant.[31] Like Kant's, Hegel's idealism elaborates the conditions for unity and hence determinacy of any possible object of thought. However, Hegel denies the claim that the reflexive nature of experience can be worked out within a model that holds that concept and intuition, sensibility and understanding, although working in concert, are independent elements and sources of knowledge. Hegel thus rejects an account of transcendental conditions and argues that reflexivity is a feature of actuality (*Wirklichkeit*). It is not until the 2008 *Hegel's Practical Philosophy*, however, that Pippin specifies Hegelian actuality as a matter of normative authority. Stressing the legacy of Kantian autonomy and its emphasis on self-legislation, Pippin argues that actuality has to do with the problem of "actual or effective normative status."[32] Hegel's idealism, Pippin clarifies, is a theory of the historical development of norms, one that supports a theory of radical conceptual change. Conceptual change is a matter of the actuality of normative commitments secured by "responsiveness to reason," that is to say, by the authority of reason.[33] Hegel's *Logic*, along these lines, raises the problem of objectivity as one of the authority—the currency or grip—of concepts within historically specific practices. It represents Hegel's "account of all possible account-givings," since it elucidates the logic of norms as self-authorizing.[34] The *Logic*, then, is ultimately an account of the "self-sufficiency of reason's own authority."[35]

For Pippin, Hegel's idealism is in the last instance a theory of institutional rationality. This follows from Hegel's emphasis on negativity, which he argues is best specified if we consider Hegel's philosophy of action. Hegel views action in light of the inseparability of the inner intention and the outer publicly performed deed.[36] Action according to Hegel, Pippin explains, entails self-negation. To act is to attempt to express an intention publicly. The determinacy of an action and the original intention is thus not up to the agent. It is rather a matter of its externality or publicity. The determinacy of deeds, moral worth, even intentions can only be established in light of the temporal extension and intersubjective character of action. For this reason, Pippin argues, the intelligibility of an action, intention, moral worth depends on historically specific institutions such as the ones discussed in the *Philosophy of Right* under the banner of *Sittlichkeit* (family, civil society, the state). Indeed, intelligibility is a matter of a "coherent social context and appropriate social reception."[37] Accordingly, contestation depends on the fact that "such a context can be shown to have intelligible form." The determinacy of a deed can only be established retrospectively, then, in light of the intelligibility that an institutional context provides.

Like Pippin, Brandom stresses Kantian autonomy for an understanding of Hegel's idealism. Hegel transforms Kant's account of the normative character of mind, meaning, and rationality, he argues, such that normative statuses are social statuses. They are a matter of *Geist*. Kantian judgment involves commitments, Brandom suggests. It is a type of endorsement that entails an exercise of authority, which makes one liable to normative assessment. Judging is therefore a kind of responsibility.[38] For these reasons, judging is a form of *binding*—one binds oneself to what a norm entails.[39] Kant understands this logic of authority–responsibility as a matter of a single individual. The "I think" must accompany all my representations, Brandom argues, because I must integrate present and future endorsements with previous ones.[40] In contrast, Hegel argues that a logic of authority–responsibility is a matter of recognition (*Annerkennung*). The authority of the application of a concept depends on the recognition of others who administer the application. Such administration assumes a "realm of the normative," namely *Geist*, which Brandom glosses as the community of "all who have normative statuses" and their "normatively significant activities." The question of authority is thus a question of authorization over time by negotiating subjects within a normative order. An intersubjective logic of authority-responsibility, then, accounts for the historical revisability of norms and explains their bindingness within a given shape of *Geist*.

While both Pippin and Brandom have gone a long way toward clarifying Hegel's transformation of Kant's critical philosophy, they do not fully draw the implications of their own accounts. This book shows that Hegel's emphasis on negativity suggests a deeper transformation of Kant's idealism. The theory of normative authority distinctive of Hegel's idealism is a theory of normative precariousness and normative ambivalence that calls into question the possibility of a fully stable normative order. Hegelian negativity, as we will see, exceeds an account of conceptual change based on the reconciliation of competing views that thereby restores the stability of a normative order. It sustains an account of normative reversal as well as coextensive incompatible meanings and valences when a norm is not in question. Even when enjoying normative authority, a normative order and its central commitments are precarious and ambivalent.

In contrast to these Kantian readings, deconstructive readings of Hegel have powerfully articulated the consequences of Hegelian negativity. They have thematized the consequences of an irreducible negativity, namely, the lack of stability or full authority of any normative commitment, practice, or institution. Derrida famously acknowledges the proximity of deconstruction to Hegelian dialectics while seeking to clarify the irreconcilable difference between the two. He states that *différance* would have to be defined as "the limit, the interruption, the destruction of Hegelian *relève wherever* it operates."[41] Unlike deconstruction, according to Derrida, Hegelian negativity seeks to establish the "Idea's return to self-presence."[42] Rather than assuming that division can be resolved into unity, Derrida suggests against Hegel that division is irreducible. In his seminal 1968 essay "*Différance*," he describes *différance* as a movement that produces differences. *Différance* is the very origin of differences.[43] It is the delay and deferral that follows from the very structure of time as negativity.[44] Such delay that is also a deferral makes it impossible for anything to be in itself. Division rather than unity is not only at the origin of identity. It cannot be reduced to or resolved into unity.

Karin de Boer's *On Hegel: The Sway of the Negative* is the most systematic deconstructive treatment of Hegel's corpus. She works within deconstruction's ambivalent relationship to Hegel in order to "set free the critical force of Hegel's method." She distinguishes what she sees as the tragic and dialectical strands of Hegel's treatment of logic, nature, and history.[45] While the dialectical strand in Hegel leads to a comprehensive philosophical system, the tragic strand expresses a "logic of entanglement [*Verwicklung*]" present in *and* suppressed by Hegel's system. The tragic strand of Hegel's thought explores and affirms the structure of Greek tragedy. The insight of Greek tragedy is that it places the mutual implication of contrary determinations at the origin of opposition. On the model of Greek tragedy, opposition is the result of the negation of mutual implication. Hegel turned the structure of Greek tragedy into the principle of his philosophical method, however, by transforming tragic negativity into absolute negativity.[46] Unlike tragic negativity and its logic of entanglement, Hegel's absolute negativity and its speculative dialectics *resolves* tragic conflicts by establishing one of the poles of the opposition as the true principle of both.[47] Whereas absolute negativity "pertains to the *relation* between contrary moments," tragic negativity "pertains to the self-undermining *dynamic* that haunts their efforts at self-actualization."[48] Reading Hegel against Hegel, then, a logic of entanglement brings into focus the structure rather than the outcome of opposition.[49]

De Boer's distinction between the dialectical and tragic strands of Hegel's idealism structures her reading of the *Logic*. The *Logic* ought to be understood, she argues, as a non-metaphysical ontology, since it is concerned with the concepts that allow something to become an object at all.[50] Hegel's treatment of being, essence, and the concept in the *Logic* are thus "ontological perspectives" on determinacy. The three ontological perspectives are modes in which thinking actualized itself within the history of philosophy. Because the *Logic* articulates the sequence of pure concepts through a consideration of how each incorporates its contrary determination, absolute negativity is "the methodological principle of the *Logic* as a whole."[51] The Doctrines of Being, Essence, and the Concept, then, correspond to the ways in which abstract, contradictory, and absolute negativity each constitutes a "particular guise of absolute negativity." This sequence overcomes "the tragic conflict between their contrary determinations."[52] The crucial point is that absolute negativity yields the absolute idea's return to self-presence. Within and beyond the *Logic*, then, Hegel's dialectical treatment of binary oppositions suppresses the undecidability that follows from his own account of tragic entanglement.

Although de Boer has gone a long way toward articulating the structure and consequences of Hegelian negativity, she suppresses her own powerful account by failing to consider the *status* of Hegel's notion of the absolute idea and, especially, the absolute idea as method. Rather than ontological, the idea as method is a philosophical perspective that elaborates that negativity is irreducible. This philosophical perspective develops a principle that establishes that undecidability is an irreducible feature of intelligibility precisely because this principle is not itself undecidable. It elaborates the negativity of form and the necessity of content, which indicates the necessity of the historicity of intelligibility as well as the necessity of the precariousness and ambivalence of any concrete form of intelligibility. Rather than a perspective that secures full reconciliation in the idea, then, Hegel's dialectics makes negativity and its consequences into the principle of intelligibility.

ROADMAP OF THE ARGUMENT

The reading of Hegel's *Science of Logic* that this book offers contextualizes key concepts in Hegel's dense and difficult corpus—ideality (*Idealität*), actuality (*Wirklichkeit*), and the absolute idea (*die absolute Idee*). It thereby clarifies the relationship between determinacy and intelligibility worked out in the *Logic* and assumed in the rest of the system.

Part 1 contextualizes Hegel's theory of determinacy within Kant's critical epistemology and Fichte's post-critical idealism. I argue that the key to Hegel's idealism and its emphasis on negativity is his treatment of the Kantian problem of synthesis. Kant accounts for the unity of the object of experience and experience in general as a synthesis of manifold representations. Hegel inherits the Kantian focus on unity as a matter of synthesis, yet he rejects Kant's emphasis on epistemic objectivity. Synthesis, according to Hegel, is a matter of actual determination within what he calls *Geist*. It is the work of practices of rendering intelligible. As we shall see, Hegel's solution to the Kantian problem of synthesis follows Fichte's suggestion that determinacy is a matter of positing (*Setzen*) and transforms Fichtean opposition (*Entgegensetzen*) into determinate negation (*bestimmte Negation*).

In order to establish the outlines of the problem of synthesis that provide the starting point for Hegel's theory of intelligibility, part 1 offers a reading of the Transcendental Aesthetic and the Transcendental Analytic in Kant's *Critique of Pure Reason*. I move on to examine the 1797 Introductions to Fichte's *Wissenschaftslehre* and part 1 of the 1794 version of the same work in order to specify Fichte's engagement with Kant. I then turn to Hegel's *Faith and Knowledge*, the Preface to the *Phenomenology of Spirit*, and the Preface to the Subjective Logic in the *Science of Logic* in order to assess Hegel's critique of Kant and Fichte as subjectivist and formal. While these texts introduce Hegel's notion of the idea as the notion that inherits Kantian synthesis via Fichtean positing, I defer a full treatment of the idea to the third part of the book. I turn instead to Hegel's discussion of reason and *Geist* in the *Phenomenology* in order to establish Hegel's transformation of the Kantian project from a critical epistemology to a post-Kantian philosophy of *Geist*. I clarify the logic of actualization (*Verwirklichung*) elaborated through the discussion of reason and *Geist* in the Preface and examine Hegel's concept of history in the chapter on Absolute Knowing. I thereby argue that Hegel transforms the Kantian problem of synthesis into a matter of recollection (*Erinnerung/Er-innerung*) by and within *Geist*.

Part 2 begins a reconstruction of the main argument of the *Logic* by examining Hegel's critique of traditional ontology and philosophies of reflection in the Objective Logic. I analyze Hegel's rejection of two forms of metaphysical foundationalism—realism and dualism—and trace both positions to reified understandings of mediation. I explain the stakes of Hegel's move from ideality (*Idealität*), the structure of self-relation involved in qualitative difference, to reciprocity (*Wechselwirkung*), the reflexive structure involved in actuality (*Wirklichkeit*). This move comprises Hegel's distinctive understanding of actuality as a process of actualization (*Verwirklichung*), which is clarified in normative rather than ontological terms in the Doctrine of the Concept.

Part 2 argues that the opening of the *Logic* is not the beginning of a post-Kantian ontology but rather the first move of Hegel's systematic *reductio* of realism. I examine Hegel's famous discussion of true infinity (*wahrhafte Unendlichkeit*), and show that it is central to begin grasping his understanding of ideality as a question of normative authority. I turn to Hegel's notion of actuality (*Wirklichkeit*), which I analyze as the retrospective logic of positing–presupposing implicit in philosophies of reflection. This retrospective logic is central to actualization—a process of externalization (*Äußerung*) and recollection (*Erinnerung*) distinctive of Hegelian mediation. Externality refers us to existent conditions, establishing that modes of recollection are articulated by those conditions. I conclude part 2 by drawing the implications of the reading of actuality offered for understanding the structure of Hegel's *Philosophy of Right*.

The Doctrine of the Concept rewrites the notion of actuality as a matter of normative authority under the heading of the idea (*die Idee*). Part 3 accordingly examines Hegel's account of the actualization of reason developed in the Subjective Logic. I assess two crucial moments in the Subjective Logic: Hegel's discussion of Subjectivity (*Subjektivität*) and the idea of cognition (*Erkennen*). These discussions together with the final chapter of the *Logic* on the absolute idea (*die absolut Idee*) elaborate a post-critical understanding of determinacy central to Hegel's distinctive understanding of intelligibility. The absolute idea and the absolute idea as method articulate the strictures of any given form of rationality.

Chapter 6 examines Hegel's treatment of concept, judgment, and the syllogism. Hegel's treatment provides a critique of notions of unity as exempt from negativity. It indicates that negativity is irreducible. It thereby establishes that form is nothing but negativity. The negativity of form, in turn, indicates the necessity of content. Hegel moves from an atomistic notion of the concept to a notion of judgment as division implied in the concept itself. The syllogism is implicit in judgment, establishing mediation as ongoing. Inferential patterns based on relations of negation articulate what something is. A totality of existent conditions here understood in terms of their content articulates the concept of what a thing is and what it should be on the basis of what it is not. Form and content, then, articulate the determinacy of matters themselves. Determinacy is a matter of normativity, since it depends on distinctions articulated by matters themselves.

Hegel's move from a theory of determinacy to a theory of normative authority at the end of the *Logic* is the basis for his post-critical philosophy of *Geist*. Normative distinctions are articulated within and by practices and institutions of rendering intelligible that comprise a historically specific form of life. Chapter 7 accordingly assesses Hegel's insistence on the unity of the theoretical and the practical in the notion of the absolute idea. This insistence indicates the structural relation between determinacy and normative authority that establishes the historicity of intelligibility. The absolute idea as method, however, adds an important dimension to the claim that intelligibility is necessarily historical. It thematizes the work of dialectics, which is central to Hegel's understanding of the relation between ideality and reality. Method thereby allows us to draw the implications of negativity for the theory of normative authority offered under the banner of the absolute idea. Determinacy is precarious, since it depends on historically specific practices that maintain or debunk modes of intelligibility. But it is also ambivalent, since any normative distinction contains within itself both positive and negative valences, thereby producing coextensive positive and negative effects even when enjoying normative authority.

The book ends with a discussion of the three syllogisms of philosophy with which the *Encyclopedia of the Philosophical Sciences* comes to a close. The conclusion argues that the syllogisms of philosophy are three distinct combinations of logic, nature, and *Geist*. The combinations represent three distinct philosophical perspectives from which to understand the relation between logic, nature, and *Geist*. The syllogisms, however, also represent philosophical perspectives that allow a critical history of the development of a practice or institution, since they make possible different perspectives from which a normative commitment is assessed. The syllogisms make possible an assessment of the history of a normative commitment along with the awareness of the irreducible precariousness and ambivalence of any given commitment.

* 1 *

Hegel's Logic of Actualization

Hegel is commonly known as a thinker of becoming. Against the Parmenedean One, Hegel defends the Heraclitean concept of absolute becoming—"all flows, that is, all is becoming."[1] His famous emphasis on contradiction has accordingly been understood as the basis for his insistence on dynamic movement, on the dialectical character of all that is. Revisionary readings of Hegel have thus attempted to curb the metaphysical, ontotheological, and Eurocentric conclusions of Hegel's notorious notion of the idea by emphasizing his treatment of contradiction. Hegel's dialectics challenges the classical notion of identity based on the principle of noncontradiction. The principle of identity, for Hegel, underlies all foundationalist metaphysics, epistemology, and socio-political theory.[2] Oppositional thinking and a two-world metaphysics generated by a thinking of identity, Hegel time and again shows, are self-undermining positions. While the letter of Hegel's corpus suggests that contradiction sustains a teleology of reason developing in being, nature, and history, the spirit of Hegelian contradiction, revisionists have argued, suggests that Hegel's philosophy of becoming does not secure the eternal self-relating movement of the idea.[3]

Rather than his investment in becoming, I will argue that the key to a revisionist reading of Hegel is his treatment of the problem of *synthesis*.[4] In section 10 of the B edition of the *Critique of Pure Reason*, Kant defines synthesis as "the act of putting different representations together with each other and comprehending their manifoldness in one cognition."[5] Synthesis, for Kant, is a matter of gathering what is manifold into a unity ("one cognition") through which what is manifold gains determinacy and hence intelligibility.[6] Hegel inherits the Kantian problem of synthesis, yet argues that Kant's narrow emphasis on epistemic objectivity misconstrues the status of determinacy.[7] Like Kant, Hegel understands synthesis as a matter of unifying what is manifold. Like Kant, Hegel maintains that the work of synthesis is what makes possible determinacy in the first place. Unlike Kant, however, Hegel conceives of determinacy as a problem of *actual* rather than possible determination within what he calls *Geist*. *Geist*, an elusive notion that I will discuss in chapter 3, rivals Kant's focus on the single epistemic subject, and suggests that synthesis is the work of practices of rendering intelligible that comprise a shape (*Gestalt*) of a world.

To be sure, from his earliest theological writings to his mature system, Hegel argued *against* fixity. He consistently pointed out the falsity and perils of reified categories, laws, identities, and institutions. Hegel's early socio-political and religious writings examine the problem of "positivity"—of a reified law that commands without sensitivity to feeling, context, community. Hegel thus argued against religion and morality based on external authority.[8] From his Frankfurt and Jena writings up to his Berlin lectures, Hegel's metaphysics sought to transform the Platonic and Kantian notions of dialectics from a method of detecting falsity to a method of truth.[9] Against Plato and Kant, Hegel argued that, rather than prompting cancellation, dialectics returns fixed determinations to their fluid, altering character.[10] In the Preface to the *Phenomenology of Spirit*, for example, Hegel writes that the task of philosophy is to "set fixed thoughts into fluid motion."[11] In the *Science of Logic*, he argues that the task of a logic of the concept is to make thinking "fluid again," "to revive the concept" from the "ossified, material" of a logic of being and essence.[12]

Although it is clear that Hegel's main critical target is fixity, Hegel's own position is *not* a defense of mere fluidity and change. Synthesis is the central problem of Hegel's idealism, given the status of *division* within his theoretical and practical philosophy. Hegel's metaphysics (what he calls "logic"), epistemology, and social-political philosophy can be understood as responses to the problem of division. As a social-political category, division is a matter of *diremption* (*Entzweiung*), which Hegel glosses as the specifically modern experience of alienation. As an epistemological category, division is a matter of *mediation* (*Vermittlung*), which Hegel develops in order to manage the skepticism raised by Kant's Copernican Turn.[13] As a logical category, division is a matter of *determinate negation* (*bestimmte Negation*), which Hegel elaborates as the successor concept to Kantian judgment and Fichtean positing.

Negation is at work in all senses of division, however. Hegel's central contribution to the legacy of critical philosophy develops, as he puts it, "the logical principle that negation is equally positive."[14] Negation is always negation of something—a concrete determination, whether a logical category, a philosophical position, a historically specific identity or institution.[15] Negation, however, yields an alternative determination. It is never mere negativity, sheer destruction (which Hegel calls "abstract negativity"). It is an exclusion that sets or posits alternative boundaries and hence a relation of something and its now established other. Logically, then, negation requires content in order to be negation. Now negation, Hegel time and again stresses, is not a function imposed externally by an epistemic subject. It is the work of articulation within and by a practice that sets boundaries thereby instituting unity. Concrete determinations are for this reason in a process of *self*-negation. Any thing or identity is such because it has boundaries, and maintains itself (determines itself) by asserting its boundaries. A boundary, however, is something that marks a limit. Marking a limit, Hegel emphasizes, is coextensively transgressing it. A boundary marks what some thing is on the basis of what it is not, and hence establishes its opposite as intrinsic to it. Because any identity is *both* itself *and* its other, any concrete identity—any individual—is subject to a logic of ambivalence. If understood as exempt from ambivalence, any given identity is but reified—an abstract, one-sided determination.

It is thus a mistake to conflate Hegelian negativity with ontological change.[16] Determinate negation does not sustain a view of mere difference. Neither does it allow Hegel to theorize sheer dynamism. Change and dynamic movement are perfectly compatible with the Parmenedean One and any philosophy of pure immanence, which would establish that all is conserved in a movement that serves the completion of the One. It is also a mistake to understand negativity as synonymous with contradiction and, furthermore, contradiction as the motor of speculative-dialectical thinking.[17] Hegelian negativity so understood would privilege the very notion of opposition that Hegel is arguing against, since it would be a notion of opposition between two self-standing yet contradictory determinations. Hegel's attack on oppositional thinking and the logic of identity underlying it is precisely an attack on self-subsistent identities that could be opposed to an other given their integrity.[18] An understanding of Hegel's idealism as a post-critical ontology exacerbates these interpretive options. The textbook interpretation of Hegel as a thinker of cosmic spirit, of the teleology of reason developing in being, nature, and history, is supported rather than challenged by understanding contradiction and change ontologically.

That negation—and hence division—is irreducible in Hegel's thought suggests that the *work* of synthesis is key. It suggests the necessity of synthesis, which Hegel understands as a matter of what he calls recollection (*Erinerrung*,

Er-innerung). Synthesis is thus crucial to specifying the *status* of Hegel's idealism. The chapters that follow argue that the problem of synthesis is central to Hegel's transformation of the critical project into a post-critical philosophy of *Geist*. My aim in these chapters, then, is to situate Hegel's theory of determinacy within Kant's critical epistemology and sketch the ways in which Hegel's idealism inherits the specifically Kantian problem of synthesis. Chapter 1 delineates the problem of synthesis in Kant's *Critique of Pure Reason*, specifically in the Aesthetic and the Analytic. My discussion of Kant in chapter 1 is not exhaustive, to be sure. Chapters 2 and 3 continue to discuss aspects of Kant's Aesthetic and Analytic. Chapter 2 discusses Fichte's solution to the Kantian problem of synthesis by developing a logic of positing. Chapter 3 examines Hegel's transformation of the problem of synthesis into a logic of actualization, which should ultimately be understood as a matter of *Geist*.

CHAPTER 1

Synthesis: Kant

Hegel inherits the Kantian problem of synthesis, as noted in the introduction to part 1, yet he argues that Kant's emphasis on epistemic objectivity misconstrues the status of determinacy. Hegel transforms Kant's focus on a single epistemic or moral subject by arguing that synthesis, determinacy, and ultimately intelligibility are a matter of *Geist*. In order to accomplish this transformation, Hegel calls into question two crucial aspects of Kant's transcendental idealism. Although Hegel agrees that determinacy and intelligibility are a matter of unity, first, he inverts the logical priority of division and unity within Kant's critical epistemology. This inversion, second, allows Hegel to call into question the assumption that unity requires a condition or principle that is not itself a synthesis, thereby developing a more consistent account of mediation than Kant's Copernican Turn elaborates. In order to reconstruct and assess Hegel's transformation, we must first sketch the problem of synthesis in Kant's *Critique of Pure Reason*.

Kant's critical epistemology is grounded on the claim that knowledge is a matter of experience, which involves the receptivity of impressions and the spontaneity of concepts.[1] Cognition accordingly involves sensibility, the capacity to be "affected in some way," and the understanding, the capacity to "bring[] forth representations itself."[2] Through sensibility an object is *given* (*gegeben*); through the understanding the object is "thought in relation to that representation (as a mere determination of the mind)."[3] Experience accordingly involves two heterogeneous elements: the sensible given and nonempirical constraints (rules for determinacy: concepts, principles, postulates). Sensibility and understanding are heterogeneous, thus irreducible to each other. Although they "cannot exchange their function," they refer us to elements whose *joint* contribution makes experience possible. Kant's strategy for establishing the objectivity of cognition in the first *Critique* is hence to account for the activity of receptivity and spontaneity, rather than the structure of the sensible and the intelligible. Accounting for the capacity to be affected and to cognize an object by way of judgment establishes that what is given in sensation is subject to nonempirical constraints on experience and, vice versa, that nonempirical constraints yield objective determinations of what is given in sensation.[4]

Division is thus the starting point in Kant's critical epistemology. It follows from the claim that cognition involves two heterogeneous capacities that provide unity to an undetermined manifold given in sensation in distinctive ways. Division, therefore, follows from the duality of the sources of cognition and from the indeterminacy of the given matter of cognition. Heterogeneity and indeterminacy suggest that unity is a matter of combination ("conjunctio"), and that synthesis is the key to the unity of any object of experience and any experience in general. Determinacy thus depends on the relation between receptivity and spontaneity of the mind, which will in turn account for the relation between intuition and concept (a singular representation of sensation and a rule for universal determination of manifold representations into an objective representation). Kant is thus immediately confronted with accounting for unity on two registers.[5] First, he must establish the work of gathering distinctive of sensibility and of unifying distinctive of the understanding, since it is what makes possible *taking* what is given in sensation *as* something given and what is determined by concepts *as* an object of experience (or an event). Second, Kant must establish unity as a matter of the relation between concept and intuition, and must therefore show that the categories apply to appearances and that appearances are subject to the categories. While the transcendental deduction addresses the second problem, the distinction between a transcendental aesthetic and a transcendental analytic addresses the first.

RECEPTIVITY AND SYNTHESIS

In the Transcendental Aesthetic, Kant sets out to give an account of the capacity for receptivity, which involves establishing the conditions of possibility for being affected.[6] Kant is clear that sensibility is a "passive faculty," that it is preconceptual, and that therefore it does not combine the manifold given in sensation. However, his discussion of space and time shows that sensibility involves an *uptake* that makes possible taking an undetermined manifold given in sensation *as* an *appearance*, as some undetermined thing given somewhere and somewhen. While Kant's discussion of sensibility has to do with givenness itself and hence with passivity in sensation, his argument concerns the very possibility of reception, of taking something as given. Sensibility can therefore also be said to provide minimal order albeit preconceptually.[7] The properly unifying activity of the understanding, to be sure, makes possible taking a manifold of representations *as* an *object* of experience, as some determinate thing or event. Yet taking what is given as given requires a form of gathering that, although preconceptual and hence pre-objective, is synthetic nonetheless.

Within the Aesthetic, the problem of division and synthesis arises in ways specific to Kant's understating of space as the form of outer sense and time as the form of inner sense. Division is a matter of externality and succession, while synthesis is a matter of an intuition of the totality of space and the duration of experience in time. As the form of outer sense, space establishes exteriority as irreducible to interiority. Synthesis accordingly concerns space as itself an intuition of a whole that makes possible distinguishing myself from other things as well as the relation between things outside of me.[8] Because space is nothing but sense of the outer as outer, it establishes the very possibility of givenness, of being affected by something that is not me. This is a crucial point for Kant's discursive model of the mind. It helps Kant contrast between a mind like ours that depends on independently given sense content and a nondiscursive mind that can know objects that are merely thinkable, which is to say, that can intuit objects that are merely logically possible.[9] A mind that can create rather than be affected by an object is no longer discursive, but rather intuitive—a god's mind.[10] Although Kant's notion of affection leads to deep inconsistencies in the basic tenet of his transcendental idealism (to wit: it implies causality, when what is affecting the mind are purportedly things in themselves and hence not subject to the categories), the point here is that the very possibility of receptivity requires more than sensation, than the alteration of sensory organs. Taking something as affecting me rather than being created by me requires the distinction between the inner and the outer and determinate relations between things outside of me in the first place.

As the form of inner sense, time establishes succession as irreducible to duration. Inner sense is a flow of moments that come into being and pass away, which establishes the necessity of synthesis to sustain a temporal continuum. Retention of what is past in the present and possibly the future is the result of synthetic activity. The possibility of continuity in and of experience depends on synthetic activity that makes possible the experience of before and after. The irreversibility of temporal succession depends on time as the form of inner sense—which is a crucial aspect of the argument of the Second Analogy and its defense of causality. Time as the form of inner sense, then, establishes that experience itself is subject to succession, to the structure of an event. The temporal structure of experience is linear, since a moment passes as soon as it comes into being, establishing that an event cannot be returned to without it being another time. Retention of moments past required for the unity of experience over time will therefore require not just memory but also imagination and ultimately self-consciousness. Imagination and self-consciousness, as we will see, are conditions of possibility of experience precisely because they make possible iterability and synthesis.

Kant's understanding of space and time as pure forms of intuition, then, suggests that they provide minimal organizing 'principles' of uptake. Specifically prediscursive, givenness is nonetheless possible thanks to ordering spatial and temporal principles. Kant indeed glosses the aesthetic as the "science of rules of sensibility," and space and time (the "two pure forms of sensible intuition") "as principles of *a priori* cognition" given the structural role that simultaneity and succession play in experience.[11] Appearances spread themselves around us, which requires the experience of simultaneity, and occur in an ordered series, which requires the experience of succession. It is only on the basis of the inner/outer distinction and as succession/duration that appearances are taken as appearances.[12] Registering an undetermined object of sensation as precisely that, something given in sensation, implies externality and duration. The manifold given in sensation is only given as some indeterminate thing or event somewhere and somewhen. Uptake, then, is here a matter of reception, of being affected. But what is given in sensation (which is by definition empirical, material, *a posteriori*) is only received as, taken as, an indeterminate object by being some thing somewhere and somewhen. Anything given can be received insofar as it is spatially and temporally located in relation to a perceiving subject.[13] Space and time are therefore forms of sense in the dual sense of sensation and minimal intelligibility. They make possible being affected by giving minimal form to what is an undetermined object of sensation.

SPONTANEITY AND SYNTHESIS

Something is a *determinate* such-and-such, however, when a manifold given in sensation is unified into one "objective representation."[14] To take something as a determinate such-and-such is to give form to an undetermined object (an appearance) given as an indiscriminate sensation. *Form-giving* is an activity of concept application by a self-conscious subject. The understanding is the capacity to unify a manifold by means of a rule (a concept) by a self-conscious subject.[15] In the Analytic, synthesis is thus a matter of subjecting the manifold of intuition to a rule, while division is a feature of the indeterminateness of the manifold. An appearance, the undetermined 'object' of intuition, is only an objective representation and hence an object of experience thanks to the synthesis of concepts in judgment.[16] The determinacy of the manifold given in sensation therefore depends on nonempirical constraints, on rules for determinacy—which Kant calls pure concepts of the understanding (*reinen Verstandesbegriffe*). To be sure, the determinacy of any possible object of experience and of any possible experience requires the categories. More significantly, however, it requires the capacity for concept-application, for judging, as well as for self-consciousness, for awareness that any such experience of an object or an event is my own. Ultimately self-ascription, not merely concept-application, makes cognition possible.[17]

Kant's strategy in the metaphysical deduction—the move from general to transcendental logic—is thus crucial.[18] The metaphysical deduction takes general logic to be the "clue" to "finding" functions of unity—rules for combining concepts and representations, the categories—by focusing on *function* itself.[19] Kant transitions from the forms of judging catalogued by classical Aristotelian logic to the rule implicit in the specific forms of judging, what following Aristotle Kant calls categories (*Kategorien*). To judge hypothetically, for example, involves conjoining two propositions on the assumption that the truth of the one justifies the inference to the other.[20] The rule involved in such an inference is the relation of ground to consequent.[21] Although the relation of ground and consequent is not equivalent to the causal relation, as Allison notes, it is "arguably a necessary condition of the possession of the latter concept."[22] The point is that, for Kant, form is a matter of rule-governance. It is a matter of normativity—of concepts that function as rules for judgment. The move from general to transcendental logic is thus a move from an account of the combination of concepts in judgments and judgments in syllogisms to the combination of representations and hence the transcendental function of synthesis.[23] Although the metaphysical deduction moves from forms of judgment to the categories, the move is in fact from the logical forms of judgment (e.g., the universal judgment: All S is P) to the transcendental function of judging (synthesizing a manifold, whether pure or empirical). It is a move, in other words, to the capacity to judge.[24] The metaphysical deduction, then, establishes that unity is the result of synthesis, and that judging is the activity *sine qua non* for the determinacy of an object of experience and for experience itself.

Now, in the metaphysical deduction and in both the A and B versions of the transcendental deduction, Kant argues that cognition is the result of three—not two—powers of the mind: sensibility, the imagination, and the understanding. In all three discussions, Kant maintains that the synthesizing activity of the three faculties is cumulative and lays out a sequence for the process of cognition.[25] In logical rather than temporal order, cognition is the result of a process of determination that involves gathering, synthesis, and unity. The transcendental function of these faculties is accordingly only "concerned with form." Gathering, synthesis, unity are all forms of form-giving.[26] The discussion of the three faculties, however, specifies the notion of synthetic unity that Kant argues is presupposed in each differentiated synthesizing activity. We have already seen the activity of gathering involved in sensibility. Crucial here is the form of synthesis proper to the imagination and the understanding.

In the metaphysical deduction, Kant argues that the spontaneity of thought "requires that this manifold first be gone through, taken up, and combined in a certain way in order for a cognition to be made out of it."[27] This going through, gathering, combining a manifold requires a faculty whose transcendental function bridges the sensible and intelligible, intuition and concept. This capacity is the imagination. Synthesis *in general*, Kant proposes, is a function of this "blind though indispensable function of the soul without which we would have no cognition at all, but of which we are seldom even conscious."[28] The unity of the manifold in a concept requires self-consciousness, but the synthesis of the manifold prior to its proper unity is unconscious gathering. The imagination effects preconceptual yet no longer merely sensible synthetic unity of the manifold.[29] Synthesis or combination proper, synthetic unity proper, Kant argues, requires concept-application by a self-conscious subject.[30] Indeed, Kant maintains that "all synthesis, *through which even perception itself becomes possible*, stands under the categories."[31]

In the B edition deduction Kant calls the imagination figurative synthesis (*synthesis speciosa*) and distinguishes it from intellectual synthesis (*synthesis intellectualis*) in order to establish the relation between the imagination and the understanding.[32] Here again the distinction is drawn in terms of self-consciousness and the possibility of self-ascription. The *synthetic unity of consciousness* is the "objective condition of all cognition," because it is something "under which every intuition must stand **in order to become an object for me**."[33] The B edition deduction accordingly begins with the crucial definition of synthesis proper, which requires the possibility of self-ascription. "[W]e can represent nothing as combined in the object," Kant famously writes, "without having previously combined it ourselves, and that among all representations **combination** is the only one that is not given through objects but can be executed only by the subject itself, since it is an act of its self-activity."[34] The understanding brings the manifold of given representations "under the unity of apperception."[35]

Now, Kant moves on to argue that it is under the assumption not of synthesizing activity but of a synthetic unity underlying all synthesizing activity that a manifold given in sensation can be united under the concept of an object.[36] The concept of the manifold and of its unity presupposes the concept of the unity of the manifold, of synthetic unity.[37] However, the notion of synthetic unity is presupposed in the unity of the concepts, of the rules that provide the unity of the object. This synthetic unity, which grounds the unity of the concepts as rules for determinacy, is the transcendental unity of apperception. The unity of experience, the possibility of ascribing a representation as my own, is necessary for the unifying capacity of the categories, since without the possibility of incorporating a given representation into the continuity of my own experience, there would be no application of a rule to a manifold. Thus, Kant argues that the "I think must **be able** to accompany all my representations; for otherwise something would be represented in me that could not be thought at all, which is as much to say that the representation would be either impossible or else at least would be nothing for me."[38] The unity of synthesis is "through original apperception."[39] In the A deduction, Kant calls transcendental apperception "pure, original, unchanging consciousness."

In the *Science of Logic*, Hegel takes issue with Kant's narrow epistemic, hence "subjectivist" and "formal," understanding of synthesis.[40] He transforms the problem of synthesis into one that acknowledges that negativity—division—is irreducible. Negativity establishes that synthesis is ongoing, which requires rejecting Kant's insistence on a "pure, original, unchanging consciousness," on a unity that is "not itself a synthesis," as Hegel says.[41] Hegel thus reverses the role that division and synthesis play in Kant without abandoning the problem of synthesis. Before turning to Hegel, however, it is important to consider Fichte's response to the Kantian problem of synthesis, since Hegel is indebted to Fichte's reading of Kant on three counts. First, Fichte's investment in making explicit the metaphysical presuppositions of the Copernican Turn also reverses the priority of division over unity in Kant. Like Kant, however, he retains the view that determinacy requires absolute unity. Second, Hegel inherits Fichte's transformation of the Kantian notion of mediation into a logic of positing. Third, Fichte's account of the logic of opposition involved in the Copernican Turn is the conceptual predecessor of Hegel's notion of determinate negation.

CHAPTER 2

Positing: Fichte

Fichte's rewriting of the Kantian problem of synthesis is an indispensable clue for a proper understanding of Hegel's idealism.[1] From the *Differenzschrift* and *Glauben und Wissen* to the *Science of Logic* and the Berlin lectures on the history of philosophy, Hegel distanced himself from Fichte's idealism, characterizing it as a radicalization of Kant's narrow focus on the epistemic subject.[2] Fichte's idealism, in short, is even more formal and more subjective than Kant's. Nevertheless, Hegel develops rather than merely rejects Fichte's rewriting of Kant's critical epistemology.[3] Hegel inherits Fichte's understanding of synthesis as a matter of positing—instituting—the very distinction between the subject and the object that Kant merely presupposes. Rather than subsumption, synthesis involves the opposition between I and not-I instituted by the I in the first place. Key here is Fichte's transformation of Kant's notion of intellectual intuition. Hegel follows Fichte in arguing that determinacy is a matter of self-determination and intelligibility a matter of the distinction between I and not-I drawn by reason itself. Hegel's signature emphasis on negativity and his concept of determinate negation, furthermore, are worked out in light of the understanding of opposition central to Fichte's theory of positing.[4]

INTELLECTUAL INTUITION

In the introduction to the 1794 *Wissenschaftslehre*, Fichte famously writes that, although it differs in method and mode of presentation, his "system in nothing other than the *Kantian*."[5] He aims to present in the most consistent form

Kant's main insight that "the object shall be posited and determined by the cognitive faculty, and not the cognitive faculty by the object."[6] Kant's task in the first *Critique*, as we saw in chapter 1, is to account for the possibility of determinacy in light of a purportedly irreducible division. Determinacy for Kant is a matter of synthesis, given the division that follows from the sources of human, finite cognition. Division is primary for at least two reasons: it is a feature of the two sources of cognition (intuition and concept) and their ordering capacities (receptivity and spontaneity), and it is also a consequence of the indeterminacy of the given. The determinacy of an object of experience requires the activity of gathering (by sensibility), synthesizing (by the imagination), unifying (by the understanding). Ultimately, the transcendental unity of apperception, the capacity to ascribe any given representation as my own, is the ground of the unity and hence determinacy of the object of experience. What Kant does not explain, what is hence merely presupposed in the Copernican Turn, Fichte argues, is the distinction between the I and the not-I.[7]

Like Jacobi, Fichte notes that passing over in silence a discussion of the assumptions underlying the distinction between what is in itself and what is for us amounts to inconsistency at best and failure at worst. It is a form of inconsistency, since the very idea of givenness and the doctrine of affection that it involves is in effect a positive assertion about things in themselves. The doctrine of affection seems to assume, at the very least, that what is given in sensibility is subject to causality. Unlike Jacobi, who argued that without the presupposition of the thing in itself he could not enter the system but with it he could not stay within it, Fichte's critique of the thing in itself leads him to elaborate the assumptions left implicit in Kant's account of spontaneity in general and apperception in particular.[8] As we will see, Fichte's rejection of the thing in itself leads him to a normative rather than ontological account of positing, which he maintains involves a logic of opposition.

Fichte transforms the problem of division and synthesis in decisive ways. Division is secondary—it follows from unity—since the opposition presupposed in Kant's account of cognition is itself the result of the unified activity of the self.[9] Fichte's reversal of the logical priority of division and unity is tied to his insistence on action as primary and existence as derivative.[10] In the Second 1797 Introduction to the *Wissenschaftslehre*, Fichte glosses the nature of self-consciousness as an activity in which the self *comes into being*. He writes:

> The self, we say, reverts *into itself*. So it is not therefore already present for itself before the occurrence of this reversion and independently thereof? Must it

> not already be there for itself in order that it may take itself the object of an act? And if so, doesn't your philosophy in that case already presuppose what it was meant to explain?
>
> I answer: Not at all. It is only through this act, and first by means of it, by an act upon an act itself, which specific act is preceded by no other whatever, that the self *originally* come to exist for itself.[11]

This act of reversion to self in which the self comes into being "precedes and conditions," Fichte argues, all acts of consciousness. For this reason, it is originary and indeed must be thought of as "the most primordial act of the subject."[12] To recall, Kant argues that self-consciousness is the primordial condition of possibility for experience, since representation itself requires that I take any given representation as my own.[13] Otherwise it would be nothing for me, which is to say, it would not be determinate. Kant, to be sure, argues that the I think is an "original unity," given that without a unified self experience would not be continuous and the object of experience would not be determinate. The I think is a condition for unity and in that sense an "originary" unity. Now, Kant forgoes an account of the structure of self-ascription, the act of self-reversion, implied in apperception. Kant resists a positive account of self-ascription, since doing so would transgress the limits set by the critical project. Fichte, in contrast, sets out to give such an account albeit within the context of the critical project. To this end, he takes Kant's regressive argument one level deeper or, to use a different metaphor, to "higher-level altitude."[14] Kant's theory of apperception presupposes that the self is pure activity, sheer spontaneity, which *comes into being* in acting.[15] There is no I before the activity of positing, Fichte argues, there is no condition before acting. Activity is the condition that makes possible an I. The self can ascribe to itself its own representations (it is self-conscious) *only* as a result of its own activity.

This activity of the self, Fichte explains, is both a fact (I immediately exist for myself) and an expression of freedom (I immediately exist for myself by having "come about for myself through acting").[16] For this reason, this act cannot be understood as a matter of discursivity, of subsuming under a concept a manifold given in sensation. Rather, it is a matter of *pure* spontaneity, of positing (*Setzen*). The activity of the self is pure, for Fichte, since it "presupposes no object, but itself produces it, and in . . . the acting, therefore, immediately becomes the deed."[17] The originary act of the self is a *Tathandlung*.[18] This self-reverting activity, as an action that becomes the deed, is the basis for Fichte's understanding the self as coming into being in acting and the relation between the subject and the object as a "subject-objectivity."[19] The self, as a transcendental condition, presupposes the coming into being of the self in its own activity of sheer spontaneity, pure positing. But this means that any possible object of experience is also contingent on the instituting and hence productive activity of the self. If there is no self before positing, then there is no object of experience before positing. Thus, as we will see below, the self also posits the not-self. This relation of the self and the not-self is what makes possible Kant's account of the object of experience as depending on the unity of experience in the first place. For this reason, Fichte maintains, Kant's articulation of apperception and, more generally, the understanding is insufficient. Fichte thus shifts Kant's constructivist language of objectivity to an account of the *production* of the object based on the production of the subject by the subject.

Fichte boldly reaches for Kant's notion of intellectual intuition (*intellektuelle Anschauung*) and maintains that it is "the only firm standpoint for all philosophy."[20] For Kant, in order to account for the strictures of finite cognition, we must contrast between a discursive understanding and an "intuitive understanding," a mind that would "not represent given objects, but through whose representation the objects would themselves at the same time be given, or produced."[21] Kant is careful to stress that the notion of an intellectual intuition is a limit concept, which serves the aim of sketching the limits of a discursive mind.[22] For Fichte, Kant's notion of intellectual intuition provides the appropriate model for articulating what is presupposed in apperception, in the very possibility of self-ascription.[23] Given that the activity of self-consciousness is not a matter of the application of concepts on a sensible given, and hence that this activity yields an immediate relation-to-self, Fichte argues, self-consciousness must be understood as a form of intuition. What is more, given that the activity of the self is productive of the self, it is also productive of the not-self, of the object of its experience. The object of experience is possible by *positing* the not-self, the not-I. With the notion of intellectual intuition, then, Fichte is arguing that discursivity presupposes nondiscursive activity. In the last instance, determinacy is dependent on nondiscursive activity. The structure of self-consciousness itself, Fichte therefore maintains, should be understood on the model of intellectual intuition.

Although famous for its blatant transgression of the limits set by the critical enterprise, Fichte's appropriation of the notion of intellectual intuition is in line with some of the most significant aspects of Kant's theory of pure apperception.[24] Crucial here is the *status* of this activity—of positing *both* the self and the not-self—since it is a claim about existence that dispels the notion of a original unified self opposed to a thing in itself. As Terry Pinkard (following Pippin) has argued, Fichte's point is *not* ontological but rather normative.[25] However, Fichte understands normativity in Kant's critical epistemology through Kantian morality, specifically his notion of autonomy as self-legislation.[26] Especially in the *Groundwork*, Kant glosses autonomy on the basis of authorship when he argues that self-legislation is a matter of the will's own giving universal law.[27] Autonomous willing requires being governed by a norm that one is coextensively instituting, but as binding for any rational creature. Fichte's insistence on self-activity and hence positing reformulates normativity such that it now refers to *instituting* a distinction, a norm, rather than *applying* a rule to a manifold of intuition. Like Kantian autonomy, the institution of this distinction is also the institution of a norm that guides such distinction.

Normativity is no longer a matter of a rule that unifies a manifold into an objective representation—an appearance into an object of experience. It is therefore no longer a matter of the capacity to judge. In Fichte's idealism, normativity is the institution of a distinction between what is given and what is discursively articulated in the first place. This distinction is both the result of the acting self as well as the action of the self distinguishing itself from what it cannot *ontologically* produce—material reality. Fichte's point, then, is that the distinction between the self and the not-self *requires* the institution of a normative order based on a boundary between I and not-I. Intellectual intuition is thus Fichte's way of elaborating the simultaneous institution-subjection of the self and the not-self in acting.[28] The institution of such a distinction is the product *and* guide over the self. For this reason, Fichte argues that self-consciousness is properly understood as an activity of *self-determination*. The "self is determined only by itself," and it is thereby "absolutely determined."[29]

Recall that, in section 3 of the *Groundwork*, Kant argues that the distinction between the sensible and the intelligible is itself made possible by reason. "Reason," Kant writes, "must consider itself as the author of its own principles."[30] It is "pure self-activity," which "proves its highest occupation in distinguishing the world of sense and the world of understanding from each other."[31] Fichte follows Kant when, in a crucial passage, he argues that

> reason is absolutely self-sufficient; it exists only for itself. But nothing exists for reason except reason itself. It follows that everything reason is must have its foundation in reason itself and must be explicable solely on the basis of reason itself and not on the basis of anything outside reason, for reason could not get outside of itself without renouncing itself.[32]

The notion of self-determination developed here—the notion central to Hegel's own idealism—does not support an unbridled idealism wherein the self produces empirical reality. As we will see, positing involves what Fichte calls "mutual limitation" (*gegenseitigen Einschränkbarkeit*).[33] Indeed, Fichte does not maintain that the activity of the self is *ontologically* unrestricted. Here again the claim is normative. In arguing that the ground of the distinction between I and not-I is reason, Fichte aims to elaborate a more consistent critical philosophy. The notion of positing—and the structure of self-determination involved in positing—seeks to deny an appeal to a ground or foundation other than the instituting-authoring activity of reason. It is a metatheoretical claim about the *status* of the ground of the distinction between the I and the not-I. The ground of this distinction is distinction-making itself. It is nothing but the activity of reason.

ABSOLUTE POSITING, OPPOSITION, LIMITATION

The very project of a science of knowledge, as we have seen, makes explicit the implicit presuppositions of Kant's transcendental philosophy. The task of the *Wissenschaftslehre*, Fichte explains, is to "*discover* the primordial, absolutely unconditioned first principle of human knowledge," and he immediately adds that this principle "is intended to express that *act* which does not and cannot appear among the empirical states of consciousness but rather lies at the basis of all consciousness and alone makes it possible."[34] Fichte's discussion of the three fundamental principles of the *Wissenschaftslehre* in part 1 of the book articulates the strictures of self-positing (*Selbstsetzung*), opposition (*Entgegensetzen*) (positing of the not-self in positing the self), and mutual limitation (*gegenseitigen Einschränkbarkeit*). As Pippin argues, the first part proceeds regressively, thereby functioning as a transcendental argument.[35] While the first principle establishes the absolute positing of the self implicit in the principle of identity, the second establishes that in positing itself, the self posits the not-self. The very idea of positing accordingly involves a logic of opposition. The third principle addresses the structure of opposition in order to show that it must be understood as limitation rather than annihilation of the not-self by the self and vice versa.

The first principle reads as follows: "The self begins by an absolute positing of its own existence."[36] Like Kant's strategy in the metaphysical deduction, Fichte's discussion of the first principle begins with a logical principle and shows the transcendental structure that it presupposes. Accordingly, Fichte begins the discussion by considering the principle of identity, A=A. He notes that this proposition is not a mere statement of existence—"A is A is by no means equivalent to A exists, or there is an A."[37] It expresses a relation of entailment: "*If* A exists, *then* A exists." The principle of identity implies a "necessary connection," which Fichte will speak of as "absolute."[38] Its absolute status resides in the fact that the very possibility of identity requires an inference concerning persistence throughout time, as Pippin explains. The problem is, in other words, the Kantian problem of unity in light of succession. The necessary connection involved in "If A exists, then A exists" has no other ground. Fichte calls it X. "X is," Fichte writes, "at least *in* the self," since this relation is a judgment that expresses a relation of entailment. The formal relation rather than the existence itself is what interests Fichte here, since as we have seen existence follows from the positing of the self.[39] The relation of entailment leads to the self, given that persistence throughout time requires synthesis by the act of self-ascription—apperception.[40] The crucial point is that it is by means of X that A exists for the self. For this reason, Fichte argues, X is nothing but the activity of positing of the self. "I am I is unconditionally and absolutely valid, since it is equivalent to the proposition X."[41] "I am" is the absolute ground of judgment, here no longer as a matter of a logical principle but a transcendental condition. A=A, then, presupposes I=I. The inference involved in the principle of identity implies the activity of self-ascription that is itself the result of the act of positing, of the self that posits itself.

Although the first principle establishes that identity presupposes the absolute activity of the self, it cannot account for determinacy or intelligibility since they involve the distinction between the activity of positing and the object of theoretical or practical intending.[42] Fichte must hence explain the distinction between the I and the not-I that he argues Kant tacitly assumes. The second principle articulates the thought that the absolute positing of the self is coextensively an institution or positing of the not-self. The principle reads: "As surely as the absolute certainty of the proposition '−A is not equal to A' is unconditionally admitted among the facts of empirical consciousness, *so surely is a not-self opposed absolutely to the self*."[43] Although still regressive, notice that Fichte's argument is here moving differently. Rather than moving from a logical principle to epistemic conditions, Fichte's discussion of the second principle moves from an epistemic relation to a principle of opposition. In positing itself, Fichte argues, the self opposes itself to the not-I. He writes: "By means, therefore, and only by means, of this absolute act, the opposite is posited, so far as it is opposed (as a mere contrary in general)."[44] The point here is *not* that the self posits the not-I—an ontological entity or the authoritative normative status of an entity—but rather *opposition in general*. "Every opposite," Fichte adds, "so far as it is so, is so absolutely, by virtue of an act of the self, and for no other reason. Opposition in general is posited absolutely by the self."[45] Absolute positing involves an opposition, since in bringing into being the self it simultaneously excludes that which it is not. The coming-into-being of the self is, in other words, establishing a distinction between itself and what it is not. Concretely, it means establishing the activity of self-ascription and the representation being ascribed as my own. In positing itself, the self posits the not-self *überhaupt*. Positing institutes a normative order structured on the basis of the distinction between the self and the not-self, the I and the not-I.

Although self-positing is "absolute," although the production of the self and the not-self depends on this originary activity, the not-self is *not* a mere ontological creation or full normative determination. Self-positing *discloses* the not-self. Fichte writes:

> If I am to present anything at all, I must oppose it to the presenting self. Now within the object of presentation there can and must be an X of some sort, whereby it discloses itself as something to be presented, and not as that which presents. But *that* everything, wherein this X may be, is not that which presents, but an item to be presented, is something that no object can teach me; for merely in order to set something as an *object*, I have to know this already; hence it must lie in myself, the presenter, in advance of any possible experience.[46]

The not-self must represent a *limit* to the self, if the self's positing is to be an opposition that establishes a distinction rather than mere annihilation. Although the I posits the not-I as limiting its own activity, and hence serves as a primordial condition for the presentation of any not-I, such positing must include the limiting act of the not-I. Rewriting Kant's dictum "thoughts without content are empty, intuitions without concepts are blind," Fichte argues that without limitation, positing would be empty.[47] The first two principles are therefore insufficient for establishing how absolute positing and the positing of absolute opposition does not entail the mutual annihilation the self and the not-self. "How can A and −A," Fichte writes, "being and nonbeing, reality and negation, be thought together without mutual elimination and destruction?"[48] To annihilate the not-self is to annihilate the content of any ascription, and hence the very possibility of a self.[49] Yet to not have established that the not-self is precisely not the absolute positing of the self is to allow for the possibility of the annihilation of the self by the not-self. But this cannot be the case, given the absolute status of the self in the originary act of positing. As Pippin puts it, "Fichte is fully aware of the problem . . . that a posited not-self is not a *not*-self, and that if the not-self is not posited as such by the self, it cannot count as a not-*self*; it is just whatever it is, and does not, of itself, 'oppose' anything."[50] The third principle, the principle of *mutual limitation* (also mutual determination), addresses this concern.

Fichte calls the absolute, originary act of self-positing X. Y, he now argues, is the act of mutual limitation that establishes opposition as negation, which makes possible thinking of opposition as the basis for determination. "The act Y," Fichte writes, "will be a *limiting* of each opposite by the other; and X will denote the *limits* [*die Schranken*]."[51] Key here is that the mutual limitation of each other presupposes the mutual *divisibility* of each. It is necessary that the self and the not-self be divisible, if opposition is not sheer annihilation. "To *limit* something," Fichte writes, "is to abolish its reality, not *wholly* but in *part* only, by negation."[52] In order for opposition to be an activity of determination, any assumption of the self-standing integrity of the self and the not-self must be called into question. Both are determinate or intelligible given the relation to the other. Both are subject to the other on the basis of a relation of dependency; neither is self-subsistent. Opposition functions as determination, then, because both the self and the not-self depend on each other—without the not-self, the self cannot function as an activity of ascribing representations to itself, and without the self that is doing the ascribing, the not-self is not determinate, intelligible.[53] Only by mutually limiting each other, mutually negating each other, can self-ascription be at the same time the production of the object. The third principle accordingly reads as follows: "In the self I oppose a divisible not-self to the divisible self."[54] However, given divisibility, the third principle can also be understood as a principle of combination. It has established the unity of opposites on the basis of the divisibility of each. "In the third principle," Fichte writes, "we have established a synthesis between two opposites, self and not-self, by postulating them each to be divisible."[55]

Now, Fichte argues that both the self and the not-self are *simultaneously* posited and posited as divisible: opposition that is negation rather than annihilation requires division, but this divisibility itself presupposes the unity of that which is divided.[56] "The self," Fichte concludes, "is to be equated with, and yet opposed to, itself. But in regard to consciousness it is equal to itself, for consciousness is one: but in this consciousness the absolute self is posited as indivisible, whereas the self to which the not-self is opposed is posited as divisible. Hence, insofar as there is a not-self opposed to it, the self is itself in opposition to the absolute self."[57] Instead of a dualism of cognition and the thing in itself, divisibility of self and not-self is grounded in an opposition to an absolute self-positing, which Fichte glosses as "absolute indivisibility."

Divisibility assumes the primary unity, indivisibility, of absolute positing. Division, then, entails a previous unity that is revealed *after the fact*, as a result of negation. Positing, in other words, establishes *after the fact* the originary unity of the self as an activity—a thought that elaborates what is tacitly assumed in the B deduction. Primordial unity is the basis for combination. Fichte has therefore transformed the Kantian notion of synthesis by inverting the priority of division and unity. Opposition rather than subsumption becomes the basis for determinacy, given the necessary divisibility of self and not-self, subject and object, posited by the absolute self. The problem of synthesis is now understood as a matter of the reciprocal determination of the I and the not-I, an opposition itself instituted by the I.

Fichte's transformation of the problem of synthesis into a logic of posting is key to Hegel's idealism. Fichtean positing shifts the terms of Kant's critical philosophy, since it makes explicit the institution of the I and the not-I implicit in the Copernican Turn. He shows that the institution of this distinction makes possible not only the determinacy of an object of experience but also its intelligibility as the not-I disclosed by the activity of the I. By the same token, such institution makes possible not only self-ascription but also the intelligibility of the I as the structure of self-reversion that produces the I. Fichte, then, rejects the givenness of the manifold. To say that what is given in sensation must be *taken as* an indeterminate object (something somewhere and somewhen) is to say that what is given is posited by the I, since it is disclosed by the activity of the I in the first place. The mutual determination of the I and the not-I thus replaces Kantian subsumption. Synthesis is not a matter of unifying a manifold but rather of an opposition that sustains the reciprocal determination between the I and the not-I. Although Hegel adopts the Fichtean notion of positing and its emphasis on opposition and negation, he rejects absolute indivisibility. For Hegel, the work of synthesis is irreducible.

CHAPTER 3

Actualization: Hegel

The status of Hegel's idealism shifts dramatically from the 1802 *Faith and Knowledge* to the 1807 *Phenomenology* and the 1812–16 *Logic*. In *Faith and Knowledge*, Hegel develops Kant's insight in terms of the ontological relation between thought and being. In the *Logic*, Hegel develops a post-critical understanding of the relation between concept (*Begriff*) and objectivity (*der Objektivität*)—a distinction that rewrites the Kantian focus on cognition and object, as I will argue in detail in part 3 of this book.[1] This signals a shift from an ontological logic to a theory of normative authority. Hegel's engagement with Kant and Fichte in *Faith and Knowledge* is nonetheless the necessary starting point for considering the legacy of Kantian synthesis in his philosophy, since it sets conditions for the mature theories of determinacy and intelligibility elaborated in the *Logic*. First, Hegel must specify the notion of unity without relying on a theory of self-consciousness understood as transcendental subjectivity or absolute positing. Unity, for Hegel, is a matter of practices of rendering intelligible—*Geist*. Second, he must clarify that determinacy is a matter of division, thereby integrating a transformed understanding of Fichtean positing. Division, for Hegel, refers to the institution of a distinction that coextensively begins a process of *actualization* (*Verwirklichung*).

A POST-CRITICAL NOTION OF REASON

In *Faith and Knowledge*, Hegel credits Kantian philosophy for "being idealism because it [shows] that neither the concept in isolation nor intuition in isolation is anything at all; that intuition by itself is blind and the concept by itself is empty; and that what is called experience, i.e., the final identity of both in consciousness is not a rational cognition either."[2] Although Kant establishes the inseparability of concept and intuition, he betrays his brilliant insight by affirming that it is a description of *finite* cognition.[3] Kant, according to Hegel, turns the "abstractly idealistic side . . . into that which is in itself."[4] Rather than a description of finite cognition, the inseparability of concept and intuition must count as a "definition of the absolute," to use the language of the *Logic*.[5] Kant's critical epistemology *already* articulates the relation between thought and being that the critical project relegates to mere faith. Taking as his point of departure the central question of the first *Critique*, "How are synthetic *a priori* judgments possible?," Hegel argues that the unity of subject and predicate, concept and intuition, is an absolute ontological identity.[6] "[T]hese heterogeneous elements," Hegel writes, "the subject which is the particular and in the form of being, and the predicate which is the universal and in the form of thought, are at the same time absolutely identical."[7]

Kant's insistence on the heterogeneity of sensibility and understanding, concept and intuition, according to Hegel, bespeaks a metaphysical dualism that cannot be maintained on the basis of Kant's own critical epistemology. Already sensibility performs an ordering function, as we have seen, leading Kant to acknowledge that the activity of concept application by a self-conscious subject is involved in intuition. Following Fichte, Hegel argues that the distinction between cognition and object presupposes a distinction between the I and the not-I that, on the basis of the critical project, can only be conceived as the result of the activity of the I. A logic of positing institutes the opposition between subject and object, to use Hegel's terms. In Hegel's mature work, this is no longer a claim about epistemic objectivity that requires ontological grounding. It depends on a broader understanding of normativity, one that traces the distinction at work in Kant's critical epistemology to a distinction instituted by reason itself. We have seen that Fichte develops Kant's notion of autonomy as the structure of self-determination involved in positing. Reason posits the opposition of the I and the not-I. Hegel follows Fichte's reading of Kantian autonomy, yet he stresses that positing is a matter of *actualization*, which he understands in terms of normative authority. The activity of reason is a matter of distinction-making by and within a shape of *Geist*. The actuality of any given distinction is a matter of concrete conditions that make up a distinctive form of rationality or intelligibility. Hegel thereby expands the subject matter of a critical philosophy to an exposition of forms of rationality authoritative within a *Gestalt des Geistes*.

In *Faith and Knowledge*, however, Hegel argues that Kant's account implies ontological continuity, which is the ground for the unifying activity of transcendental subjectivity. Kant's language of "isolated faculties" is accordingly inappropriate. Reading Kant against Kant, Hegel turns to the notion of the productive imagination to develop the unity of thought and being. "Here," Hegel writes, "the original synthetic unity of apperception is recognized also as the principle of the figurative synthesis, i.e., of the forms of intuition; space and time are themselves conceived as synthetic unities, and spontaneity, the absolute synthetic activity of the productive imagination, is conceived as the principle of the very sensibility which was previously characterized only as receptivity."[8] In the first *Critique*, Kant elaborated the notion of productive imagination as a form of synthesis—*synthesis speciosa*. Kant explains that this type of synthesis is determining and hence a product of spontaneity, which means that it can "determine the form of sense *a priori* in accordance with the unity of apperception."[9] However, as the work of the imagination, rather than the understanding, this type of synthesis gathers and unifies the sensible manifold immanently. The figurative synthesis, Kant writes, "is an effect of the understanding on sensibility and its *first* application (*and at the same time the ground of all others*) to objects of the intuition that is possible for us."[10] The transcendental imagination is a mediating faculty, which functions as spontaneous synthetic activity albeit within sensibility. It makes possible the determination of the sensible given by the understanding. *Synthesis speciosa* is a *form* of form-giving that is neither associative (hence empirical) nor merely discursive. It makes possible *figures of determination*, which Kant ultimately calls "schemata."[11]

Kant's notions of apperception and figurative synthesis overlap, given that they are both forms of *spontaneity*. Hegel focuses on this overlap in order to bring into focus the *form of synthesis* Kant elaborated despite himself—one that is not based on a model of subsumption. The form of synthetic unity that the transcendental imagination makes possible is a form of spontaneity immanent in the sensible and hence also at work in receptivity. Synthesis is thus no longer a matter of bridging the sensible and the intelligible. It is a two-sided activity. On the side of the sensible, the synthesis is "blind" albeit synthesis nonetheless, while on the side of the intelligible, synthesis is "posited."[12] On the side of the sensible, synthesis is "immersed in difference," while on the side of the intelligible synthesis is the result of an activity of self-ascription. The "power of the productive imagination," Hegel concludes, is "the original two-sided identity."[13] The figurative synthesis articulates a notion of synthesis that follows a model of identity within difference, which Hegel argues makes sense of the inseparability of concept and intuition at the heart of Kant's critical philosophy. Synthetic unity, accordingly, must be understood not as "produced out of opposites" but rather as an "original identity of opposites."[14]

By emphasizing the productive imagination, Hegel is arguing for the priority of unity over division. Kant ultimately showed the originary status of identity, Hegel argues, in maintaining that the division involved in the subject and predicate, concept and intuition distinction is "posited" by self-consciousness.[15] Recognizing this inadvertent upshot of Kant's critical epistemology, Hegel poses the question "How are synthetic a priori judgments possible?" once more. He now replies: "They are possible through the original, absolute identity of the heterogeneous. This identity, as the unconditioned, sunders itself, and appears as separated into the form of a judgment, as subject and predicate, or particular and universal."[16] The elements of judgment that for Kant are heterogeneous, Hegel suggests, follow from a separation that institutes the distinction between subject and predicate, particular (intuition) and universal (concept) in the first place. It is the activity of distinction (or separation), its presupposed unity, and its entailed work of synthesis that Hegel is here beginning to elaborate. Hegel adds: "The productive imagination must rather be recognized as primary and original, as that out of which subjective ego and objective world first sunder themselves into necessarily bipartite appearance and product, and the sole in-Itself."[17] Unity is originary, given that it is presupposed in the opposition not only between subject and predicate, but also subject and object here understood as *subjective ego* and *objective world*.

The originary positing is originary, then, given that the distinction between the subject and the object is itself an institution, not a given. Unlike Fichte, Hegel maintains that such a primordial unity must not be understood on the side of apperception. According to Hegel, Fichte merely radicalizes Kant's subjectivism and formalism by focusing on the activity of self-consciousness now understood as positing. This leads Fichte to argue that the sensible is an external check (*Anstoß*) on the subject's activity of positing.[18] It further deepens Kant's dualism, Hegel maintains, since it dichotomizes the activity of positing and an absolute externality. "[T]he one side is absolutely not what the other is," Hegel explains in his engagement with Fichte in *Faith and Knowledge*, "and no genuine identity emerges from any linkage between them."[19] The assumption of unity within a logic of opposition that Fichte attempted to elaborate in effect affirms the Kantian notion of synthesis as *linking*, *bridging* two absolutely heterogeneous elements. The activity of positing is accordingly elaborated as "mere form, in abstraction of all content," and thus unable to give an account of actual or concrete determination.[20]

In *Faith and Knowledge*, Hegel emphasizes that "being and thought are one"—language akin to the pre-critical rationalist tradition.[21] Nevertheless, we get a glimpse of Hegel's mature understanding of intelligibility in his comments on reason. Recall that Hegel suggests that the transcendental unity of apperception and the figurative synthesis are one and the same synthetic unity. Hegel calls this one and the same synthetic unity "reason." In fact, he argues that "the imagination is nothing but reason itself."[22] "[T]he rational," Hegel adds, "or, as Kant calls it, the *a priori* nature of this judgment, the absolute identity as the mediating concept [*Mittlebegriff*] manifests itself, not in the judgment but in the [syllogistic] inference."[23] Reason for Hegel, I want to suggest, is neither an epistemic faculty nor an ontological principle. It is the *work of synthesis*. Although the details of this argument are worked out in the *Logic*, judgment is the division—the negation—of what is immediate whereby its boundary is transgressed and a new boundary is instituted. Negation institutes a boundary between a determination and its now established other. It thereby institutes an alternative unity, a new form of immediacy albeit a mediated immediacy. Patterns of inferences—the syllogism, the rational—are the basis for unity *in light of* this logic of boundary. A totality of relations of negation is gathered together by inferential patterns that thereby institute a concrete determination of reason. Reason can thus be thought of as concrete forms, figures, or shapes of rationality articulated by a process of actualization. For this reason, Hegel argues that the syllogism is the minimum unit of analysis for understanding individuality. Rather than a singular epistemic subject, then, patterns of rationality are the basis for unity or determinacy. Shapes of rationality, as we will see below, are concrete shapes of *Geist*. Patterns of rationality establish intelligibility at a given moment in time, given a logic of actualization.

Hegel's conception of reason—of *rational form*—in the *Logic* is developed under the banner of the idea (*die Idee*). The notion of the absolute idea that brings the *Logic* to a close and that I will consider in part 3 of this book transforms Kant's inseparability thesis from a matter of epistemic determinacy to a matter of normative authority. What is crucial here, however, is Hegel's *rejection* of an absolute unity. Such rejection represents a turning away from Kant and Fichte's understanding of synthesis and positing as requiring an originary unity. In the preface to the Subjective Logic, "The Concept in General," Hegel argues that although Kant has introduced "the extremely important thought that there are synthetic judgments *a priori*," and although he has proposed "one of the most profound principles for speculative development," namely, the "original synthesis of apperception," his notion of the concept is that of an "*empty identity or abstract universality which is not within itself a synthesis.*"[24] As an empty identity—crucially: *something that is not itself a synthesis*—apperception cannot account for the unity of that which is absolutely other to it. The unity between concept and sensuous reality is considered "*external* unity and a *mere combination* of entities that are *intrinsically separate*," which leads Hegel to argue that Kant has merely offered a faculty psychology.[25]

In contrast, Hegel argues that "the concept is to be regarded . . . not just as a subjective presupposition but as absolute foundation; but it cannot be the latter except to the extent that it has made itself into one."[26] The concept is not a presupposed foundation; it is not a unity that is not itself the result of synthetic activity. It is *made into* a foundation, it *counts* as a foundation, when it adequately expresses a form of rationality specific to concrete conditions at hand. The concept must make itself into a foundation, must establish itself as authoritative, given that it itself is a synthetic unity, a concrete form of rationality specific to the context at hand. Determinacy is not the result of the work of the concept, then, if we understand by concept an abstract rule or norm that makes possible the unity of an object of experience. It is a matter of distinctions articulated by and within specific concrete conditions—conditions that refer us to a specific shape of *Geist*. Any determination is maintained or debunked by the ongoing work of synthesis within and by concrete practices, discourses, institutions that comprise a shape of a world. But these practices and institutions are themselves synthetic unities. They are themselves sustained by forms of rationality and hence articulated by historically specific conditions. The concept must make itself into the foundation, then, because the normative commitment at work in the determinacy of any way of life is itself a concrete form of rationality that may or may not express or capture the conditions at hand. It may or may not be actual or, as we will see, authoritative.

Hegel's account of the actualization of the idea is the proper inheritor of the Kantian view of synthesis. The strictures of the actualization of the idea are elaborated in the *Logic* at a formal register, bracketing a substantive reference to *Geist* as the concrete ground of actualization. Parts 2 and 3 of this book are dedicated to explicating and assessing these strictures by focusing on the relation between determinacy and intelligibility developed in the *Logic*. While Hegel's theory of intelligibility is developed as a theory of normative authority under the banner of the idea, his theory of determinacy establishes the inseparability of form and content crucial for clarifying his view of the actualization of the idea. A logic of actualization indicates that intelligibility is not only historically specific but also precarious and ambivalent. The system as a whole—logic, nature, *Geist*—provides the context for fully elaborating *Geist* as the concrete ground of actualization. Such a task is beyond the bounds of this book. Hegel's metaphenomenological—philosophical—discussion of actualization, subjectivity, and history in the 1807 *Phenomenology of Spirit*, however, is a compact statement of the logic of actualization and its relation to *Geist*.[27] Turning to this discussion before moving on to the *Logic* allows us to see in nuce Hegel's understanding of *Geist* as the concrete ground of actualization. It thereby helps specify concretely Hegel's distinctive transformation of Kant's critical idealism.

SUBJECTIVITY, NEGATIVITY, GEIST

From the *Phenomenology* onward, Hegel understands division and synthesis as a process of actualization that entails externalization (*Entäußerung*) and recollection (*Erinnerung/Er-innerung*). Unity or determinacy, according to Hegel, is a matter of concreteness. Concreteness is the *result* of a process by which matters themselves—things, events, ideas, institutions—gather themselves out of their externality. As we will see throughout this book, externality refers to the totality of existent conditions that produce matters in the first place. The determinacy of matters themselves is accordingly the result of a process of instituting a boundary that establishes it as an individual *in light of* a totality of existent conditions that exceed it. That a thing, event, idea is always already outside of itself—determined by material, social, historical conditions that exceed it—is not to the detriment of the thing. Rather, it is the thing's way of becoming what it is. Hegel's signature argument is thus that the *self-negation* of any thing makes possible its actuality (*Wirklichkeit*). Actualization (*Verwirklichung*) is for this reason a process of "becoming other" that is also a "taking back" (*zurückgenommen*).[28]

In the Preface to the *Phenomenology*, Hegel's elaborates a conception of reason in light of this logic of actualization and develops his distinctive notion of subjectivity as negativity itself and as *Geist*. Key here is Hegel's insistence on understanding reason in terms of its actualization by characterizing reason as "purposive activity."[29] Hegel does not articulate reason's purposiveness in terms of a goal that is unambiguously actualized, thereby affirming a classical teleology of reason. Hegel argues that reason is purposive "in the sense in which Aristotle also determines nature as purposive activity."[30] But "purpose," he clarifies, "is the immediate, is what is at rest, is self-moving, that is, it is subject."[31] Reason is purposive activity in being nothing but the thing, event, idea's "power to move." The thing's power to move—its being-at-work—is its *subjectivity*. What does this mean?

In the Preface, Hegel speaks of subjectivity as "pure *simple negativity*."[32] It is "the bifurcation of the simple," he argues. As such, "it is the doubling which sets up opposition, and then again the negation of this indifferent diversity and its antithesis." Subjectivity is the activity of negation that divides what appears as an immediate unity. This division—this self-negation—is the dispersal of the previous unity into an opposition. This opposition reveals that the externality of what was seen as an immediate identity ("the simple") is essential to it. It reveals that such unity, which comprises a thing's intelligibility, is in fact a matter of a totality of existent conditions that exceed it. In dividing the simple, negativity makes possible instituting new boundaries and hence an alternative determination. It makes possible negating the "indifferent diversity" of a now dispersed identity, thereby establishing an alternative determination—a concrete unity. Precisely because a new determination is established, negativity can be understood as an activity that returns-to-self. It is because negativity establishes new boundaries that it can be understood as a process of actualization—a process whereby a thing, event, idea "becomes other" thereby "returning-to-self."

The crucial point is that negativity makes possible "*being-for-itself*."[33] Matters themselves are produced by a totality of existent conditions, yet they nevertheless express a *rational form* or, more precisely, a *form of rationality*. The universality that matters bear in their individuality depends on particular conditions at hand. Actuality should therefore be understood as a concrete form of rationality. But because the intelligibility of any thing depends on the concrete conditions that produce it in the first place, its form of rationality should be understood in terms of the self-determination of the thing itself. The form of rationality that things express, Hegel therefore argues, is their *subjectivity*. The "tremendous power of the negative" is accordingly the capacity of things to unfold in and through conditions that exceed them thereby exhibiting their own rationality—their subjectivity.[34] Because things themselves have the power to move themselves, to develop themselves through their own self-negation, they are forms of subjectivity. The actualization of reason is the *subjectivity* of things themselves.

This logic of actualization is crucial for understanding the central claim of the Preface to the *Phenomenology* and indeed of Hegel's idealism in general. In the Preface, Hegel famously argues that "everything turns on grasping and expressing the true not only as substance, but equally as subject."[35]

Becoming-other and returning-to-self is the process whereby, as Hegel writes, "being is absolutely mediated" and therefore it is "equally immediately the possession of the I, is self-like, that is, is the concept."[36] Actualization, then, is a process of "mediation" (*Vermittlung*).[37] We saw above that Hegel speaks of actuality as the subjectivity of things themselves. "Subject," accordingly, does not refer to a single epistemic, moral, social individual. It is the process of actualization. Things themselves articulate their rationality in light of conditions that produce, sustain, or call them into question. That being is mediated warrants that it is understood as subject—as that which determines itself through its self-negation.[38] Substance should be understood as subject. Hegel now adds that subjectivity refers to the process of actualization distinctive of *Geist*. Indeed, in the Preface, Hegel makes the very abstract logic of actualization much more concrete when he argues that subjectivity can also be called *Geist*. "[T]hat substance is essentially subject," Hegel writes, "is expressed in the representation that articulates the absolute as *Geist*—the most sublime concept and the one which belongs to modernity and its religion."[39]

Geist is not a "cosmic entity" or an "ontological principle."[40] Robert Brandom explains that *Geist* is "Hegel's term for everything that has a *history* rather than a *nature*—or, put otherwise, everything whose nature is essentially historical."[41] Taking Brandom's suggestion further, I argue that Hegel's logic of actualization should be understood as a matter of *Geist*. Rendering intelligible is a matter of historically specific practices that establish any distinction between nature and history expressed in Brandom's gloss. Accordingly, *Geist* is Hegel's term for historically specific commitments, practices, institutions that render nature, self, society intelligible. They establish the nature of nature, self, society within a specific context at a specific moment in time. Substance is subject insofar as existence is always already mediated—articulated—within and by commitments, practices, and institutions that comprise a specific *Gestalt des Geistes*. However, commitments, practices, institutions that make up a shape of *Geist* are themselves concrete forms of rationality, forms of mediation that depend on existent conditions. As a logic of *Geist*, then, actualization is an ongoing process of articulation through self-negation and return-to-self by and within practices and institutions that are themselves articulations, forms of rationality. It is a process of distinction-making and remaking that establishes forms of intelligibility specific to a form of life. In the Preface, Hegel speaks of *Geist* abstractly, as a process of actualization through self-negation. In the last chapter of the *Phenomenology*—"Absolute Knowing"—Hegel speaks of this process concretely via a discussion of history.

HISTORY

In the chapter on Absolute Knowing, recollection (*Erinnerung*) is tied to history as the process of externalization (*Entäußerung*) and inwardization (*Er-Innerung*). Hegel's notion of recollection in this chapter is both an account of the main normative commitment (freedom as self-determination) structuring a historically specific way of life (modernity) *and* the self-knowing involved in making explicit this normative commitment as a structuring commitment (philosophical reflection). Recollection is the activity of synthesis in two senses, then. First, recollection is the account of freedom as the main normative commitment at work in distinction-making and remaking within Western modernity. Freedom is thus understood as structural to intelligibility within this specific shape of *Geist*. Second, recollection is the philosophical work that the *Phenomenology* achieves.[42] The last chapter is a mode of "absolute knowing," since the philosophical reflection achieved represents modernity's assessment of its own commitment to freedom. Knowing is absolute, since it represents modernity's self-consciousness.[43] *Geist* knows itself as *Geist*, as Hegel says in the Preface.[44]

Hegel's notions of *wirkliche Geschichte* (history in its actuality) and *begriffne Geschichte* (conceptual history) are the central philosophical categories for understanding what Hegel calls absolute knowing. Conceptual history is history comprehended from the standpoint of absolute knowing, of *Geist* knowing itself as *Geist*.[45] History is conceptually grasped—*begriffne*—in three ways. These are three philosophical insights that represent different ways in which *Geist* knows itself as *Geist*. They are different aspects of the mode of self-knowing that Hegel calls absolute knowing. First, *Geist* comprehends itself as a specific form of life, as a specific *Gestalt des Geistes*. This comprehension involves the work of recollection: gathering, ordering, and hence determining events, ideas, norms, institutions as contributions to this specific *Gestalt des Geistes*. Second, *Geist* comprehends the work of gathering itself and thus the logic of a phenomenology of spirit. This insight transforms the phenomenology of spirit into a *science* of phenomenal knowledge (*die Wissenschaft des erscheinenden Wissens*). Third, *Geist* comprehends itself as the author of this way of life, which is to say that *Geist* realizes that its activity is constitutive of its shape. This insight, however, is not a metaphysical realization. It is the philosophical articulation of self-determination as the central normative commitment of modernity together with an assessment of freedom as self-determination in light of modernity's concrete development. Hegel explicitly discusses the first two modes of self-knowing under the banner of conceptual history and the third under the banner of history in its actuality also crucial to conceptual history.[46]

The notion of conceptual history that appears in the final lines of the *Phenomenology* is the philosophical articulation of the structure of recollection, which develops further the movement of externalization and inwardization that comprises the process of actualization. First and foremost, history is *Geist* in its temporal contingency, *Geist* in its *mere* existence.[47] Time, for Hegel, is nothing but the self-negation of something. Time itself is sheer negativity, mere vanishing.[48] In its "freestanding existence," a thing or event is something that comes to be and passes away. The externality of *Geist—Geist* in its temporal contingency—is thus existence that is *dispersed*. Scattered events have no authoritative meaning. In their isolation, events are not ideal. They are not understood *as* a part of a history. As such, they have not exceeded their momentary and necessarily destructible existence. They have not cheated their own demise ("annulled time," as Hegel provocatively says) by being gathered into a history.[49] An event is said to be contingent, then, if it is not considered as a moment in the development of a history, if it is not *taken as* part of the history of the present shape of *Geist*.

The crucial point here is that ideality—intelligibility—is the result of the work of *Erinnerung*. Recollection is a gathering of what is contingent into a sequence that makes up a history. History is a "succession of spirits, a gallery of pictures," each of which are "endowed with the entire wealth of *Geist*."[50] Now, *Erinnerung* is a reconstruction of the past from the perspective of the present that turns past events into a past, into a history. It orders moments that have been pointed out as significant contributions to a tradition or legacy. The perspective of the present—of present commitments—establishes an event, idea, norm as authoritative. History is thus existence or reality that has gained ideality, rather than reason that has realized itself in history. Events cheat the destruction of time, but they only do so by gaining normative authority. Although an event may survive its momentary existence by becoming a legacy, by becoming part of a history, its authority may collapse in the future. The work of recollection cannot secure the fate of the finite beyond all destruction and loss. Normative authority is never final or fully authorized. It is precarious and ambivalent. The *Phenomenology* itself, as we will see, documents the ways in which the authority of shapes of *Geist* collapses.

In becoming part of a history, an event becomes part of the "*conscious* self-*mediating* coming-to-be" of *Geist* in its contingency.[51] History is "conscious" and "self-mediating," for Hegel, because the activity of gathering makes possible *Geist*'s self-knowing. Absolute knowing, Hegel thus writes, "*gather*[s] *together* the individual moments, each of which in its principle exhibits the life of the whole *Geist*."[52] *Geist* knows itself—a form of life knows itself—by gathering itself into a narrative about how it has become what it is. Recollection, Hegel accordingly argues, is an inward movement (*in-sich-gehen*) and, ultimately, inwardization (*Er-innerung*). In gathering itself, *Geist* forsakes its *mere* existence. It reflectively understands how it has become *this* particular shape of *Geist*. Furthermore, it understands that recollection is its own activity and therefore that it is fundamentally historical. With these insights, history is no longer a gallery of images, a succession of events that reconstructs *Geist*'s becoming. History is now conceptually grasped—*begriffne Geschichte*. Absolute knowing is absolute, then, insofar as it is *Geist*'s knowledge of its history, the structure of ordering or form-giving, and its fundamentally historical character.[53]

The *Phenomenology* itself, as I mentioned above, reconstructs the idea of freedom central to modernity.[54] It is an account that gathers together moments in Western culture that according to Hegel contributed to an understanding of freedom as self-determination. As reconstructed in the *Phenomenology*, the history of *Geist* is the history of a *specific tradition*: the Western understanding of freedom. It is a history of the idea of freedom as autonomy or self-determination. Hegel thus submits to critical scrutiny epistemological paradigms, Roman philosophical positions, the medieval Catholic Church, eighteenth- and nineteenth-century scientific paradigms, Greek tragedy, the Enlightenment, the French Revolution, Kantian morality, versions of an ethics of conscience, and religions. As isolated positions, these shapes of consciousness (*Gestalten des Bewußtseins*) and shapes of *Geist* (*Gestalten des Geistes*) are untenable.[55] However, combined they are reconciled in or make up the history of this shape of *Geist*.[56] In the last chapter of the book, Hegel recounts the concrete development of this history in nuce. Moving away from a phenomenological treatment of these shapes of consciousness and shapes of *Geist*, Hegel's philosophical review of the development in this chapter adds crucial aspects to *Geist*'s knowledge of itself. The concrete development of modernity reveals not only the fundamentally historical character of *Geist* but also the structural precariousness and ambivalence of any shape of *Geist*.

Hegel opens the last chapter of the *Phenomenology* by recounting the most significant moments of a phenomenology of *Geist*.[57] The contribution of Kantian *Moralität* and an ethics of conscience, Hegel argues, are decisive.[58] Hegel is critical of both, but he argues that they contribute something crucial to an understanding of freedom as self-determination. How they fail is equally important. Their failure reveals structural features of the actualization of any shape of *Geist*. The earlier chapter on *Geist* ends with a scene of denied recognition, one that entails a form of reconciliation that Hegel calls forgiveness (*Verzeihung*). Conscience is a figure of acting consciousness (*das handelnde Bewußtsein*) whose moral ambiguity resides in claiming universal validity for her particular action. It is considered to be evil by judging consciousness (*das beurteilende Bewußtsein*), one among various versions of the figure of the beautiful soul that Hegel examines, since it aims at retaining moral purity and, to that end, is willing to withhold action. In an attempt to gain recognition of her conscientious act, acting consciousness articulates its position to judging consciousness.[59] In publicly declaring reasons for its action, acting consciousness submits to universal assessment. Acting consciousness confesses and expects judging consciousness to return recognition. Judging consciousness, however, refuses recognition and expects such refusal to be understood as evidence of *its* conscientiousness.[60] It thereby reveals itself to be base, vain, and hypocritical. Both acting and judging consciousness thus find their self-understanding *reversed*. These reversals establish, according to Hegel, that a consistent account of freedom requires abandoning the idea that self-determination is a matter of the absolute authority of the individual. It requires abandoning the fantasy of sovereign subjectivity.[61]

The reversals that acting and judging consciousness undergo are experienced as forms of injury, since they represent a violation of reciprocal recognition (*Anerkennung*). The back-and-forth between both positions, however, attests to *systematic* misrecognition and denied recognition. The scene of misrecognition and denied recognition is one that exhibits a logic of sheer or abstract negativity.[62] Oscillating between misrecognition and denial of recognition—perpetuating injury—allows for neither a shared past nor a shared future. Forgiveness, Hegel thus argues, breaks what would otherwise sustain a logic of injury indefinitely. In a scene of systematic misrecognition, forgiveness makes possible moving forward. The breaking of the hard heart is an act of *self-renunciation*—the hard heart lets go of itself, Hegel says—that makes possible reconciliation of two one-sided positions.[63] Forgiveness is a letting go of the other, and a finding oneself in this act of letting go. It is reciprocal recognition, which Hegel calls absolute *Geist*.[64] In negating abstract negation, the "reconciling yes" (*das versöhnende* Ja) that follows the breaking of the hard heart makes possible history. It makes possible determining a past as a past. Hegel thus provocatively says that the "wounds of *Geist* heal and leave no scars behind."[65] The wounds of *Geist* heal insofar as *geistige* creatures are the kinds of creatures that can convert the past into a past.[66]

Similarly, in the chapter on Absolute Knowing, Hegel states that forgiveness is a "giving up of self-sufficiency."[67] The point of returning to the notion of forgiveness, however, is *not* to say that history is modeled on a logic of forgiveness.[68] Hegel's reference to the earlier phenomenological treatment of forgiveness functions as a transition to a *philosophical* exposition of history. In this context, giving up of self-sufficiency is a recognition of a structural instability not only in action but also in the normative commitment that purports to make moral action intelligible—self-determination. Indeed, Hegel ends the book by arguing that recollection refers to the normative structure of history and incorporates what is revealed by the concrete development of the modern commitment to freedom into his account of the normative structure of history.[69] Absolute knowing is thus more precisely understood as the self-consciousness of modernity in its concrete unfolding. "The movement of propelling forward the form of its self-knowledge," Hegel writes, "is the work which spirit accomplishes as *actual history*."[70] Crucial here, then, is Hegel's discussion of *wirkliche Geschichte*.

History is actual, *wirklich,* when *Geist* knows itself as *Geist*. Hegel is here more precise than in his discussion of conceptual history, since he specifies that *Geist* knows itself as *Geist* when it grasps the main normative commitment structuring its specific shape. Note that Hegel ties the discussion of *wirkliche Geschichte* to the central gamble of the book—everything hinges on understanding substance as subject.[71] In the chapter on Absolute Knowing, Hegel argues that grasping substance as subject is an historical achievement. "[A]s long as spirit has not *in itself* brought itself to consummation as *Weltgeist*," Hegel writes, "it cannot attain its consummation as *self-conscious* spirit."[72] History in its actuality, Hegel goes on to argue, is achieved once we have overcome the religious representation of *Geist*. Religion is an institution, practice, and a mode of self-understanding that represents *Geist* to itself inadequately. In religion, *Geist* mistakes its own activity for that of an absolute other beyond this world.[73] *Geist* knows itself as *Geist* when it comprehends that its own activity is constitutive of its different *Gestalten*. *Geist* knows itself as *Geist*, in other words, when it knows itself to be the author of its institutions and modes of self-understanding. A philosophical rather than religious understanding of *Geist* is adequate, then, because it allows *Geist* to understand itself in light of its main normative commitment: freedom. History is *wirkliche Geschichte*, accordingly, when it makes possible *Geist*'s knowing itself as *this* specific shape of *Geist*, as a way of life structured by *this* particular normative commitment, modernity and freedom respectively.

By reconstructing freedom as the main normative commitment of modernity, a phenomenology of *Geist* allows self-understanding on the basis of this commitment. By giving an account of the normative structure of history, a *science* of phenomenal knowledge articulates that the norm central to this particular shape of *Geist* is not insulated from the effects of negativity. Rather than the unambiguous unfolding of modernity whereby freedom is brought to fruition, the concrete *actualization* of modernity expresses a structural precariousness and ambivalence. Indeed, throughout the *Phenomenology* we learn that the norm at work in recollection implies a forgetting. Consolidating a history on the basis of normative commitments entails that some events, institutions, modes of understanding are forgotten, buried, or made invisible. *Gestalten des Bewußtseins* and *Gestalten des Geistes* go under, are left behind, or do not at all appear in the book. Forgetting is not the only negative effect coextensive with recollection. Events, norms, modes of self-understanding may be pathologized, appear as deviant, evil, irrational: Antigone becomes a criminal, conscience becomes evil.[74] The norm itself may also legitimize institutions and modes of self-understanding opposite to the norm at hand: freedom turns into Terror in the French Revolution.[75] Even when enjoying normative authority, normative commitments suffer reversals into the very opposite of what they purport to represent, entail a correlative exclusion that compromises their identity, generate contradictions that sustain misrecognition. As the self-consciousness of modernity, then, absolute knowing makes explicit that precariousness and ambivalence are structural features of *Geist*.

At this point, Hegel's transformation of Kantian synthesis is in full view. A logic of actualization elaborates the Kantian problem of synthesis in a radical new direction. Mediation is understood in light of an irreducible negativity and negativity a matter of *Geist*. With these two claims, Hegel has resisted Kant's understanding of mediation in light of transcendental conditions that are not themselves forms of mediation, forms of synthesis. Additionally, Hegel has resisted Kant's insistence on the first-person perspective of a single epistemic or moral subject. For Hegel, then, there is no metaphysical principle or transcendental condition that is not itself a synthesis. Synthesis can only be properly understood in terms of historically specific commitments, practices, institutions that articulate the nature of nature, self, society. Hegel's post-critical philosophy of *Geist*, however, requires an account of rational form that accounts for intelligibility as a matter of actualization. This is the task of the *Science of Logic*.

* 2 *

Hegel's Critique of Reflection

The philosophies of Kant and Fichte, Hegel argues in *Faith and Knowledge*, give an account of faith rather than knowledge. Both Kant and Fichte pursue an account of determinacy based on the human standpoint, but end up giving up on knowledge altogether. For Kant, an emphasis on the human standpoint entails forgoing the task of elaborating the metaphysical assumptions implied by his sketch of the limits of finite cognition. Although Fichte's idealism aims to give such an account, he does not question the central assumption of Kant's idealism, namely, that the human standpoint can be surmised from the perspective of the single individual.[1] It is precisely the assumption that an affirmation of finitude requires privileging the first-person perspective that leads Kant and Fichte astray, according to Hegel. It leads both Kant and Fichte to an untenable metaphysical assumption—the absolute heterogeneity of the I and not-I. The philosophies of Kant and Fichte, then, express the opposite of philosophical humility. They reflect a culture committed to the thought that the authority of any epistemic or moral claim depends on the finite standpoint, but which ends up absolutizing finitude.[2]

Kant's transcendental idealism and Fichte's post-critical idealism, according to Hegel, are philosophies of reflection. They are committed to the Cartesian understanding of the subject as the ground for an account of objectivity. They maintain that determinacy is the result of structures of reflection that refer to the subject—for Kant, transcendental subjectivity, for Fichte, the absolute positing. Kant and Fichte's insistence on finitude, however, bespeaks a pernicious subjectivism. Their accounts of subjectivity imply an ontological dualism that compromises the very possibility of giving an account of determinacy and intelligibility. It reifies the distinction between mind and world, I and not-I, making it impossible to consistently account for the relation between the I and the not-I.[3] The absolute heterogeneity of I and not-I turn both into self-standing identities—givens, something beyond reason itself. They are unities that are not themselves syntheses, to recall the discussion of part 1 of this book. "The main principle common to the philosophies of Kant . . . and Fichte," Hegel writes, "is, then, the absoluteness of finitude and, resulting from it, the absolute antithesis of finitude and infinity, reality and ideality, the sensuous and the supersensuous, and the beyondness of what is truly real and absolute."[4]

Philosophically, then, the problem with the philosophies of Kant and Fichte is their inconsistency. Kant and Fichte affirm the opposite of what they set out to show. They affirm that the finite is absolute, but both actually show that the infinite is absolute. In affirming that human cognition cannot know things in themselves, that the truth is unknowable, Kant and Fichte in fact affirm that the unknowable is the true, that the infinite is the ground of the finite, that the infinite is in fact the absolute. This inversion, Hegel argues, is symptomatic of Kant and Fichte's philosophical treatments of determinacy and intelligibility. Despite their own accounts of reason, they fail to realize that the distinction between the finite and the infinite is a distinction drawn by reason itself. They fail to realize that conceptions of the finite and the infinite are conceptions of reason. Reason, Hegel argues in contrast, is the true infinite (*das wahrhafte Unendliche*). Not only is the distinction between I and the not-I instituted by reason itself. Reason is involved in making explicit that such distinction is its own institution.[5]

Hegel's rejection of the absolute as an infinite beyond (whether under the guise of the finite or the infinite) is crucial to specifying the *status* of Hegel's conception of reason as the true infinite. Under the banner of the true infinite, Hegel develops the thought that any concrete determination bears the structure of *self-relation* (*Beziehung-auf-sich*). Determinacy is the result of a structure of reflexivity that is not reducible to the subject. It is the result of a process of self-negation and return-to-self of matters themselves—*die Sache selbst*.[6] As we will see in part 3, in the Subjective Logic Hegel speaks of the rationality of matters themselves as their subjectivity. The Objective Logic, however, traces the failures of understanding mediation first as ideality (*Idealität*) in the Doctrine of Being and second as actuality (*Wirklichkeit*) in the Doctrine of Essence. Although the Doctrine of Being and the Doctrine of Essence cannot be equated, neither with respect to the position that each expresses nor the details of such positions, Hegel's critique of a *Seinslogik* and a

Wesenslogik overlap. Both misconstrue reflexivity.[7] Both reify the distinction between reflexivity and the individual thing, event, idea. As we will see, Hegel's critique of a logic of being and a logic of essence are critiques of realist and dualist metaphysics respectively. The former fails to recognize the role of mediation and hence reflexivity in the determinacy of an individual, while the latter does not recognize that reflexivity is not a matter of the imposition of intelligible form on indeterminate matter. Realism and dualism are thus, according to Hegel, forms of foundationalism.[8] Implicitly or explicitly, they understand reflexivity—mediation—in light of immediacy, of a merely given, of that which is in itself. They rely on a conception of mediation that is not itself mediated, of unity that is not itself a synthesis.

A logic of being and a logic of essence comprise "an immediate *ontology*," Hegel argues in the introduction to the *Logic*. They represent an investigation of the "nature of *ens*" and an investigation of "such particular substrata, originally drawn from the imagination, as the soul, the world, and God."[9] An Objective Logic, "*uncritically*" reifies being itself (*ens*) as well as essence (a psychological, cosmological, or theological principle of explanation). A doctrine of being and a doctrine of essence fail to consider the necessary relation of being and essence. They thereby fail to give a consistent account of determinacy—of the strictures of individuation. They take being and essence to be realities unto themselves, thereby failing to give an account of mediation. Unlike this "former metaphysics," "logic" investigates the "nature and worth" of conceptions of reality and ideality on the basis of their own assumptions. Logic, in the Hegelian sense, "considers them, not according to the abstract form of the *a priori* as contrasted with the *a posteriori*, but in themselves according to their particular content."[10] Logic brackets epistemological and ontological considerations and examines *conceptions* of the ideal and the real in order to assess the metaphysical position that such conceptions express. The first part of a science of logic is thus a "genuine critique" of the metaphysical assumptions of classical ontology and philosophies of reflection.

The Objective Logic is an immanent critique of a logic of being and a logic of essence through a *reductio* of the metaphysical positions that they represent. Hegel shows that the assumptions underlying each account are untenable. While a logic of being expresses an untenable realism by claiming that determinacy is an unmediated feature of being itself, a logic of essence expresses an untenable dualism by claiming that determinacy is mediated by a principle or activity external to being itself. A logic of being cannot adequately explain determinacy without appealing to structures of reflexivity that mediate what exists. Its claim to immediacy is shown to be inconsistent with itself. A logic of essence cannot account for determinacy without making sense of the reciprocal determination of reality and ideality involved in reflexivity itself. Its emphasis on the irreducibility of both ideality and reality is shown to be inconsistent with itself. "The subjective logic," Hegel argues in contrast, "is the logic of the concept—of essence which has sublated its relation to a being or to its *Schein*, and in its determination is no longer external but something subjective, freely self-subsisting, self-determining, or rather it is subject itself."[11] As we will see in part 3 of this book, the structure of self-relation that goes unaccounted for by a logic of being and a logic of essence is clarified under the banner of the concept in the Doctrine of the Concept.

Here I will consider Hegel's critique of reflection in the Objective Logic by examining his assessment of two key notions: ideality (*Idealität*) and actuality (*Wirklichkeit*). I will track Hegel's move from an account of ideality as the structure of self-relation involved in qualitative difference to reciprocity (*Wechselwirkung*) as the reflexive structure involved in actuality. This will provide a context for assessing the logic of the concept developed in the Doctrine of the Concept. Hegel's critique of reflection in the Doctrine of Essence begins to articulate Hegel's distinctive understanding of actuality as a process of actualization (*Verwirklichung*), which he glosses as a movement of externalization and recollection. What is significant about the account of actuality in the Doctrine of Essence is Hegel's stress on the reciprocal structure of externalization and recollection. The notion of reciprocity is thus key. Hegel's understanding of reflexivity as a reciprocal determination begins to establish that actualization is a process of matters themselves. The move from a logic of essence to a logic of the concept is hence a move from understanding reciprocity ontologically and toward a theory of normative authority. To begin, however, it is helpful to examine Hegel's notion of ideality in the Doctrine of Being. Ideality accounts for the structure of self-relation that Hegel ultimately calls the idea (*die Idee*). Hegel's notion of the true infinite—and its elaboration in the notion of ideality—is the first articulation of the reflexive structure of any given determination. It also accounts for the reflective standpoint of reason involved in any account of ideality or, in a logic of essence, actuality. The true infinite, then, begins to explain the structure of reflexivity involved in any individual as well as the reflection involved in a philosophical account of the strictures of individuation.

CHAPTER 4

Ideality

Famously, true infinity is "true," for Hegel, because it does not fall into the problems of the "bad infinite" (*das schlechte Unendliche*): an endless series or infinite progress that renders infinity finite. While the bad infinite as an endless series is best represented by the mathematical infinite, the bad infinite as endless progress is analyzed as the structure of Kantian and Fichtean morality.[1] As endless displacement perpetuated either by a sequence that proceeds to an infinitely smaller amount or by a ceaseless striving to a goal that is forever beyond reach, infinity is limited. For in being beyond reach, infinity itself cannot relate to the finite. What results from this becoming-infinite of the finite and the becoming-finite of the infinite is a ceaseless alternation between both—a back and forth between two forms of finitude. This alternation is held in check by the true infinite. In stopping an infinite regress or progress, the true infinite secures the possibility of the true and the good.[2] Hegel thus notoriously argues that "it is not the finite which is the real, but rather the infinite."[3]

The influential dialectic of the finite and the infinite in the opening chapters of the Doctrine of Being is a systematic undermining of an oppositional understanding of finitude and infinity. Bad infinity is the effect of understanding finitude and infinity in absolutely oppositional terms. The claims of absolute finitude and infinity collapse, since each in effect reverts into the other. This reversal reveals that each is dependent on the other. In thematizing their inseparability, Hegel maintains, true infinity resolves the contradiction that is generated by an oppositional understanding of these notions. Such resolution, however, represents the comprehension that neither finitude nor infinity can be held as absolute, pure notions, since neither is self-subsistent.

By undermining absolute conceptions of finitude and infinity, Hegel takes issue with, on the one hand, reductive accounts of finitude which deny the ideality of reality and, on the other hand, reductive accounts of the infinite which establish it as beyond being. These accounts not only imply a metaphysical dualism. They distort our understanding of the relation between reality and ideality. They, for example, sustain an untenable view of action, self, and society based on an appeal to a given, whether an immediate reality or an immediate beyond. Absolute notions of finitude and infinity also misconstrue the status of ideality, leading to an untenable view of the relation between philosophy and what Hegel calls "real science" (*Realphilosophie*). To think finitude consistently, Hegel argues in contrast, involves thinking infinity. To think reality consistently involves a notion of ideality.

Stephen Houlgate has given a powerful defense of Hegel's notion of the true infinite. According to Houlgate, if one wishes to successfully challenge Hegel's notion of true infinity as itself an ontological notion that develops the rationality of being in itself, one must show that "being is consigned to endless finitude and repetition or conditioned by irreducible differences that render its union with itself impossible."[4] Houlgate declines pursuing this strategy, however, for methodological reasons. It is "less critical" than Hegel's presuppositionless philosophy.[5] In focusing on mediation and mediating conditions (e.g., time, history, so on), other thinkers "take more for granted" than Hegel. They assume rather than show that being is conditioned by irreducible difference. In contrast, Hegel refuses to begin with presuppositions about being. The self-relating and hence self-uniting idea is not a founding premise but the logical consequence of the ontological category of being.

Houlgate is among the most sophisticated Hegel commentators who have focused on the opening of the *Logic* as the locus for understanding Hegel's idealism. Since Schelling's critique of Hegel, the opening of the *Logic* has received considerable attention, thus putting in the shadow Hegel's own theory of determinacy elaborated in the Doctrine of the Concept. By opening the *Logic* with the thought of pure being, Houlgate argues, Hegel is able to arrive at the nature of being. This establishes, according to Houlgate, that Hegel's speculative logic spells out what is logically entailed by thought's awareness of sheer being, which is further extended to a claim about the rationality of being itself.[6] What is made explicit in thought thinking itself is thus not merely a category of thought. It is also a structure of being. The structure of self-relation that Hegel calls the true infinite is accordingly the ontological structure of self-relating being logically implied in the preservation of being despite the demise of finite things. "[T]ruly infinite being," Houlgate writes, "is simply the process whereby being unites with itself through the demise of finite things."[7]

While Houlgate's reading of the opening of the *Logic* is unmatched in its clarity and precision, his commitment to reading the *Logic* as both a logic and an ontology leads to an understanding of the true infinite that gives new grounds for reading Hegel as a pre-critical thinker.[8] Houlgate's gloss on ideality helps specify what he takes self-relating being to be for Hegel. Ideality, he maintains, implies the "self-determination of logos or the Idea at work" in the finite.[9] This claim is not restricted to a moderately rationalist view that determinacy involves the contribution of nonempirical constraints (concepts, principles) or that intelligibility is a matter of discursive articulation by and within practices and institutions. The claim is rather that nature and spirit *are* rational thanks to the self-determination of logos, which remains unscathed throughout the demise of finite natural or *geistige* things. The latter point is key. As will become clear below in the discussions of essence and, ultimately, the idea, the logos at work in the finite is nothing but the self-articulation of things themselves. Such self-articulation—the subjectivity of matters themselves—is ultimately a matter of *Geist*. Houlgate, too, suggests looking ahead within Hegel's system to shed light on his understanding of ideality. He also clarifies the notion of ideality by turning to Hegel's notion of *Geist*. For Houlgate, *Geist* follows the development of the idea, which "cannot be controlled or manipulated by human beings."[10] I will argue in contrast that rather than ontologically self-determining, the rationality or subjectivity of things themselves is a matter of historically specific commitments, practices, institutions. Lacking authority, the rationality of a thing, event, or way of life collapses. Thus, the idea or logos cannot remain unscathed. Indeed, Hegel understands ideality as a question of normative authority that is precarious and ambivalent.

THE CONTRADICTION OF BAD INFINITY

The most productive route to clarifying the status of Hegel's claim that finitude and infinity are inseparable is articulating the nature of the contradiction that is bad infinity. I will therefore track the series of reversals that lead to the bad infinite and, eventually, to its resolution in the true infinite. We must recall, however, the context of the dialectic of the finite and the infinite. It is part of Hegel's discussion of quality (*Qualität*) which first articulates the notion of determinatness (*Bestimmtheit*). It comes after Hegel's famous introductory remarks on the very beginning of a science of logic. I will not rehearse these famous arguments here, since they have framed the reading of the *Logic* in ways that obscure Hegel's overall treatment of determinacy in the Doctrine of the Concept.[11] What cannot be passed over in silence, however, is Hegel's insistence on beginning with a notion of immediacy—being (*Sein*). Immediacy, as we will see, not only fails as a stable starting point, but fails to be a coherent notion overall.

The *Logic* begins with the following *fragment*: "being, pure being—without any further determination."[12] The pure indeterminacy of being is but pure emptiness; nothing is intuited in this empty thought. Pure being is "nothing more nor less than *nothing*." However, in trying to think pure being, we find ourselves thinking nothing. Nothing, however, has a "meaning"—it *is*, or rather is being thought. To think nothing is accordingly to think something that *is*, although something that is purely indeterminate, which is to say: pure being. "Nothing is therefore," Hegel writes, "the same determination or rather absence of determination, and thus altogether the same as what pure *being* is."[13] This passing over of one into the other does not collapse one into the other, however. Being and nothing are distinct, though *inseparable* (*untrennbar*). Hegel describes this passing over as "vanishing" (*Verschwindens*) of one into the other, and argues that "[t]heir truth is, therefore . . . *becoming*, a movement in which the two are distinguished, but by a difference which has just immediately dissolved itself."[14] Becoming—the inseparability of being and nothing—is a "*determinate* unity, or one in which there being and nothing equally *are*."[15]

As Robert Pippin has convincingly argued, Hegel is here rehearsing the main tenet of the Copernican Turn—the irreducibility of mediation. Hegel begins the *Logic* by undermining the very possibility of thinking pure being. For this reason, the dialectic of becoming represents the first move in Hegel's *reductio* of realism. Hegel is here, then, not doing much.[16] For Houlgate, the suggestion that Hegel is offering a *reductio* is incompatible with the project of presuppositionless philosophy. A *reductio* would imply that Hegel is executing a strategy to prove what he has already understood determinacy to be. Being turns out to be becoming on its own accord, Houlgate argues, and thought realizes that this is the case by *attending to* the logical mutation of being into nothing and, ultimately, into becoming. What we are aware of is sheer indeterminate being; but being *shows itself* to also be a vanishing into nothing, and then to be becoming, and so on. Becoming eventually turns out to be nature and *Geist*.[17] Pure being is therefore not a mere category of thought or an untenable philosophical position.

I will discuss Houlgate's reading of Hegel's *Logic* throughout the next two sections. At this point, however, it is crucial to note that the mere thought of being represents sheer instability. It merely turns into nothing begetting a logic of becoming. A logic of becoming is burdened with the instability of a blind flip back and forth from being to nothing. In establishing that immediacy is untenable, becoming presses us to rethink the basis for qualitative determination. A logic of being does not appeal to a structure of reflection in accounting for qualitative determination. On the model of being, then, the most sophisticated determination is *Dasein*—existence, determinate being. Some thing (*Etwas*) is a finite thing that is subject to coming into being and passing away. Finitude is thus the first determination that gives content to the logic of becoming. It is a candidate for establishing the determinacy of being itself.

Now, the reversal of being into nothing leading to a logic of becoming sets the tone for the subsequent reversals in the Doctrine of Being and especially in the section on infinity.[18] The logical character of becoming is methodologically important, however, given the character of the reversals that take place: what is meant by the category of finitude is not what is actually said.[19] Hegel will exploit the inversion of what is said (*sagt*) and what is meant (*gemeint*) throughout the dialectic of the finite and the infinite. He transitions from bad infinity to true infinity by noting that one must only be aware of what one is saying in order to grasp the notion of true infinity already present before us.[20] Rather than pointing to the role of language in *Logic*, reversals of the said and the meant answer to the philosophical strategy of the *Logic*.[21] If absolute claims revert to their opposite, then the challenge lies in thinking them together.[22]

A finite something, Hegel tells us, is that which finds its truth in its *end*, in the fact that it will inevitably cease-to-be or perish (*Vergehen*). "When we say of things that *they are finite*," Hegel writes, "we understand by this that . . . nonbeing constitutes their nature, their being."[23] Thus understood, finitude is "negation driven to the extreme," which reinstates the "opposition of nothing and perishing to being," an opposition which gives rise to the dialectic of being and nothing with which the Doctrine of Being begins. Like the category of nothing, finitude is here "fixed negation," sheer negativity.[24] The nature of the finite, we are led to believe, derives from it having no affirmative moment. Accordingly, the nonbeing of the finite is made "imperishable and absolute."[25] What is said when finitude is understood as absolute—incorruptible negativity—is, in effect, the infinite: To say that perishing is the finite's "unalterable quality" is to say that the nonbeing of the finite is "eternal."[26]

For Hegel, the reversal of absolute finitude into absolute infinity—of perishing into eternity—needs to be further clarified.[27] "But all depends on," Hegel writes, "whether in one's view of *finitude* its *being* is insisted on, and the *transitoriness* thus persists, or whether the *transitoriness* and the *perishing perish*."[28] Hegel takes this to make explicit not that finitude is itself beholden to its own demise, and hence is itself so conditioned, but rather that sheer negation is negated. It is crucial to see why he thinks this. In holding on to a notion of sheer annihilation, pure nothing resurfaces. Yet Hegel has already shown that pure nothing is an impossible category, since its assertion is but an assertion of pure being.[29] For this reason, Hegel explains that finitude implies a logic of boundary that specifies the negativity of any finite thing as a matter of self-negation.

The finite, for Hegel, is fundamentally self-transcending. A finite thing can only be taken as such if it has a boundary (*Grenze*). By virtue of having a boundary, any finite thing posits itself *and* its other. In so doing, it has transgressed its limit. Yet a finite thing is such if it is *not* some other thing. The notion of a limitation (*Schranke*) follows from the notion of a boundary (*Grenze*). Some thing is limited—it both is and ceases to be itself—by having delineated what is beyond it. Any boundary traces what is on the basis of what it is not. This already announces the notion of *das Sollen*, since to say that something both is and is not is to establish what it is in relation to what it should be. What it is not has been established as essential to it. However, a mere ought cannot establish the determinacy of an individual insofar as the finite would always reach for an essence now deemed to be beyond it.[30] Still, the notion of boundary is key to understanding negativity as a matter of self-negation. Determinacy cannot be a matter of absolute self-identity. The determinacy of any finite thing must negotiate its unity on the basis of a boundary that immediately transgresses its own limit.

The negation of absolute finitude as sheer annihilation is the transition to a consideration of infinity. In denying any affirmative character to the finite, we cannot account for finitude, that is, for the continuation of the finite. According to Houlgate, Hegel here is noting that, in its demise, a finite thing leaves a trace of itself.[31] This trace is a negative that is also a positive. A finite thing's demise generates other finite things. When we burn a piece of wood, for example, it is not nothing that comes of it, but smoke, ashes, etc.[32] The wood is no longer, but it leaves a negative of itself in smoke, which is another, positive finite thing: smoke. The demise of a finite something gives way to another finite something that comes-to-be of it, and so on to infinity. This endless continuation implies a preservation of the finite in its transformation into other finite things. Preservation implies the infinite.

All of this assumes, however, that Hegel's exposition makes an ontological claim about the alteration of things,[33] rather than a claim about what is implied in actual determination.[34] Houlgate takes the explication of the constitutive alterability of the finite to show the ontological construction of infinite being out of the demise of the finite. Unlike Houlgate, I argue that Hegel is questioning the cogency of the category of finitude understood as absolute. Hegel is spelling out what is implicit in the notion of finitude in order to think finitude consistently. Thus far the claim is that a consistent thinking of finitude involves more than sheer demise. Understanding finitude as sheer negativity cannot be maintained.

Although we are confronted with the fact that thinking finitude involves thinking infinity, this insight first leads us to construe endless finitude as a *qualitatively* different type of being. Thinking of a finite something involves thinking of a process of coming-to-be and passing away that exceeds it.[35] Unlike the finite, endless finitude is purportedly invulnerable to ceasing. In being invulnerable to ceasing, "[b]eing, absolute being, is ascribed to the infinite. The finite remains held fast over against it as its negative."[36] Infinity is construed as affirmative being. Through the negation of negation it has gained identity with itself.[37] Infinity is therefore the "other of the finite," and hence is "burdened with the opposition to the finite."[38] Both finitude and infinity are understood as absolute at this point: The finite is finite only insofar as its nature is nonbeing, and the infinite is infinite only insofar as its nature is being. The finite is the "series of existent determinacies, of realities," and infinity is the "indeterminate emptiness, the beyond of the finite."[39]

The result of this opposition is the alternating movement between finitude and infinity that comprises bad infinity. Hegel characterizes this movement as "tedious" and states that it is "only repetitious monotony."[40] It is the alternation of *one and the same content* because, in asserting that the infinite is the beyond of the finite, they are in effect "two finites."[41] Since neither finitude nor infinity reaches the other, these two absolutes, these two infinites, are rather two finites. While, as we saw above, the reversal of finitude into infinity questioned the notion of absolute finitude, the reversal of absolute infinity into finitude calls into question the notion of absolute infinity.

Bad infinity, then, is a twofold contradiction: understanding infinity as beyond the nonbeing of the finite reverses infinity to the negative of the finite, a nothing, an "indeterminate emptiness." In holding on to the claim that they are absolutely opposed, the finite and the infinite reveal that they are bound to each other, that the identity of each is dependent on the other. Bad infinity makes explicit that neither absolute finitude nor absolute infinity can be maintained in its purity because the alternation reveals that "each is in and through its determination the positing of its other."[42] In order to assert its own being, the other must emerge as other to it (endlessly).[43] The reversal of otherness into dependence reveals the entanglement between the finite and the infinite. What is recognized is their inseparability, which had been "*concealed* in their *qualitative* otherness."[44] True infinity is "implicitly present and all that is required is to take up what is before us."[45]

The crucial question, however, is how the inseparability of finitude and infinity should be understood. Houlgate argues that "truly infinite being is nothing apart from finitude but is simply the process whereby finite things constitute being that unites with itself."[46] Although he is correct to note that Hegel is taking issue with dualist conceptions of infinity, which would hold that the infinite transcends the realm of the finite and thereby exists separately from the finite, true infinity should not be understood as the process whereby being unites with itself. It is rather the comprehension of the inseparability of the notions of finitude and infinity. Hegel glosses this comprehension as the becoming infinite of the finite, and as the becoming ideal of the real.[47] The becoming infinite of the finite is a movement toward a consistent way of thinking finitude and away from thinking infinity as an ontological notion of being that is beyond the finite.

Now, Hegel speaks of the true infinite as a return to self and hence a restoration of being.[48] Such "restoration" should be understood as reality that is determinate, hence reflexive. This mediation is what Hegel speaks of as the ideality of reality. True infinity is a restoration because the entanglement of the finite and the infinite is a finding of "its own self in the other of itself."[49] Hegel takes this finding of the one in the other to collapse the dualism of the finite and the infinite. However, this is a return to self of *both* the finite and the infinite, so there is still some work to be done to collapse and not reinstate the duality. "[T]he finite and the infinite," Hegel writes, "are both this *movement* of each returning to itself through its negation; they are only as implicit mediation, and the affirmative of each contains the negative of each, and is the negation of the negation."[50] This return to self, Hegel argues, is a negation of the negation that each is for the other.[51] What does this mean?

Recall that Hegel characterizes the dualism of the finite and the finite infinite as the duality between determinateness (or reality) and the indeterminate emptiness. Accordingly, Hegel characterized the finite infinite as the negation of the finite. We arrived at a notion of infinity as that which is beyond the finite by rejecting our initial notion of finitude as sheer annihilation. This is crucial for understanding Hegel's obscure suggestion that we think of infinity as a return-to-self through a negation of *this* negation. Because the finite infinite—the infinite qua the beyond of the finite—is but the negation of finitude as sheer annihilation, the negation of the negation is a rejection of infinity as beyond the finite. This double negation is a return to the finite, to *reality*. It is, however, a restoration because the finite is now understood as ideal. "[T]he idealized is the finite as it is in the true infinite—as a determination, a content, a distinct but not a subsistent existent, a moment rather."[52] That reality is ultimately ideal answers to Hegel's insistence that determinacy involves more than the finite as the merely perishable. Determinacy is a product of nonempirical constraints that exceed yet make possible individuation—nonempirical constraints that, because of their iterability, exceed the finite qua merely perishing or vanishing.

Hegel accordingly argues that "true infinity, thus taken in general as *existence* posited as *affirmative* in contrast to abstract negation, is *reality* in a higher sense than it was earlier as *simply* determined; it has now obtained a concrete content."[53] Understanding Hegel's provocative claim that true infinity is "reality in a higher sense" is crucial. It is misleading to claim, as Houlgate does, that in characterizing the true infinite as reality in a higher sense Hegel is suggesting that there is a "nisus toward self-consciousness within the logical structure of being."[54] Being itself would prove to be rational and contain the germ of self-consciousness. I argue in contrast that the true infinite is reality in a "higher sense" insofar as it is the consistent thinking of finitude, whereby the rationality or subjectivity of the reflexive character of being is subject to destruction. The qualitative shift from bad infinity to true infinity is a transition from a dualistic understanding of finitude and infinity to a consistent understanding of finitude.

This qualitative shift allows us to avoid reinstating the ontological duality that we have seen Hegel criticizes through the notion of the bad infinite, since it is a "change in standpoint" for understanding the relation between the finite and the infinite, or the real and the ideal.[55] True infinity in effect allows the comprehension and thus resolution of the inconsistencies of absolute notions of finitude and infinity. True infinity clarifies what it means to think *finitude* consistently, since it articulates the constitutive perishing or vanishing of the finite together with its iterability and alterability. To say that true infinity is a consistent thinking of finitude thus means that the notion of finitude also involves the notion of infinity, that the notion of reality implies a notion of the ideality of reality. In thematizing the ideality of reality, true infinity is a metalogical standpoint that raises the status of thinking from finite to infinite.

Ideality, then, is the finite qua moment of a process that exceeds it. Note that to contrast the ideal and the real by aligning the former with the infinite and the latter with the finite would lead us back to the one-sidedness that the notion of the true infinite is supposed to resolve.[56] For this reason, Hegel is here calling into question the strict opposition between reality and ideality.

The crucial point is that implicit in such an opposition are incoherent notions of finitude and infinity. By undermining absolute conceptions of finitude and infinity, Hegel takes issue with reductive accounts of finitude that, in thinking finitude on the basis of annihilation, deny the ideality of reality. Hegel furthermore takes issue with reductive accounts of the infinite that establish it as the absolute other of the finite and hence as beyond being. For Hegel, such notions of finitude and infinity distort our understanding of the relation between reality and ideality.

IDEALITY: FINITUDE AND INFINITY OF AGENCY

At his point, it is helpful to turn to Hegel's philosophy of action for an illustration of such distortions.[57] Hegel's philosophy of action provides instructive examples of what he takes to be reductive notions of finitude and infinity. As we will see, Houlgate too follows this strategy. To begin, Hegel takes issue with reductive notions of individuality that do not take into account the *infinity* of agency. Hegel's famous critique of physiognomy and phrenology in the *Phenomenology of Spirit* is here relevant. It shows the distortion that occurs when the finite is severed from the infinite. Specifying the character and the behavior of a person by referring to physiological aspects alone in effect *reduces* the character of an agent to her immediate corporeality. Physiognomy and phrenology seek to establish a law-like relation between an individual's inner states and her organic nature. The mental, they suggest, is in a strict causal relation with the physical. Physiognomy seeks to establish a causal relation between an agent's facial expressions and her character. Phrenology seeks to establish a causal relation between the brain and spinal cord or the skull and the individual's dispositions. The "actuality and existence" of an agent is thereby, Hegel argues, reduced to a "thing."[58]

Against such a reductive view, Hegel argues that human action is *inexhaustible*.[59] Human action cannot be explained merely on the basis of a science of capacities, inclinations, and propensities.[60] Indeed, it cannot be explained only on the basis of the body.[61] These sciences cannot capture the complexity of an individual life extended throughout time and subject to change and alteration in light of variable social conditions.[62] In contrast, Hegel argues that individuality is the *result* of action. "The *true being* of a person," Hegel writes, "is rather *his deed*. Individuality is *actual* in the deed."[63] The crucial point, however, is that the determinacy of a deed depends on its reception within social space, in addition to depending on the agent's description of her actions. It is only through intersubjective uptake and public accountability of an initial intention unfolded publicly over time that an action (what was really done) and an agent's character can be determined. Accordingly, the character of a person can only be described and furthermore assessed in light of actual deeds. The temporal extension of a deed and the intersubjective nature of what was done establish that agency is *infinite*.

Agency is infinite, furthermore, given the normative expectations involved in establishing actions as intelligible. Institutions and modes of individual and collective self-understanding, Hegel argues, are crucial for establishing what was done and for establishing what was done as right or wrong, normal or deviant, in compliance or subversive. Yet the normative expectations structuring institutions are themselves never fully determined. They are revisable in light of internal contradictions that lead to the collapse of their normative authority. They are also reversible, given that they can generate opposite meanings and effects. In Hegel's famous account of Sophocles' *Antigone* in the chapter on *Geist* we see that Antigone and Creon act on the basis of normative expectations within Greek *Sittlichkeit*.[64] Creon forbids Polynices' burial, thus transgressing divine law, the law of the family. Following the divine law, Antigone buries her brother, yet such an act is a transgression of the law of the *polis*. It is only on the basis of the reversals that both Antigone and Creon suffer that their character or, in the case of Antigone, individuality, is determined.[65] Both act in accordance to expectations that structure their social roles, yet both find the meaning and effects of their actions reversed. The inexhaustibility of action as well as of the normative expectations that structure the social context in which an individual acts establish the infinity of finite agency.

Similarly, we find examples of what Hegel takes to be reductive notions of infinity in his critique of that which is beyond rational articulation or intersubjective authorization. Revelation and moral intuition are ways of thinking of the infinite reductively, since they are cut off from the possibility of giving reasons as the source of their normative authority. Hegel's most nuanced account is his critique of the beautiful soul in the *Phenomenology*. The moral genius, one version of the figure of the beautiful soul, is most relevant here, since it is a figure of radical subjectivism.[66] An ethics of conscience, Hegel argues, maintains that duty is "the law that exists for the sake of the self, not the self that exists for the sake of the law."[67] The moral genius emphasizes his capacity for binding himself to *any* maxim of his choosing.[68] In fact, the moral genius takes his capacity for binding as *divine*.[69] He contemplates the divinity of his actions as his own divinity. Now, the moral genius insists on absolute purity as a form of authenticity. Thus, he retreats from everyday life. The worship of the moral genius, however, requires life within a community of moral geniuses, where absolute sincerity is purportedly possible.[70] The moral genius is for this reason a form of religious fanaticism.[71] Yet the community of moral geniuses is the inverse of the unhappy consciousness. Rather than placing all authority in another world beyond this one, moral geniuses place all authority in their own selves. In so doing, they take themselves to be beyond rational articulation and intersubjective authorization.

Like any agent, however, the moral genius must *act*—"something must be determined by the individual."[72] Yet action compromises moral purity and, moreover, the absolute authority of the self. In the dialectic of acting consciousness and judging consciousness that continues Hegel's critique of the beautiful soul, Hegel makes explicit the failures of radical subjectivism. Judging consciousness (a version of the beautiful soul) regards acting consciousness as evil because, in acting, she has asserted her particularity but demanded universal recognition. In denying recognition to acting consciousness, the beautiful soul reveals himself to be hypocritical, since he regards this denial as evidence of his own conscientiousness.[73] The contradiction between his insistence on purity and the irreducibility of action, however, leads the beautiful soul to madness.[74] Indeed, the beautiful soul understands that, in action, purity and authority are compromised. In addition to hypocritical, the beautiful soul has revealed himself to be the ultimate expression of the "narcissism of the moral standpoint."[75] His insistence on authenticity, on absolute purity, has been shown to be a form of self-involvement. Rather than responsiveness to others, moral authenticity has led to moral indifference. The crucial point is that agents reveal themselves in action, and hence retrospectively, rather than in intention, and hence *ex ante*.[76] They are not the sole interpreters of their deeds; they cannot give final meaning to their actions. The infinity of radical subjectivism is thus shown to be *finite*, irreducibly dependent on intersubjective determination.

Houlgate also finds examples of ideality by turning to Hegel's notion of *Geist*. Recall that Houlgate glosses true infinity as the truth of the finite insofar as "all finite things are moments of the process of uniting-with-itself that being proves to be."[77] He adds that true infinity can be illustrated by Hegel's account of marriage or the state, which are "self-relating wholes" or "processes" in which an individual, by coming to form intimate bonds with others, acquires a new quality.[78] Presumably this means that one is not only an individual but also a citizen and a wife, since these institutions articulate social expectations and entitlements. They thereby provide the basis for accounts of individuals that exceed an order of explanation qua natural being. This would mean that an account of one's actions would refer to one's standing as a citizen or wife, rather than to one's standing as a natural creature. Houlgate, however, explains his reading of infinity by appealing to the idea as the self-determining logos that although immanent in the finite is not compromised by finitude. In fact, Houlgate writes that the logos "cannot be controlled or manipulated by human beings."[79]

To be sure, Houlgate does not argue that Hegel maintains that the finite and the infinite exist separately, since this would reinstate the dualism that Hegel has collapsed. Houlgate rather argues that the infinity of reason exists unscathed within the realm of the finite.[80] In contrast, I argue that rather than the self-determination of logos at work in the finite, the inseparability of the finite and the infinite establishes the precariousness and ambivalence of the ideal itself. This is not to say that ideality is precarious and ambivalent because it is corrupted or compromised by reality—by action, for example. The infinity of finite agency is nothing but the inexhaustibility of action as well as of the normative expectations that structure the social context in which an action is done. The finitude of infinite agency is nothing but the irreducible dependence on externality—on intersubjective recognition—that may challenge one's sense of self. Hegel's point is that ideality itself is finite, subject to the fate of the finite, since it is nothing but the *mediated* or *reflexive* character of the finite.[81] It is nothing but a set of commitments, practices, and institutions authoritative at a given moment in time. These commitments, practices, and institutions cease with the demise of the finite conditions that sustain them.

Reflection, Hegel argues in the *Logic*, refers to the reflexive character of actuality. Any given thing, event, idea is the result of concrete conditions that can be identified as essential only *after the fact*. Reflection should thus be understood in terms of a totality of conditions that produce a concrete determination but that can only be identified as necessary after the fact. This retrospective logic is appropriate for understanding the infinity of finite agency, the ideality of reality. It is only by acting, by externalizing one's intention in a public space, that the determinacy of what was done and who one is on the basis of what was done can be established. It is only after the fact that intentions can be specified—in light of competing interpretations of actions, of substantive misfires in action, so on.

Hegel's treatment of reflection in the Doctrine of Essence specifies determinacy as a matter of reflexivity. In the Doctrine of Essence, Hegel seeks to dispel the view that reflexivity—mediation, what Hegel calls "positedness" (*Gesetzsein*)—is the result of external reflection. The move from a logic of being to a logic of essence, as we will see, therefore consists in the transformation of negativity from qualitative difference to posited negation. This transformation of negativity signals a move from determinate being or existence (*Dasein*), developed in terms of the notion of ideality (*Idealität*), to posited being or positedness (*Gesetzsein*), developed in terms of the notion of actuality (*Wirklichkeit*). Negativity is now understood as externalization (*Entäußerung*) and self-relation as the result of the recollection (*Erinnerung*). The Doctrine of Essence, then, elaborates the strictures of the process of actualization (*Verwirklichung*) that we began to see in part 1 above and that is central to Hegel's logic of the concept that I will discuss in part 3 below.

CHAPTER 5

Actuality

What is under consideration in the Doctrine of Essence, Hegel writes, is "reflection generally."[1] Philosophies of reflection articulate mediation according to a metaphysics of essence. A logic of essence is a metaphysical position that understands the ground of phenomena in a principle or faculty beyond the phenomena at hand. Philosophies of reflection misconstrue reflexivity by understanding it as *external reflection*—as the result of an epistemic faculty or a metaphysical principle external to the phenomenon at hand or, more precisely, the matter at hand (*die Sache*). Disentangling our understanding of reflexivity from the dualism implied by a metaphysics of essence is the task of the second part of the Objective Logic. As becomes clear by the end of the Doctrine of Essence, reflexivity according to Hegel refers to the totality of conditions producing a concrete determination. A determination is therefore never a mere given but always already articulated by existent conditions. Reflection must thus be understood as the reflexive character of things themselves, rather than the activity of an I or the determining power of an extrasensuous principle. Reflexivity, in a word, is a feature of actuality (*Wirklichkeit*).

Hegel develops his distinctive understanding of reflexivity by elaborating a notion of actuality based on the idea of reciprocity (*die Wechselwirkung*). Reflexivity requires rethinking causality in a way that can account for the retrospective logic of positing (*setzen*). Positing is Hegel's term for the activity of mediation, while positedness (*Gesetzsein*) is that which has a concrete determinacy—that which is mediated. Positedness is a matter of concrete conditions that produce the thing itself (*die Sache selbst*). Reciprocity accordingly refers to the fact that the ground or cause of any given determination can only be specified *after the fact*. It elaborates the idea that cause and the effect fundamentally depend on each other. They are inseparable, albeit distinguishable. Distinguishing between cause and effect can only be done after the fact because their relation can be surmised once the process of actualization of the thing itself has come to its end. Hegel thus shows in the Doctrine of Essence that retrospectivity is an essential feature of reflexivity, of mediation. Ideality, for this reason, must be understood as the result of existent conditions.

Although a metaphysics of essence misconstrues reflexivity, a critical assessment of external reflection is important for understanding the work of negation in determination. It represents a move away from understanding negativity merely on the basis of the logic of the boundary. As we saw above, the logic of the boundary examined in the Doctrine of Being introduces the properly Hegelian notion of negation as self-negation. Any identity is such because it has boundaries and maintains itself by asserting its boundaries. A boundary, however, is something that marks a limit. Marking a limit is coextensively transgressing it. A boundary marks what some thing is on the basis of what it is not, establishing its opposite as intrinsic to it. Yet the logic of boundary only accounts for qualitative and quantitative difference, thereby failing to properly articulate the strictures of mediation. The logic of boundary cannot properly account for mediation, since the determinacy of an individual would be based on an infinity of possible rather than actual determinations. The determinacy of an individual could never be established if its qualitative or quantitative features solely depended on negative relations to others because it would have to be contrasted with an infinity of others, e.g., a finite thing that has the quality red entails that it is not yellow, violet, green, and so on.[2] A logic of boundary, in sum, cannot articulate the *self-relating* moment necessary for individuation.[3]

In the Doctrine of Essence, Hegel argues that ideality involves "immanently reflected being." Hegel characterizes qualitative difference as "existent negation," while he specifies positedness as "immanently reflected being."[4] "Quality, through its relation, passes over into an other," Hegel writes; "its alteration begins in its relation." "The determination of reflection, on the contrary," Hegel adds, "has taken its otherness back into itself. It is *positedness*—negation, which has however deflected the relation to another into itself, and negation which, equal to itself, is the unity of itself and its other."[5] In contrast to mere self-negation, reflexivity depends on existent conditions that articulate the singular determination in its externality. Concrete conditions are the source of relation-to-self. Mediation is thus a deflection—a turning or bending-backwards-into-self—from concrete conditions. Self-negation is accordingly a matter of *externalization*. What externalizes itself, however, gathers or recollects itself into a concrete determination. For this reason, it depends on the totality of concrete conditions that in effect sustain it. Mediation, then, is a process of externalization and inwardization. This establishes existent, concrete conditions as the essence of a given determination. Ideality cannot be specified *a priori*, then. Determinacy depends on conditions that are not only existent, but that can only be established as conditions after the fact. Because dependence on existent conditions makes possible a concrete determination, reflexivity can never be a matter of external reflection. It cannot be a matter of *possibility*, of an infinity of relations. It is a matter of *actuality*, of concrete conditions.

"Actuality" is the heading of the third section of the Doctrine of Essence. This third section is comprised of chapters on "The Absolute," "Actuality," and "The Absolute Relation." The most important discussion here is Hegel's defense of reciprocity in the chapter on the absolute relation. Now, the section on actuality is preceded, first, by a section on "Essence as Reflection Within" and, second, a section on "Appearance." The first section moves from a critique of external reflection that takes issue with Kant's notion of judgment in the *Critique of Pure Reason* and the *Critique of Judgment*, to an exposition of the determinations of reflection that takes issue with Kant's account of the Amphiboly of Reflection in the *Critique of Pure Reason*, culminating with an account of ground that explains what he calls the emergence of *die Sache* (the matter, the thing) into existence entirely on the basis of its own conditions.[6] The second section on appearance criticizes the distinction between reality and appearance by showing that the essential relation is a matter of the reciprocal relation between the outer and the inner, thus articulating the strictures of the classical distinction between appearance and reality as one that follows a logic of externalization and inwardization. Before turning to the section on actuality, then, it is instructive to recall the critique of external reflection. This discussion will help specify the logic of externalization and recollection that Hegel suggests in opposition to external reflection.

CRITIQUE OF EXTERNAL REFLECTION

In the section on *Schein*, Hegel writes that "essence is being that has been sublated in and for itself," and hence what "stands over against it is only *Schein*."[7] The opposition implied by this "confrontation" means, for Hegel, that essence determines being as the inessential. The truth of this opposition, however, is that being is determined not as the inessential but as illusory. In order for essence to be the truer, however, essence relies on being. This leads to the conclusion that essence rather than being is the illusory. Rather than the extrasensuous true, Hegel argues, essence is "absolute negativity." Essence is nothing but the negation of mere immediacy, of *Dasein*, of what is merely there. Philosophies of reflection, however, take essence to be form over against mere *Dasein*—the true over against merely illusory being, matter, sensuousness. The reflexive character of an individual is accordingly taken to be *opposed to* its being-there, its existence, its reality.

Essence, however, is "not being determined only as other," as it was in the Doctrine of Being; "it is being rather that has sublated itself both as immediate and as immediate negation, as the negation which is affected by an otherness."[8] This means that in being opposed to *Dasein*, essence too is an immediate and it too is opposed to its other. Essence therefore is also infected by the other, by being, by its dependence on being. A metaphysical or physical principle, for example, would be considered as the "truth" of nature, but in being understood as *opposed* to nature, it is a mere law infected by its instantiation in nature.[9] This conceptual confusion, Hegel argues, cannot make sense of the relation between law and nature. Law cannot explain the phenomenon that it purports to explain if it is taken to be external to it. Hegel's point here is that the opposition reduces negation, that is to say, form (the metaphysical or physical principle), to illusion itself. The reduction of not only being but also essence to illusion is the result of the notion of reflection at work—external reflection.[10]

The section on reflection is accordingly an account of the retrospective logic of positing developed out of the failure of external reflection. Unlike a logic of essence, which in effect establishes that both the essence and being are illusory, the notion of reflection maintains that immediacy is nothing but negation that has "returned-to-itself." "The self-relation of the negative is . . . its turning back into itself," Hegel writes; "it is immediacy as the sublating of the negative, but immediacy simply and solely as this relation or as *turning back from a one,* and hence as self-sublating immediacy. This is *positedness,* immediacy purely as *determinateness* or as self-reflecting."[11] The crucial point, however, is to understand the "self-relation of the negative" as a movement that is not imposed on *Dasein*. To begin, note that Hegel argues that reflection is *negated negativity*. It thus appears as a form of *immediacy*—a *congealed* mediation or determination. Hegel points out that this immediacy is simply a presupposition (*voraussetzen*). External reflection, in other words, is but a conceptual confusion. Hegel's point here is fairly simple. Negation implies negation of something. This something is an immediate determination; it bears an identity, it is an individual. Here, however, is precisely where the confusion of external reflection begins.[12] Because the activity of negation presupposes something that is negated, reflection is understood as beginning from rather than culminating in an immediate determination. It is therefore misconstrued as the imposition of form on an immediate determination, as the negation of something that is self-standing.[13] This fails to recognize that the negated negativity is an activity of *Dasein* itself.

Kant's insistence on understanding immediacy (what is given in sensation) and reflection (the nonempirical constraints on experience, e.g., the categories, the transcendental unity of apperception) as heterogeneous is perhaps Hegel's most obvious critical target.[14] For Kant, reflection is understood subjectively, as a function of the capacity to judge. Whether determining or reflective judgment, reflection in Kant is nothing but the negation of immediacy by an epistemic subject. Kant's revision of judgment in the *Critique of Judgment*, where he argues for a notion of reflection based on finding the rule (the universal) in the particular, rather than subsuming the particular under the universal, does not advance an understanding of determinacy.[15] Both models are based on the need to bridge the universal, aligned with the epistemic faculty, and the particular, understood as the sensible given. "[A] closer consideration of the action of external reflection," Hegel argues in contrast,

> shows it to be . . . a positing of the immediate, which consequently becomes the negative or the determinate; but external reflection is immediately also the sublating of this its positing; for it *pre*supposes the immediate; in negating, it is the negating of this negating. But in so doing it is immediately equally a *positing*, a sublating of the immediate negatively related to it, and this immediate from which it seemed to start as from something alien, *is* only in this its beginning.[16]

What is there, the given, is not actually an immediacy. It is always already posited, mediated, a "positedness." The immediate is not merely a presupposition of the activity of reflection. It is the product of the *ongoing* mediation of *Dasein* itself. Immediacy is posited being, and thus mediated being. Positedness has the character of an immediate, given determination in being the presupposition of the activity of negation, yet it is nothing but the result of mediation.

Self-relating negativity, then, is a notion that rivals the infinite beyond the finite of the logic of being. It is not an external ideality over against the finite. Rather, it is the self-gathering or self-articulation of the conditions that make up the thing itself. This ordering of the conditions of the thing itself is congealed into what appears as immediate determination, one that does not express the process of mediation that has produced it. For this reason, Hegel maintains that any account of determinacy must work *backwards*—it must reconstruct conditions of *actual* determination.[17] Contra Kant, then, Hegel maintains that determinacy is based not on necessary conditions of possibility, but rather on *sufficient* conditions of actuality. While the former sketches formal conditions that determine an indeterminate sensuous given, for example, the latter recounts the existent conditions that make up or produce a singular determination—an individual. An account of determinacy answers to the question *how actual*, rather than how possible.[18]

While reflection is "pure mediation in general," *ground* is "real mediation of essence with itself."[19] Hegel's discussion of ground is a transformation of the Leibnizian principle of sufficient reason. Leibniz's formulation of the principle of sufficient reason (to recall: nothing happens without a reason) is formal, according to Hegel.[20] The Leibnizian formulation takes the principle to be the ground of being as such. For Hegel, this is but another version of an external principle imposed on *Dasein*. In so being, it cannot account for actual conditions that can, in effect, count as a reason for an event or a determination. Such a ground, Hegel anticipates, is the concept.[21] I will come back to Hegel's notion of the concept in part 3 below. Here the point is that ground must be thought of as *determinate* ground. For this reason, Hegel moves on to show that the classical distinction between form and matter is spurious. The collapse of the distinction between form and matter will entail, Hegel will argue, a move to a consideration of the relation between form and content—a rewriting central to the Subjective Logic. Indeed, the move to the language of form and content is central to Hegel's signature notion of absolute form (*absolute Form*).

Form "presupposes matter as its other," Hegel argues, and for this reason is considered as the "active principle" that forms or informs matter.[22] Here again we see that philosophies of reflection fall into a simple conceptual confusion. Because form is an idea of the activity of form-giving necessary for determinacy, it presupposes a previously indeterminate matter. For Hegel, such a notion of form is self-defeating. It hinges on an understanding of form as self-subsistent, yet at the same time affirms that form is dependent on a presupposition: matter.[23] What is in effect established by the distinction between form and matter, Hegel argues, is their inseparability. For this reason, Hegel maintains that the activity of form is a movement belonging to matter itself. Matter is thus "just as much self-determined" as the purportedly self-subsistent activity of form. The unity of form and matter can be appreciated in light of the retrospective logic of positing that I discussed above. It is nothing but the positedness of matter. It is nothing but the form-determination of matter itself. The very notion of matter only comes into focus in light of being distinguished from or related to the notion of form. Any account of matter implicitly appeals to a metaphysical or physical understanding of this notion: as that which is indeterminate, for example.[24]

Rather than a distinction between form and matter, then, the philosophically significant distinction should be form and content. Content, according to Hegel, is the "identical" or "shared determinateness" of form and matter. It is the notion that articulates the inseparability of form and matter.[25] The notion of content replaces an appeal to matter on its own—without a consideration of how the notion of matter is already informed by physical or metaphysical assumptions about the relation between form and matter. I will say much more about the inseparability of form and content in part 3 of this book. For the moment, it is crucial to highlight that the move from matter to content allows Hegel to specify the ground-relation as a matter of conditions that bring into existence the thing, or matter, *die Sache*. The language of "bringing into existence" should not be read ontologically, however. Throughout the Objective Logic, as we have seen, Hegel criticizes the reification of conceptual confusions concerning classical metaphysical notions—essence, ground, so on. "Bringing into existence" refers to actual conditions that produce the thing itself, the concept of which must resist a dualism of form and matter if it is to be consistent.

Hegel accordingly argues that the relation of entailment—of condition and conditioned—is distorted when understood in terms of conditions and the *un*conditioned. Here again we have a version of the distinction between essence and reality, form and matter, metaphysical principle and sensuous reality germane to external reflection. Hegel's critique suggests rethinking ground in terms of a totality of conditions that "are in fact present."[26] The totality of conditions that must be present in order for the thing to come into being, to gain or have determinacy, refers us to the work of *recollection*, of *inwardization*, that results in any given concrete determination.[27] The unity of a manifold of conditions that make up the existence of the thing collapses the idea of an unconditioned condition. For this reason, Hegel argues that the matter at hand, the thing itself, is unconditioned—groundless: There is nothing behind it, no essence that determines a thing from behind or above, but the totality of conditions that are actually present.[28] In being nothing but the entirety of present conditions, *die Sache* is *thoroughly conditioned*, or what is the same according to Hegel, it is unconditioned. This alternative understanding of the notion of a ground shifts the Kantian emphasis on necessary conditions of possibility to sufficient conditions for actuality.

ACTUALITY AS ACTUALIZATION

Actuality, Hegel argues, is more precisely understood as a process of *actualization*.[29] Actuality is a process of actualization that reformulates the Kantian insistence on mediation from a model of subsumption to a model of recollection. Central to Hegelian actuality is the dialectic of the inner and the outer and, more specifically, the process of externalization (*Entäußerung*) and inwardization (*Erinnerung*).[30] Positedness is the result of the double movement of externalization and inwardization, self-negation and return-to-self. Hegel writes:

> Quite in general, everything real is at its beginning only an immediate identity of this sort, for at this stage it has not yet opposed and developed its moments; on the one hand, it has not yet inwardly recollected [*erinnert*] itself from externality; on the other, it has not yet *externalized* [*entäußert*] its inwardness, not yet produced itself out of it.[31]

Hegel speaks of this movement of externalization and inwardization as manifestation (*Manifestation*), but it is crucial to realize that manifestation here is not revelation or development of what is already presupposed as essential to the actual.[32] Hegel's notion of manifestation refers to the necessity of externality—to the fact that determinacy depends on existent conditions that can never be contained in or be merely internal to a determination *a priori* or, more precisely, *ex ante*. Hegel's thought is that any determination, any individual, is a determinate such-and-such by being outside of itself. My discussion of Hegel's philosophy of action in chapter 4 helps specify the point. The determinacy of what was done as well as the moral worth of the agent is not up to the agent or her intentions, but rather to conditions that are beyond her control—external to her, such as misfires, competing interpretations of her action, institutionalized normative expectations, so on. The temporal and spatial extension of an action is what establishes what the action really is as well as what it should have been. It is only through a development that goes beyond itself that the determinacy of an action and of an agent can be established. The idea that determinacy is the result of externality is key for understanding Hegel's notion of absolute form, as we will see in part 3. "Also, as the *manifestation* that it is nothing, that it has no content, save to be the manifestation of itself," Hegel writes, "the absolute is *absolute form.*"[33] Absolute form is decidedly a nonmetaphysical notion. It captures the thought that any determination is articulated by concrete conditions that are external to it—external because they are not specified *a priori,* before a process of actualization or, what is the same, manifestation, which is to say, of recollection out of existent conditions.

The chapter on actuality is a rewriting of modality that culminates in a notion of totality of conditions, which in turn yields a notion of absolute necessity. Here it is helpful to recall that in the first *Critique*, particularly in the Postulates of Empirical Thinking, Kant defines possibility, actuality, and necessity as synthetic principles of empirical cognition. Kant writes: "Whatever agrees with the formal conditions of experience (in accordance with intuition and concepts) is *possible*; That which is connected with the material conditions of experience (of sensation) is *actual*; That whose connection with the actual is determined in accordance with general conditions of experience is (exists) *necessarily*."[34] A given object or event is possible, for Kant, if it conforms to the strictures of human cognition: the pure forms of intuition, the categories, and the transcendental unity of apperception. It would not be a possible object of experience if sensibility and the understanding could not determine its unity, fix its determinacy. That which is indeed given in sensation is accordingly actual. What is actual, in other words, is materially connected to the objects of experience.[35] What is both given in sensation and determined by the sensibility and the understanding is necessary. For Kant, then, modality concerns the mode of the object in light of the strictures of human cognition and thus concerns modal concepts as schematized categories. Notice that the possible object is possible only given necessary conditions, while the actual is based on sensation whose determinacy is granted by necessary conditions. The necessary, finally, is what follows causality. Necessity has to do with the "existence of effects from given causes according to the law of causality."[36]

Following his critique of external reflection, Hegel transforms modality in a way that responds to the notion of ground that he has developed—ground now understood as a totality of existent conditions. Modality is no longer a question of the conditions of human cognition. Rather, it is a question of a logic of *reciprocal determination*. Reciprocity (*Wechselwirkung*) will transform the relation between contingency and necessity in a way that can account for the retrospective logic of positing. It therefore also transforms the notion of causality in light of the retrospectivity that we have seen is central to the process of actualization. Positedness refers to a condition that is revealed to be logically prior after the fact. We should therefore think of cause as determined as logically prior to the effect retrospectively, as what is presupposed in an effect after the fact. Showing that the relation between cause and effect follows this retrospective logic transforms the relation between freedom and necessity, Hegel argues. Freedom and necessity will need to be rethought in light of their reciprocal determination. Hegel's notion of *reciprocity* is thus key to a move from a logic of essence to a logic of the concept, therefore to the transition to the Doctrine of the Concept. In understanding the concept in terms of freedom yet in light of a logic of reciprocity, Hegel transforms the role that freedom plays in Kant's critical epistemology. Rather than the spontaneity of concepts and self-consciousness, freedom responds to the fact that reflexivity is a feature of a totality of concrete conditions.

The chapter on actuality contains three sections: formal actuality, possibility, and necessity—contingency; real actuality, possibility, and necessity—relative necessity; and finally, absolute necessity.[37] To recall, actuality is for Hegel best understood as a process of actualization, which requires externality. A formal understanding of modality cannot make sense of the fact that actuality refers to a totality of conditions. Formal actuality is existence, being, what is given. As such, Hegel argues, it is mere possibility. "What is actual is possible," Hegel says, given that existence is implicitly the "form-unity of the in-itselfness or inwardness and externality."[38] What is there, the immediate, is not yet actualized in not having negated and gathered itself in light of a totality of concrete conditions. A formal account of actuality therefore simply maintains that "everything is possible that does not contradict itself; the realm of possibility is therefore limitless manifoldness."[39] Actuality on this view is a matter of mere logical consistency among a totality of possible relations. Formal actuality is possibility that is merely consistent with itself. But in being tied to a limitless manifoldness, actuality is here mere indeterminacy; it cannot refer to concrete conditions. Kantian morality, for example, establishes a test procedure that depends on logical consistency.[40] The categorical imperative depends on moving away from concrete conditions of the ethical situation in order to establish the universalizability of action. It thereby depends on noncontradiction to secure the objective status of a given maxim of action. Taking the formal view of actuality on its word, Hegel argues that the problem here is that such limitless manifoldness merely generates contradiction upon contradiction. It is the unrest of condition and conditioned that cannot concretely establish what is the condition and what is conditioned. It cannot, for example, establish the institutional ground for the universalizability of an action, as Hegel famously argued against Kant.[41] Actuality is here only "*through an other* or in its ground and is at the same time the positedness of this ground and its reflection into itself."[42] In other words, actuality is the restless relation of ground and grounded that does not recognize their reciprocal determination. This restlessness, this bad infinity, is only able to establish that everything is contingent. The problem here is not that everything is contingent, but rather that the relentless flip back and forth between ground and grounded cannot specify a *concrete* ground. This failure points to the notion of necessity. It posits the *relation* between ground and grounded as itself necessary.[43]

The relation between actuality and possibility, Hegel moves on to argue, is determined as "relative." Relative necessity is a matter of real actuality, possibility, and necessity. The relation between these three aspects develops the dependence on the relation between ground and grounded, actuality and possibility. The notion of relativity or dependence is here crucial. It points to the necessity of the *activity* of actualization. "What is actual *can act*," Hegel argues; "something announces its actuality *by what it produces*."[44] Actuality is the result of a process of actualization via externalization and inwardization. What is actual is the result of a relation of dependence on, Hegel writes, "the determinations, the circumstances, the conditions of a something in order to discover its possibility."[45] This means that possibility, too, is bound up with concrete determinations, circumstances, and conditions. For this reason, we are no longer speaking of formal possibility, but neither are we speaking of necessary conditions of possibility. "The real possibility of something [*einer Sache*]," Hegel writes, "is therefore the immediately existent manifoldness of circumstances that refer to it."[46] The problem of an infinity of relations that cannot concretely sustain the actuality of any individual, however, comes up again. Real possibility requires a reflexive "return back into itself." So conceived, "[r]eal possibility thus *constitutes* the *totality of conditions*, a dispersed actuality which is not reflected into itself but is determined to be the in-itself of an other."[47] Here again Hegel argues that the point is that the notions of real possibility and necessity are inseparable, since the dependence on a totality of relations is based on a contingent presupposition. This expresses the "*in itself* or *in principle*" unity of necessity and contingency, which Hegel calls "absolute actuality."[48]

"Absolute necessity," Hegel writes, "is thus the reflection or form of the absolute: the unity of being and essence, simply immediacy that is absolute negativity."[49] Immediacy is absolute negativity, since what is simply there is posited, a positedness. Being is always already mediated. Hegel's point here is that mediation is necessarily a matter of an "affirmative multiplicity."[50] But absolute necessity is the form of the absolute, since it is the "absolute conversion of its actuality into its possibility and of its possibility into actuality."[51] The form of the absolute, of what is there in its positedness, is entirely dependent on a multiplicity of conditions. Possibility and actuality must thus be understood as reciprocally determined. What is necessary is based on a totality of conditions that are themselves contingent, relative. What is possible is determined by the necessity of such a concrete totality—a totality of contingent conditions. What is actual was possible because what is possible is a matter of actuality. For this reason, absolute necessity is "blind," which is to say, it is a matter of conditions or grounds that can only be specified retrospectively.[52] Conditions are themselves deemed necessary after the fact, which is to say, once they are gathered together in a concrete determination. What is simply there, or what is a mere possibility, is mere indeterminacy (mere immediacy) since it has not yet *acted*.[53] It has not yet manifested itself by articulating itself in and through contingent conditions that will establish the necessity of its individuality. Determinacy is a matter of concrete articulation. Necessity is a matter of contingent conditions established as necessary after the fact.[54] Actualization is thus a process of self-relation or self-articulation. For this reason, Hegel refers to actualization also as "exposition" (*Darstellung*).

That actuality must be rethought as the process of actualization via externalization and inwardization presses us to rethink the notion of causality in terms of reciprocity. The last chapter of the Doctrine of Essence thus elaborates self-relation in terms of reciprocity. Kant, to be sure, moved from causality to reciprocity in the categories of relation elaborated as principles of experience in the Analogies of Experience. For Kant, one of the most significant aspects of causality is irreversibility. On the one hand, irreversibility has to do with the linear notion of time that Kant elaborates in the Transcendental Aesthetic. Time as succession entails that events in time are irreversible. We cannot go back in time or establish that future consequences determine the cause of an object of experience or an event. On the other hand, irreversibility does not itself establish causal relations. It would be fallacious to argue that a temporal antecedent is the cause of a consequent. As Kant argues in the Second Analogy, the principle of causality makes possible the objective ordering of events in time. To be sure, Hegel does not make such a serious logical mistake in rewriting causality in terms of reciprocity. Nevertheless, Hegel's insistence on reciprocity has to do with the retrospective logic of positing that we have seen he develops in the Doctrine of Essence. It is thus important to note that the chapter on absolute relation takes the form of a *reductio*, where the logic of reciprocal relation is established as implicit in the notion of causality and substance. This *reductio* allows Hegel to argue, in the famous words of the *Phenomenology*, that everything hinges on understanding substance as subject. It therefore allows Hegel to move from a logic of essence to a logic of the concept, from an objective to a subjective logic.

What is crucial about Hegel's rewriting of Kant's categories of relation and of the Analogies of Experience is the activity of self-relation germane to reciprocity.[55] Absolute necessity represents Hegel's notion of self-relation, self-mediation, and crucially *self-determination*.[56] Indeed, necessity is understood in terms of self-determination. "Absolute necessity," Hegel argues, "is not so much the *necessary*, even less *a necessary*, but *necessity*—being simply as reflection. It is relation because it is a distinguishing whose moments are themselves the whole totality of necessity."[57] Hegel's notion of absolute necessity, as we have seen, refers to the inseparability of possibility and actuality. This inseparability is not ontological, but rather responds to the inseparability of the notions of possibility and actuality. It refers to the fact that the possible can only be consistently accounted for in terms of the actual, the totality of contingent conditions, and that the actual can only be consistently accounted for in terms of an implicit possibility articulated by such a totality of conditions. Absolute necessity, Hegel maintains, can thus be called *substance*.

Because actualization is a process of ordering a totality of conditions into a concrete determination, Hegel suggests, substance should be understood as "absolute power" (*die absolut Macht*). Substance is the power of "creation and destruction" that sustains the relation between actuality and possibility.[58] To say that substance is a power is to say that it "posits *determinations* and *distinguishes them from itself*."[59] Substance is the power of mediation through self-negation and self-relation that we have examined. It mediates itself, determines itself, through its articulation or exposition in existent conditions. Substance is thus no longer a metaphysical notion of that which is ontologically unconditioned or independent. Rather, it is the notion implied in the process of actualization. To recall, already at the beginning of the Doctrine of Essence Hegel displaced the dualist notion of substance as the unconditioned by arguing that implicit in the notion of unconditioned is the entirely conditioned. Substance is a matter of a totality of concrete, which is to say contingent, conditions established as necessary for *die Sache*. Substance, Hegel now adds, involves causality. It is, in fact, a cause for itself. It is an activity or power of self-production. Thus, it implies a relation between itself as condition and its products. According to the logic of positing that we have seen, the power of substance "expounds or explicates" what is in itself or immediate (and hence indeterminate) "*posited as positedness—as effect*."[60] Substance is the cause of itself insofar as it is nothing but the activity of positing, of negativity. Its products are nothing but the mediated character of what is there.[61] Determinacy is nothing but the result of the self-mediation of things themselves.

Hegel first discusses a formal understanding of the causality of substance. In this version, causality can show the necessity of the effect on the basis of positing itself. This simply means that a notion of causality entails that the cause posits the effect and the effect is implicit in the cause. Yet the coming into being of an effect, Hegel notes, vanishes or destroys the cause, and vice versa. Only a determinate relation of causality can explain the way in which the destruction of the cause in the effect is the positing of the cause, and the extinction of the effect is also the positing of a cause. Otherwise, an infinity of causes that have no intrinsic or necessary connection with their effects is asserted. This notion of causality would not be able to account for the determinacy of an individual. Here again the point is that the inseparability of cause and effect comes into view. The inseparability of cause and effect, "which was previously only *implicit identity*, the substrate," Hegel writes, "is therefore now *determined as presupposition* or *posited as against the efficient* causality, and the *reflection hitherto only* external to the identity is now *in relation* to it."[62]

Mechanism, Hegel argues, is the externality of causality, whereby the cause is a reflection of itself in the effect but the effect passes over into another substance.[63] The formal causality of mechanism expresses a relation between cause and effect where the cause entails the effect but the effect is not recognized as implicit in the cause. In reciprocity, Hegel maintains, mechanism is sublated. "[I]t contains first the *disappearing* of that original *persistence* of immediate substantiality," Hegel writes, "and "*second,* the *coming to be* of the *cause*, and hence *originariness mediating* itself with itself through its *negation*."[64] Reciprocity expresses that mediation itself is the originary. It is the ongoing process of mediation and therefore it is that which can be said to be the cause but also the effect. Reciprocity, Hegel thus argues, is "therefore, only causality itself; the cause does not just *have* an effect, but, in the effect, refers as *cause* back to itself."[65] It is causality itself because it articulates that the cause—the "originative being," that which is responsible for the production of a given determination—is just as much in the effect as the effect is implied in the cause.[66] Hegel thus boldly argues that in the same way that the effect can only be specified after the fact, on the basis of the presupposition of the cause, the cause can only be specified after the fact, on the basis of the effect.

The reciprocal determination of cause and effect, Hegel moves on to argue, transforms our understanding of the relation between freedom and necessity. The self-negation of substance does not culminate in "self-external substances," but a self-differentiation into a totality—it is the negation of the immediate and hence indeterminate into a totality of conditions that are not indifferent to each other but can be gathered together in a concrete determination. The immediate or indeterminate is now the "universal" and that which is actual, that which is mediated, is self-consciously mediated by a totality of existent conditions. With this account, we can now account for the determinacy of an individual. Notions of ground, cause, and so on essential for accounting for the determinacy of an individual can now be deployed dialectically, rather than dualistically. The reciprocal determination of cause and effect are now understood as inseparable albeit distinguishable. Now, the reciprocal determination of that which is a condition and coextensively itself conditioned is best understood in terms of a logic of self-determination. The universality (the ground, the cause) of an individual determination is not beyond it, but rather refers to the articulation of concrete conditions. "This is the concept," Hegel writes, "the realm of *subjectivity* or *freedom*."[67]

ACTUALITY AND FREEDOM IN THE *PHILOSOPHY OF RIGHT*

Before turning to the Doctrine of the Concept, however, it is instructive to examine the relation between actuality and the idea of freedom elaborated in the 1820 *Philosophy of Right*. Although a full account of the project of the *Philosophy of Right* is beyond the bounds of the present discussion, a brief survey of its main themes will help make Hegel's very abstract argument against external reflection and in favor of reciprocity much more concrete.[68] In the Preface to the *Philosophy of Right*, Hegel refers us to the "scientific method" developed in the *Logic* for the philosophical context presupposed in his account of the idea of right.[69] Freedom—the basis of right, according to Hegel—*ought* to be read according to the analysis of actuality sketched in the *Logic*.[70] This is a contentious claim. It is precisely the connection between logic, history, and politics that has established the notoriety of Hegel's *Philosophy of Right*.[71] Commentators have read Hegel's metaphysics of the idea ontologically, thereby insisting that the *Philosophy of Right* is an indefensible defense of the Prussian State.[72] By the end of the Objective Logic, however, Hegel has done nothing but *displace* an ontological understanding of classical metaphysical concepts. As we have seen, he has criticized the ways in which reified conceptual confusions about the notion of essence, ground, cause, and so on have led to untenable metaphysical positions. The above discussion of Hegel's notion of actuality allows me to delineate a rubric for understanding anew the connection between Hegel's metaphysics of the idea and modern ethical life as the actualization of the idea of freedom.[73]

The *Philosophy of Right* is concerned with the idea of right and its actualization.[74] The idea of right is *freedom* (*Frieheit*). According to the lesson of the *Logic*, the idea of freedom is a matter of a totality of existent conditions. According to the notion of reciprocity, freedom must be comprehended in terms of the totality of conditions that articulate it and that conversely it informs or articulates. Norms, practices, and institutions articulate a concrete notion of freedom, but that notion of freedom coextensively informs these norms, practices, and institutions. Rather than an abstract ideal, then, concrete norms, practices, and institutions are the minimum unit of analysis for an assessment of the idea of freedom. The idea of self-determination that sustains norms, practices, and institutions in their specifically modern shape, conversely, is the minimum unit of analysis for an assessment of the actuality of freedom within these practices and institutions. Freedom as self-determination is accordingly a product of and sustained by the institution of right, based on the notion of property; the institution of morality, based on an ideal of conscience; and the institutions that comprise ethical life—family, the sphere of market relations (civil society), and the sphere of political relations (the state).

It is a "capital mistake," Hegel argues, to understand freedom abstractly. In the Preface to the *Philosophy of Right*, he criticizes Plato's understanding of the ideal of justice as a philosophical fantasy. It neither responds to the strictures of concrete institutions and practices nor accounts for its origin in concrete practices and institutions.[75] The Platonic understanding of right would merely express an external reflection on freedom, one to be imposed blindly on concrete conditions structured by potentially competing normative commitments. Freedom is not a merely indeterminate idea, Hegel maintains, but only truly an idea if it is concretely worked out by and within real practices and institutions. Property, an ethics of conscience, the family, civil society, and the state are concrete institutions of a society in a given moment in time and not disembodied norms that ought to be affirmed throughout all time. These concrete conditions are the "externality" of the idea of freedom. According to the lesson of the *Logic*, they are the basis for the concrete articulation of the idea of freedom and hence the basis for assessing its actuality. This concrete articulation of freedom makes possible assessment of *this* society (modern, Western, European) in this moment in time (nineteenth century).[76] "*Here* is the rose, dance *here*," Hegel suggests rewriting the saying "*Hic* Rhodus, *hic* saltus."[77] A normative commitment is articulated and must therefore be assessed in terms of the concrete conditions that express or fail to express it.[78]

The necessary externality of the concrete idea of freedom entails that both the idea as well as the institution that expresses it lack full authority or stability. Hegel does not see this lack as a corruption of the idea but rather as a necessary part of an ongoing process of concrete articulation and rearticulation. Internal to the process of actualization is freedom's reversal into its opposite and into practices that counter its purported aims. The notion of property in which freedom is embodied in the act of taking possession or that is recognized in the contract is at the same time the necessity of material existence that many times turns into coercion and crime. Conscientious moral duty turns into bad conscience, hypocrisy, subjectivism, and irony precisely because it ties all moral authority to the individual. The good of civil society and the market economy, from modern infrastructure to entry and exit of economic relations on the basis of individual interests, is inextricably bound to poverty.[79]

To be sure, Hegel gives an account of the idea of freedom that involves a consideration of the appropriate institutional embodiment of freedom as well as the appropriate understanding of freedom given available practices and institutions.[80] He is careful, for example, to speak of a state in its mere reality (*Realität*) rather than in its actuality (*Wirklichkeit*), thus referring to institutions that do not in effect express the idea of freedom.[81] Yet in the same way that Hegel argues that the negative effects of an institution or normative commitment are intrinsic to it, he suggests equally immanent responses to the lack of authority and stability of a norm or institution. While the market economy makes possible individual freedom, poverty compromises its capacity to be an actual embodiment of freedom. Relations of solidarity in the corporations modeled on medieval guilds are an example of forms of solidarity that recognize the constitutive dependence on others for the actualization of one's freedom.[82] They are an immanent response to poverty.

The idea of freedom, then, gives itself actuality by gaining *rational form*. Freedom must be a *form of rationality* and hence a form of *institutional rationality*. It can only be consistent with itself as a normative commitment if it is expressed by the institutional context that appeals to it as its grounding commitment.[83] The idea of freedom is therefore nothing but an ongoing articulation of a set of commitments expressed by material conditions either negatively (in terms of what is lacking) or positively (in terms of what is working). For Hegel, this is both a claim about reality *and* ideality. It is a claim about an idea *as* a practice and institution and, conversely, a practice or institution *as* an idea. Institutions must reflect the idea of freedom and the idea of freedom must reflect its material practices and institutions if they are to be actual, *wirklich*.

The actualization of freedom is thus the gaining concreteness of a norm in terms of the totality of conditions that sustain it, or call it into question. The concrete institutions, practices, and forms of self-understanding that sustain the idea of freedom and vice versa can only be specified *after the fact*, once such a reciprocal determination has been worked out in action by and in specific historical conditions. It is not a matter of theory and for that reason theory is always too late. It is "only when actuality has reached maturity that the ideal appears opposite to the real and reconstructs this real world," Hegel writes, "which it has grasped in its substance, in the shape of an intellectual realm."[84] Given the lack of full authority and stability of a normative commitment, given the precariousness and ambivalence of a normative commitment, it can only be specified as an "ideal" retrospectively and provisionally. "The owl of Minerva begins its flight only with the onset of dusk."[85] The idea of freedom can only be determined after the fact, concretely, once it has a history.

* 3 *

Hegel's Idealism

"To consider something rationally," Hegel writes in the Introduction to the *Philosophy of Right*,

> means not to bring reason to bear on the object from outside in order to work upon it, for the object is itself rational for itself; it is *Geist* in its freedom, the highest apex of self-conscious reason, which gives itself actuality and engenders itself as an existing world; and the sole business of science is to make conscious this work which is accomplished by the reason of the thing itself.[1]

On the whole, the *Science of Logic* is Hegel's account of reason that, on the one hand, denies that reason is external to matters themselves and, on the other hand, denies that reason is an ontological constant that shapes history irrespective of differentiated material conditions. Hegel's conception of reason, however, is only elaborated in the Doctrine of the Concept, specifically in the last section—"The Idea." A Subjective Logic responds to the failures of an Objective Logic that I discussed in part 2 of this book. It articulates an understanding of determinacy central to an account of intelligibility out of the failures of a logic of being and a logic of essence. Albeit in different ways, a logic of being and a logic of essence both ontologize conceptual confusions regarding classical metaphysical concepts such as being, finitude, infinity, ideality, essence, form, ground, cause, and so on. In the Doctrine of Being, Hegel shows that ideality involves structures of reflection that can specify concretely the self-relating character of an individual in its self-negating structure. In the Doctrine of Essence, Hegel shows that the reflexive character of any individual can only be properly explained on the basis of a retrospective logic of positing and, accordingly, the reciprocal determination of ground and grounded, cause and effect. While the Doctrine of Being shows the self-defeating character of a realist metaphysics, the Doctrine of Essence establishes the equally self-defeating character of a dualist metaphysics. By the end of the Objective Logic, Hegel has suggested that reflexivity—mediation—is an ongoing process of actualization, one that involves the externalization and recollection of matters themselves.

Determinacy, then, is the result of a process of actualization. Actuality is the reciprocal determination of a totality of existent conditions that are established as necessary after the fact. In the Doctrine of the Concept, Hegel argues that the ideality of any thing is dependent on existent conditions, yet he clarifies that conditions comprise not only what the thing is but also what it should be. The point here is that things themselves express a *rational form*. Because the determinacy they bear depends on the conditions at hand, their actuality expresses a *concrete form of rationality*. Accordingly, a subjective logic establishes that reason is nothing but the form of rationality of matters themselves. Because the determinacy of any individual depends on the conditions that produce it in the first place, its form of rationality should be understood in terms of the *self-determination* of the thing itself. The form of rationality that things express, Hegel argues, is their *subjectivity*. To say that things themselves express a form of rationality, that they are forms of subjectivity, is to say that they bear intelligibility. That Hegel calls the rationality of matters themselves their subjectivity is no small detail. In the Doctrine of the Concept, Hegel transforms the meaning of subjectivity from the Kantian epistemic subject to the form of rationality of matters themselves. The theory of determinacy necessary for an account of intelligibility must move away from a critical epistemology to a theory of normative authority in the notion of the idea (*die Idee*).[2]

Hegel's transformation of the critical project is achieved in the last sections of the *Logic*, which are devoted to an account of the idea. Keeping in mind Hegel's critique of an objective logic is crucial for specifying the *status* of Hegel's notion of the idea. Hegel glosses the idea as the unity of concept and reality (*der Einheit von Begriff und Realität*).[3] Such a unity or inseparability, however, is not to be understood as ontological adequation. It is a matter of "the more particular unity of the subjective notion and objectivity" (*den bestimmteren [Einheit] von subjektivem Begriffe und der Objektivität*).[4] Intelligibility—the rationality of things themselves—is the result of the subjective notion, the determinacy specific to conditions at hand, and objectivity, "the total concept that has withdrawn into identity with itself out of its determinateness." The idea, in other words, is the inseparability of the determinacy of matters themselves and the concept that expresses this determination as a distinctive form of rationality. Above I mentioned that in the Subjective Logic Hegel argues that the rationality of matters themselves is a matter of existent conditions that articulate not only the concept of what a thing is but also the concept of what it should be. Hegel's notion of the idea accordingly articulates the thought that a form of rationality is not only determinate but concrete—which is to say, *actual*—when authoritative. Reflexivity as subjectivity is not merely a matter of what something is on the basis of what it is not (as in a logic of being). It is not a matter of what something is on the basis of existent conditions that make possible self-relation (as in a logic of essence). Reflexivity as subjectivity is a matter of what something is on the basis of what it should be—of distinctions made possible by concrete conditions and actual by the authority of reason.

In part 1 of this book, I argued that Hegel's idealism should be understood as a post-critical philosophy of *Geist*. The closing section of the *Logic*, "The Idea," contains Hegel's justification of the normative rather than ontological ground of determinacy. This is the key argument for his insistence on the necessarily historical character of intelligibility. It articulates the one ahistorical feature of intelligibility—the historical variability of rationality. The section on the idea, as we will see, articulates the formal strictures of rational form through a rewriting of Kant's account of cognition (*Erkennen*). Hegel's critique of Kant's account of theoretical and practical cognition establishes the relation between determinacy and normative authority. Normative authority does not refer to the authorization of a volition, institution, or object of experience by an individual moral or epistemic subject. It refers to the very structure of *bindingness* that sustains a historically specific form of rationality. Concrete forms of rationality, concrete conceptions of nature, self, society, are variable throughout time because they depend on their currency within practices and institutions of rendering intelligible: science, art, religion, philosophy. In the *Logic*, Hegel elaborates the structure of bindingness through a characterization of the absolute idea as personality (*Persönlichkeit*). I will argue that Hegel's insistence on describing the absolute idea as personality inherits the structure of Kantian autonomy yet transposes this structure to *Geist*. This fully develops his distinctive use of subjectivity as the rationality of matters themselves. It establishes that intelligibility is ultimately a matter of the authority of reason or, more precisely, of forms of rationality.

While Hegel's rewriting of Kant is achieved in the discussion of the absolute idea, the *Logic* ends with an account of method. Method is the universal aspect of the idea. This discussion is crucial. It allows me to develop the consequences of negativity for Hegel's understanding of intelligibility as a matter of normative authority. What Hegel calls absolute method (*absolute Methode*), as we will see, accounts for the account given in the *Logic*. It does so in two ways. First, the *Logic* ends with a statement on method, since it must give an account of reason as self-authorizing. Reason is self-authorizing in two senses. It is presupposed in an account of itself—in a science of logic. An account of intelligibility relies on its object of study, namely, reason. The circularity of the project of a science of logic is an acknowledgment that inquiry into the nature and history of any form of rationality depends on the work of reason itself.[5] The *Logic* articulates and authorizes a distinctive form of rationality, however—Western modernity along with its commitment to autonomy. Second, the *Logic* is straightforwardly an account of its own account of intelligibility. Method clarifies the notion of reason at work in and made explicit by a science of logic. As method, the idea makes explicit its own activity of rendering intelligible and what has been revealed by this activity. It does so through a discussion of what Hegel describes as the syllogism of method. The syllogism of method thematizes the work of dialectics, which Hegel glosses as the unity of the positive and the negative. Method thereby establishes that negativity is irreducible and allows us to draw the implications of negativity for the theory of normative authority offered under the banner of the absolute idea.

Central to Hegel's notion of the idea as method is his understanding of the relation between form and content. Recall Hegel's critique of the form/matter distinction in the Doctrine of Essence. There, Hegel argued that the philosophically significant distinction should be form and content. Content, he maintained, is the shared determinateness of form and matter. It is the notion that articulates the inseparability of form and matter. Content replaces an appeal to matter without a consideration of the relation between form and matter contained in any such appeal. In the Doctrine of the Concept, the structure of the idea is understood in terms of the notion of "absolute form" (*absolute Form*). Absolute form articulates the unity of form and content, which I argue should be understood as the *negativity of form* and the *necessity of content*. Form is nothing but the negation of immediacy. It requires content in order to be negation, to negate a fixed determination. Negation, however, yields an alternative determination—an alternative content. To speak of form and content rather than the precritical form and matter or, more importantly, concept and intuition makes possible understanding reason as a form of rationality that radically depends on content.[6] Moving from form and matter to form and content makes possible grasping that any given form of rationality is dependent on existent conditions that are always already mediated. Existent conditions are concrete precisely because they are mediated by and within an institution or practice—within a shape of *Geist.* The unity of form and content thus allows for an assessment of the *actuality* of a commitment, practice, or institution on the basis of its own historicity—on the basis of the fact that it itself is the result of mediation, that it itself is a historically specific form of rationality.

Hegel's notion of absolute form provides a rubric for reading the infamous passage from logic to nature that occurs at the end of the *Logic.* It thereby provides a rubric for understanding the signature development of Hegel's system from logic to nature to *Geist.* Logic—philosophy as an activity or practice of rendering intelligible—must go outside of itself if it seeks to assess concrete determinations of nature and *Geist.* It must become a philosophy of nature or a philosophy of *Geist* if it is to assess specific forms of intelligibility. It must therefore refer to practices, discourses, and institutions that articulate the intelligibility of nature and *Geist* in a given society at a specific moment in time. The negativity of form and the necessity of content allow us to go further, however. Forms of rationality are not only a historical product, but also necessarily precarious and ambivalent. Intelligibility is precarious, since it depends on historically specific practices and institutions that maintain or debunk concrete determinations of nature and *Geist.* It is also ambivalent, since any normative distinction contains within itself both positive and negative valences. They produce coextensive positive and negative effects even when enjoying authority. Specific conceptions of nature, self, and society can only be understood as positive developments of a history retrospectively and provisionally. They cannot be understood as final or fully stable.

CHAPTER 6

Form and Content

In the opening chapter of the Doctrine of the Concept we find the following curious passage:

> The universal is . . . *free* power [*die freie* Macht]; it is itself while reaching out to its other and embracing it, but without *doing violence* to it [aber nicht als ein *Gewaltsames*]; on the contrary, it is at rest in its other as *in its* own. Just as it has been called free power, it could also be called *free love* [die *freie Liebe*] and *boundless blessedness* [*schrankenlose Seligkeit*], for it relates to *that which is distinct from it as to itself;* in it, it has returned to itself.[1]

The passage is curious, given that Hegel's invocation of the category of love in the *Logic* is rare. Hegel mentions love as an example once in the Introduction to the second edition of the *Logic* and once in the chapter on Chemism.[2] The appeal to love as an analogy for the concept (*der Begriff*), however, is the sole use of the category of love (*Liebe*) in the *Logic*. Here Hegel likens the concept to free power and clarifies that, rather than violent, the power of the concept is like the power of free love. In maintaining or preserving itself through otherness, the concept is free power.[3] Yet this power to maintain itself is like the power of love, since it has authority over the other only insofar as it does not coerce. Instead, it inspires reciprocity. In love (according to Hegel), one becomes who one is through the beloved. It is only the beloved—only another who is utterly other to oneself—who can give one back to oneself, thus consolidating one's self-relation. The other, then, is constitutive for being oneself—*im Anderen bei sich selbst sein*. In invoking love, Hegel thus aims to make concrete the abstract claim that the concept is to be understood as "self-relating determinateness" (*sich auf sich beziehende Bestimmtheit ist*), which in the introductory remarks to the Doctrine of the Concept (in *Vom Begriff im allgemeinen*) Hegel characterizes as freedom (*Freiheit*).[4]

Note that love is the central category of Hegel's first attempt at developing a post-Kantian idealism that would do justice to Kant's singular contribution to philosophy. Throughout his time in Frankfurt (1797–1800), Hegel addressed what he took to be deep inconsistencies in Kant's critical philosophy initially via the category of love. Kant's morality, Hegel argued, inadvertently reverses to legality, mere lawfulness that denies inclination and feeling.[5] Kant's theoretical philosophy, Hegel furthermore maintained, represents the violence of discursivity on the sensuous. With the category of love, Hegel set out to give an account of the *unity* of morality and *Sittlichkeit*, of reason and sensibility. Love would articulate the speculative structure of identity within difference that could explain such unity. However, as Dilthey, H. S. Harris, and Dieter Henrich have shown, Hegel abandoned his early emphasis on the category of love first in favor of the category of life (*Leben*), finally settling on the category of *Geist* most prominently in the *Phenomenology of Spirit*.[6] Indeed, the romantic elements of love once thought to be most helpful in establishing absolute idealism—the emphasis on love as analogy for intellectual intuition and the longing for a lost unity—are not only no longer found in Hegel's mature idealism. They are themselves subject to Hegel's infamous polemics already in the *Phenomenology*.[7] By 1812–16, when the *Science of Logic* appeared, Hegel had altogether abandoned love as the central category for understanding a speculative logic.

Finding love in Hegel's *Logic* should thus make us pause. In likening the concept to love, Hegel is first of all offering a key to his brand of idealism. Hegel scholars at both ends of the interpretive spectrum we have considered have offered readings of this curious passage as support for their understanding of Hegel's idealism. Houlgate, as we have seen, argues that Hegel's logic is both an ontology and a logic. Consequently, the concept should be understood as "wholly self-determining, self-developing being."[8] Along this line, love clarifies that "the concept *lets* its differences emerge from its own identity. . . . [It] enjoys its identity only in letting those differences emerge as genuine differences and so letting itself become differentiated. . . . [I]t continues itself in that particularity and individuality and so is, in its other, in peaceful communion with itself."[9] In contrast, Pippin argues that Hegel's logic should be understood as a theory of intelligibility along Kantian lines. Accordingly, Hegel's discussion of the concept raises the question of the "normative authority of any concept."[10]

Rather than an ontology of self-determining and hence rational being, freedom is here tied to the notion of self-legislation central to Kantian autonomy.[11] The free power of the concept, however, "should not be understood as something like the legislative power over something separate and resistant. What is 'other' to the concept can itself play its role as other only so conceptualized."[12] The concept and its other are inseparable, yet for normative rather than ontological reasons. In being inseparable, the power of the concept entailed by the *freedom* of the concept is like the power of love—reconciliatory.[13]

While the passage on love in the Doctrine of the Concept indeed offers a key to Hegel's idealism, this passage offers insight into Hegel's understanding of *unity* that cuts across the debate concerning the status of his idealism. In the *Logic*, Hegel develops a notion of unity that is fundamentally different from that of his youth. Rather than establishing the ontological identity of the heterogeneous—of the rational and the sensible, of the transcendental and the empirical—the notion of unity elaborated in the *Logic* corresponds to the inseparability of form and content at the heart of Hegel's idealism. Form is nothing but the negation of immediacy. Negation, then, requires content in order to be negation, to negate a fixed determinacy. Conversely, the positive that results from negation is an alternative determination. Hegel's notion of determinate negation establishes that determinacy radically *depends* on the other. Moving further along in the system, Hegel specifies the other of the concept as spatiality, materiality, nature, and eventually *Geist*.[14] Love in Hegel's *Logic* is accordingly a love that is thoroughly conditioned by the other. It is *not* the unconditional maintenance of the self through an other that is dispensed with.

Now, the *Logic* is Hegel's systematic treatise on *form*. A science of logic makes explicit the inseparability of form and content *formally*.[15] In the *Logic*, unity is rethought as the structural dependence of form on content, given the irreducible negativity of form. Establishing that form is nothing but negation is therefore the crucial move for achieving the collapse of any form/content dualism distinctive of Hegel's idealism. In the Doctrine of the Concept, Hegel's understanding of unity is initially established through a consideration of what he calls Subjectivity (*Subjektivität*). In the chapters on the concept (*der Begriff*), judgment (*das Urteil*), and the syllogism (*der Schluß*) that comprise the section on Subjectivity, Hegel treats these classical notions of formal logic. However, Hegel's discussion of concept, judgment, and the syllogism is neither an account of logical validity, nor an exposition of epistemic authority, nor an argument that sustains a rationalist ontology.[16] In these chapters, Hegel is concerned with isolating form from content in order to establish the *absolute negativity of form*.[17] The unity classically attributed to form and understood as necessary for determinacy, Hegel argues, is not to be thought as exempt from division. Indeed, Hegel provides a trenchant *critique* of unity as an instance or principle that is not subject to negativity. Division is thought as *intrinsic* to unity. Yet division does not secure the seamless unfolding of an all-powerful concept. To think of division as internal to unity is rather to thematize structural constraints that must be reckoned with, namely, precariousness and ambivalence. The unity of form and content cannot therefore be thought of as an ontological unity, but neither can it be understood as reconciliatory, given structural precariousness and ambivalence.

A MATTER OF UNITY

It would seem that such a program for reading Hegel is difficult to accomplish, if at all possible. If one were to show that for Hegel negativity is constitutive rather than something to be reduced to unity in the early parts of the Doctrine of the Concept, one would need to provide a reading of Hegel's analysis of judgment that could temper his critique of judgment in favor of the syllogism. The chapters appended to Béatrice Longuenesse's 2007 English translation of her 1981 *Hegel et la critique de la métaphysique* propose this exact challenge. Especially in the chapter entitled "Hegel on Kant on Judgment," Longuenesse launches a thoroughgoing critique of Hegel's defense of the syllogism. Longuenesse writes that "one can hail only as a strange and grandiose philosophical novel Hegel's presentation of judgment."[18] She argues that Hegel pays a high price for his defense of the syllogism, one that provides grounds for rejecting the very project of a science of logic. Hegel's defense of the syllogism serves his untenable goal of transitioning from the "standpoint of finite consciousness to the standpoint of the absolute," which represents Hegel's problematic return to a precritical rationalism. By seeking to establish knowledge from the "point of view of God" and away from the "point of view of man," Longuenesse maintains, Hegel betrays Kant's critical philosophy.[19]

Recall that, for Kant, to judge is to unify or synthesize subject and predicate, concept and intuition.[20] Judgments are accordingly "functions of unity among representations."[21] In contrast, Hegel argues that judgment is a matter of truth.[22] Judgment according to Hegel, Longuenesse maintains, is a matter of the *agreement* of form and content. In the *Logic*, Hegel writes that "judgment is the self-diremption of the concept . . . the *original division* [*Teilung*] of an originative unity."[23] The goal of the movement of judgment is to restore (*wieder herzustellen*) the original identity of the concept.[24] The truth of judgment—and, by extension, the form of truth—is the syllogism.[25] In stating that the subject *is* the predicate, the copula already announces that "subject and predicate are *in and for themselves* the totality of the concept."[26] Although the agreement between or unity of subject and predicate implicit in judgment is already expressed by the copula, such unity is only *made explicit* in the syllogism.[27] The chapters on Subjectivity accordingly provide an exposition of the concept, its self-differentiation in judgment, and its return-to-self in the syllogism. This restoration of unity culminates in Hegel's exposition of the absolute idea with which the *Logic* ends. The absolute idea establishes the inseparability of subjectivity and objectivity, of form and content. As such, the idea is the "*adequate concept*, the objectively *true*, or the *true as such*."[28]

Although there are important differences between Hegel's early discussions of judgment and those contained in the *Logic* and the *Encyclopedia Logic*, Longuenesse maintains, Hegel's argument in the Doctrine of the Concept is akin to the one he rehearsed in his 1802 *Glauben und Wissen*. In *Faith and Knowledge*, Hegel spoke of "judgment as the self-division of *being*."[29] The signature division of judgment is established only against the background of the original identity of thought and being.[30] Accordingly, the identity of subject and predicate, for Hegel, expresses the original unity of thought and being, which in turn establishes the adequacy between cognition and object.[31] Hegel's dialectical transformation of judgment thus "brings together two classical definitions of truth: truth as correspondence, according to which truth is the agreement of cognition with its object, and truth as coherence, the agreement of the predicate with the subject of a judgment."[32] In so doing, Hegel has conflated logical with ontological relations, in the vein of the amphibolous rationalism of, most prominently, Leibniz. For Kant, form refers to the manner in which the combination of concepts in a given judgment is related to the unity of thought solely, without appeal to the content of concepts and therefore without reference to their material marks.[33] In contrast, rationalism holds that the combination of concepts depends on content—on the material marks contained in the concepts combined. Viewing the content of concepts intellectually, independently of sensible conditions, leads Leibniz to illegitimately move from the logical comparison of concepts to relations of agreement or conflict between determinations of things thought under concepts.[34] In particular, for the rationalist, modality expresses relations between things rather than concepts. On the basis of the fallacy of amphiboly, Longuenesse argues, Hegel's treatment of judgment should be regarded as a mere regression to the metaphysics of a bygone age.

Hegel indeed argues that the science of logic is "the science of the *absolute form* . . . [which] has in it a content or reality of its own."[35] There are crucial reasons, however, why Hegel thinks that logic is *in effect* a logic of truth and not merely a logic of validity. Hegel's main point is deceptively simple: In giving an account of form, we inevitably make assumptions about content. Hegel's analysis of form makes explicit the implicit appeal to content that is involved in assessing the validity of an inference.[36] Hegel does not, however, maintain that an account of truth ought to begin with an account of content and thus with the material marks of concepts. Neither does Hegel argue that material marks that comprise conceptual content are constitutive of logical form.[37] Rather, Hegel maintains that content *constrains* the truth of formal relations. The combination of concepts in judgments and syllogisms accordingly depends on content. If the validity of a judgment or inference appeals to the content of the concepts involved, then an assessment of the validity of judgments or syllogisms in effect amounts to an assessment of their *truth*. Now, Hegel insists that content is central to any account of form because he understands form as irreducible negativity. Indeed, negativity establishes *why* form depends on content. As we will see, the syllogism makes explicit the dependence on content on the basis of the negativity of form: formal relations—such as categorical, hypothetical, or modal relations—are based on relations of *exclusion* that depend on the content of the concepts combined. We might thus borrow Robert Brandom's terms and refer to Hegel's discussion of judgment and the syllogism as a discussion of "material inference," and his theory of determinacy as based on relations of "material incompatibility."[38]

Hegel's critique of judgment and defense of the syllogism, however, go further. In arguing that negativity is irreducible, Hegel refashions the notion of unity in a way that goes beyond the idea that determinacy is the result of relations of material incompatibility. Hegel's notion of determinate negation sets strictures on determinacy that are themselves irreducible. Clarifying that Hegel's signature emphasis on negativity imposes strictures on determinacy is crucial for understanding Hegel's provocative claim that the syllogism, as the form of reason, restores the unity of the concept dirempted in judgment. For Brandom, the upshot of Hegel's notions of determinate negation and mediation is an account of conceptual content as a matter of socio-historical practices. Accordingly, he argues that, for Hegel, "the content of concepts are identified and individuated by the functional roles they play in historically evolving webs constituted by relations of mediation and determinate negation, that is, by their material inferential and incompatibility relations to each other."[39] Negativity, however, establishes that division is internal to the unity of any possible determination fixed by relations of material incompatibility within any given shape of *Geist*. Thus, negativity calls into question the assumption that the content of concepts retain stability when playing roles in historically specific forms of intelligibility.

JUDGMENT AS NEGATIVITY

The most productive way to assess Hegel's transformation of the notion of unity and develop the constraints that his notion of unity places on determinacy is to track his exposition of the concept, its self-differentiation in judgment, and its return to self in the syllogism. *Pace* Longuenesse, rather than representing a return to original identity, this movement is a systematic *reductio* of the very idea of unity as an instance exempt from division. Indeed, Hegel's discussion of the concept is an attempt to show the inseparability of universality, particularity, and individuality, and thus the irreducibility of division and difference.[40] Initially, the concept is understood in terms of immediate universality—"absolute self-identity," "simple determination."[41] However, precisely because of its universality, Hegel argues, a universal concept is *determinate*. The self-identity and simplicity of abstract universals is self-undermining. The determinacy of the universal qua universal shows its inseparability from the particular in the individual. The universality of the concept, Hegel maintains, is based on its function as attribute, class, and genus.[42] As Hegel puts it, the concept *gives content to itself* because it allows determinacy on the basis of attribute, class, and genus.[43] As we will see, the determinacy of the concept cannot be established without reference to the different types of judgments that Hegel examines in the chapter on judgment—the universal *red* is a quality that inheres in *rose* in the judgment "The rose is red"; the universal *flower* is the class under which *rose* is subsumed in the judgment "The rose is a flower"; finally, the universal *organism* is the genus of which *plant* is a species in the judgment "The plant is an organism."[44] As will become clear, the determinacy of the universal qua universal establishes the need to think of judgment rather than concept as the minimum unit of determinacy.[45]

Let us examine the genus–species relation, given that it is exemplary of determinate universality. As Richard Winfield explains, the universal has determinacy insofar as it is "identical with the difference it posits in virtue of being what it is."[46] The very notion of *organism*, for example, is *necessarily* pregnant with content *other* than reference to itself. In order to be universal, universal concepts—genera—must be differentiated into *particular* determinations—species. Thus, the genus *organism* is differentiated into the species *animal*, *plant*, or *single-celled life form*.[47] Genera retain their identity as universals in "remain[ing] unaltered" throughout its differentiation in species.[48] The very notion of *organism* remains self-identical because of its differentiation into particulars, but also because universal concepts can be the species of higher genera, thus, *life form*. Species, in turn, are "not different from the universal but only *from each other*."[49] We are therefore speaking of individuality, rather than particularity. Through this self-related *negativity*—the division implied by the differentia that differentiates the genus into species—the universal and particular can in fact be described as the being-for-self of this individual.[50]

The unity (or inseparability) of universal and particular in the individual is what Hegel calls "determinate universality" (*die bestimmte Allgemeinheit*).[51] Universality, particularity, individuality are moments or aspects of the concept. One should not insist on counting them, for they are neither different things nor discrete moments of the development of a thing. They are the formal aspects of universality as such.[52] The crucial point is that the concept qua universal is not divorced from content. Rather, it depends on content. This is not to say that universality is parasitic on any specific content. On the contrary, the point is a formal one—the very meaning of universality is structurally inseparable from an appeal to content, to particularity, which in turn comprises individuality. The content to which they will refer—specific class relations, for example—is not the subject matter of a science of logic. That is the subject matter of formal logic. One may analytically isolate the genus–species relations implicit in a universal concept, for example, but, on the formal register of a science of logic, the point is to make explicit the conceptual (*begriffliche*) distinctions inherent in universality as such.

Hegel argues that a discussion of the concept leads to a discussion of judgment. As I mentioned above, determinate universality establishes the need to think of judgment rather than concept as the minimum unit of determinacy. Determinate universality, Hegel tells us, is an "*immediate* unity in which none of these moments is posited as distinct or as the determinant."[53] Although the concept contains negativity and thus difference within itself, the unity of the determinate universal is understood as *immediate* (*unmittelbare Einheit*), since it "will constitute the *middle term of the formal syllogism*."[54] Objects of judgments and, furthermore, of judgments that comprise syllogisms are determinate—ultimately, concrete—universals.[55] They are totalities unto themselves, given the content contained in the concept. In Hegel's obscure words: "As individuality, the concept returns in determinateness into itself, and therewith the determinate has itself become totality. The concept's turning back into itself is thus the absolute, originative *partition of itself*, that is, as individuality it is posited as *judgment*."[56] Implicit in the discussion of the concept is the fact that the determinateness of the universal relies on a combination of concepts in judgments. Implicit in an atomistic understanding of the concept, in other words, is the combination of concepts.[57] The concept, therefore, was never a simple unity with self, but rather intrinsically divided—dependent on distinctions between concepts on the basis of their content.

Hegel thus opens the chapter on judgment by arguing that "judging is . . . *the other function* of the concept, for it is the *determining* of the concept through itself. The further progress of judgment into a diversity of judgments is this progressive determination of the concept."[58] Judgment is the function of differentiation, which determines "what kinds of determinate notions *there are*."[59] In the Analytic of Concepts, Kant argued that *any judgment* is analyzable with respect to its quantity (as universal, particular, singular), quality (as affirmative, negative, infinite), relation (as categorical, hypothetical, disjunctive), and modality (problematic, assertoric, apodeictic).[60] In contrast, Hegel maintains that there are four distinct *types* of judgments. There are distinct types of judgments because the combination of concepts in judgment depends on the content of the concepts and not solely on the form of judgment. Form *and* content characterize the four different types of judgments.[61] To be sure, Hegel himself simply rearranges Kant's own table of judgments.[62] Kant's heading of quality becomes judgment of existence (*Das Urteil des Daseins*). Under this heading, Hegel treats positive, negative, and infinite judgments that respond to immediate qualities. Thus, judgments of existence are judgments of inherence.[63] Kant's heading of quantity becomes judgment of reflection (*Das Urteil der Reflexion*). Under this heading, Hegel treats singular, particular, and universal judgments corresponding to relations of comparison, reflection, and abstraction. Judgments of reflection are thus judgments of subsumption. Kant's heading of relation becomes judgment of necessity (*Das Urteil der Notwendigkeit*), where Hegel treats categorical, hypothetical, and disjunctive judgments responding to essential or accidental relations. Hence, Hegel argues, judgments of necessity correspond to relations of genus and species. Finally, Kant's heading of modality becomes the judgment of the concept (*Das Urteil des Begriffes*), where Hegel treats assertoric, problematic, and apodeictic judgments responding to normative assessments. Judgments of the concept thus concern modality.

Longuenesse notes that the different types of judgment that Hegel analyzes "correspond to different moments in the progression towards the identity of predicate and subject in judgment and so to different contents for *both* predicate and subject."[64] She argues that these contents correspond to the determinations of *Sein* and *Wesen* laid out in the first part of the *Logic*—the Objective Logic—now "internalized within the process of self-division and return to self-identity of the concept."[65] As she reads Hegel, such a process of self-division and return to self-identity is an ontological one, not a logical one. In particular, Hegel's treatment of modality mistakes the transcendental for the empirical. For Hegel, modality pertains to the unfolding of form, different moments of the self-division of being qua concept.[66] To be sure, Hegel indeed states that the forms of judgments are "successive applications" of the categories of being, essence, and concept, thus following the overall movement of the *Science of Logic*. Yet as we have seen the movement of the *Logic* is a *critique* of realist and dualist accounts of determinacy, rather than an elaboration of the ontological identity of thought and being. The logic of the concept thematizes what is implicit in accounts of determinacy as sheer being or as the product of external reflection, as we saw in part 2. I suggest setting aside the assumption that the *Logic* offers an ontological account of the identity of thought and being, and assessing Longuenesse's critique on the basis of the notion of unity that she argues leads Hegel to commit the fallacy of amphiboly.

As Winfield suggests, the typology of universals that the taxonomy of judgment contains is the most significant aspect of Hegel's discussion of judgment.[67] The judgment of quality contains abstract universality; the judgment of quantity contains the universal of class membership; the judgment of necessity contains the genus; and, finally, the judgment of the concept contains the universal of normativity—the concrete universal. To begin, predicates of judgments of existence attribute immediately given qualities to a subject.[68] The universal—the predicate—is here merely abstract. Although it provides determinacy to the subject, it inheres in a subject whose determination is entirely different to it—for example, "The rose is red." The predicate (redness) is universal insofar as it is not reducible to the subject (the rose) that it is predicating. The universal has a determination independent of the subject and, accordingly, is susceptible to inhering in other subjects—"The car is red."[69] Subject and predicate are accordingly in a negative rather than a positive relation to each other; that is to say, they are independent from each other, indifferent to the purported identity announced by the copula. The rose is not redness; it can in fact be yellow or white. For this reason, the individual (this rose) can be said to be a particular; nothing else about it is mediated by its universal. Now, its particularity is mediated by contrastive relations—the rose is red, not yellow, not white, and so on. For this reason, qualitative judgments are infinite judgments. Given the indifference of subject and predicate in qualitative judgments, the infinity of contrastive relations can generate absurd modes of determination—"spirit is not red, yellow, etc., is not acid, not alkali, etc., or that the rose is not an elephant, the understanding is not a table, and the like."[70]

The universal of qualitative judgments, therefore, cannot provide determinacy in a satisfactory way.

The notion of an immediate universal turns out to depend on relations of class membership. Judgments of existence imply judgments of reflection, given that the individual is in relation to other individuals that fall under the same universal, the same class—red, white, yellow fall under the class color. The universal of the judgment of reflection is not merely abstract, and the individual is not merely immediate. What is more, the universal of class membership relates its members by ascribing qualities to one, some, or all members of a class—"some humans are happy"; "all human beings are mortal."[71] Belonging to a class, however, mediates the determinacy of individuals to a certain degree. Class membership leaves undetermined what other features distinguish members from one another. Judgments of existence and reflection (of quality and quantity) depend on content—on the material marks that comprise conceptual content. Judgments of reflection depend on judgments of existence, given that what defines class membership is an empirical matter, "to be decided by the corrigible labors of collection and comparison that uncover the family resemblances distinguishing natural, that is, empirically given, kinds."[72] As we have seen, attributing given qualities is the activity of judgments of existence. Judgments of existence refer to the purportedly immediate material reality of the concepts combined in the judgments. Thus, universality pertains to what is denoted rather than what is merely contained in the combined concepts. Judgments of existence and reflection thus concern the problem of observation and induction. This is not to say that Hegel has provided an account of the formation of concepts and their relation to material reality. He is rather giving an account of the logical strictures of observation and induction.

Unlike judgments of existence and reflection, judgments of necessity determine the particularity of individuality via genus and species relations, which Hegel argues are presupposed in relations of substance, cause and effect, and reciprocity.[73] The crucial point is that, in judgments of necessity, the differentia is established *a priori* rather than *a posteriori*. They express necessary relations—"the rose is a plant" rather than "the rose is red"; "gold is a metal" rather than "the ring is yellow."[74] In judgments of necessity, judgments about a determinate genus with respect to higher genera are possible.[75] The genus and its species are inseparable, yet not on the basis of dependence on material marks, although dependent on conceptual content. Conceptual content rather refers to the meaning of concepts, not to the material and thus empirical reference.[76] Content is one step removed from an account of the formation of concepts and/or their relation to material reality. The judgment of necessity thus works at an even higher level of formality than the judgments of existence and reflection. It concerns categorical, hypothetical (relations between ground and consequent),[77] and disjunctive relations (based on relations of exclusion)[78] on the basis of the meaning of concepts (and hence on conceptual content), while bracketing the question of the relation to material or empirical reality. For this reason, we can say that judgments of necessity are made on the basis of *reasons*. The appeal to content follows the strictures of neither observation nor inductive generalization. However, what establishes individuals as members of species is here, too, left undetermined. Differentiae within judgments of necessity only establish species, not individuals.[79]

In contrast, the judgment of the concept establishes the unity of universality and particularity in the individual. The judgment of the concept ties determinacy to normative judgments. This is not to say that determinacy is a matter of what ought to be the case, but rather that determinacy involves the *ought* structure, which Hegel takes to be the true relation of the object to universality or the concept.[80] What does this mean? As Longuenesse explains, "[t]he knowledge of the genus and of the way its specific differences are determined is what makes it possible to consider a thing *according to its own proper concept*."[81] The unity of universal and particular in the individual, Hegel argues, follows from understanding determinacy as *self-determination*. Understood as self-determination, determinacy is the product of an individual giving itself its own actuality. Hegel stresses that the concrete universal pertains to normative assessments that contain as "predicates *good*, *bad*, *true*, *beautiful*, *correct*, etc."[82] The crucial point, however, is the notion of self-determination at the heart of normative assessments of this kind—self-determination refers to the types of modal relations constitutive of identity and thus individuality. Modality is no longer a matter of reflective relations that establish what is possible or actual, contingent or necessary—as in a logic of essence.[83] Modality establishes identity on the basis of the *normative authority* of the concept. The determinacy of any given matter at hand (*die Sache*—the thing or the state of affairs) is established (or fails to be established, for that matter) in accordance with its own concept, rather than by appealing to immediate qualities or abstract relations of reflection. Accordingly, the universal is here not an external measure useful for testing the appropriateness of any given determination. Determinacy is the result of the normative authority of universal concepts inseparable from the particular matter at hand. The universal does not legislate *over* the particular, like free power, but rather draws its authority from its internal relation to its other, like free love.

Given the genus–species relation specified by the reflective judgment, assertoric judgments are those in which mediated or actual predicates can be asserted of subjects *immediately*: "The subject is a concrete individual in general, and the predicate expresses this same individual as the *connection* of its *actuality*, its determinateness or *constitution*, to its *concept*. ('This house is *bad*,' 'this action is *good*.')"[84] However, insofar as it remains an assertion without justification, it remains problematic—it could or could not actually be the case that the house is bad or that the action is good.[85] In other words, the judgment remains *contingent*—that is to say, *contingent on* or "*according to*" the constitution of the house, to keep with Hegel's example.[86] Such justification is provided by a consideration of the *constitution* of particular with respect to the universal. The subjectivity or actuality of any given matter at hand (of the particular) lies in its concept (in the universal). Hegel explains that "*both* sides of the subject, its concept and the way it is constituted [*Beschaffenheit*], could each be called its *subjectivity*. The concept is the universal essence of the matter at hand [*Sache*], withdrawn into itself, the matter's negative self-unity; this unity constitutes the matter's subjectivity."[87] Determinacy is established when the individual is shown to necessarily be the case on the basis of its own constitution yet at the same time in relation to its own universal aspect, its concept. This is not to say that the particular is subsumed by the universal, but rather that determinacy itself is established on the basis of the constitution of the subject matter as internally related to its own concept—"the house, as so and so constituted, is good."[88] In being able to establish that the constitution of a subject matter is in accordance with its concept, the apodeictic judgment can establish the necessity or *actuality* of the given determination.[89] In establishing that the concept or universal is authoritative, the apodeictic judgment is the "truly objective"—the "subject and predicate correspond to each other."[90]

We must keep in mind that Hegel's discussion of the judgment of the concept is not ontological or epistemological. Rather, he makes a set of claims about the logical strictures of individuality, which have to do with the normative structure of determinacy. It is also crucial to keep in mind that, in the *Logic*, Hegel is moving both progressively and regressively. The progression (or self-development) of the concept to judgment (and further the syllogism) is a regress, since it makes explicit the strictures implicit in the previous notion. The progression is also a progress insofar as what are clarified are the formal (or logical) strictures involved in determinacy.[91] Accordingly, Hegel's discussion of judgment ascends to higher levels of formality that, in effect, establish richer levels of concreteness. His treatment of judgment began with judgments that take as given the content of the concepts in reference to what they purport to denote on merely empirical bases. He then moved on to a consideration of a notion of concept containment and connection on *a priori* bases in reference to the differentiation of genera into species. Finally, he examined normative judgments that allow for determinacy on the basis of what is definitely the case, what is possibly the case, and what is necessarily the case according to the individual's *own* concept but depending on the very constitution of the matter at hand.[92] The apodeictic judgment thus arrives at much richer levels of concreteness than the judgments of existence in their supposed immediacy: the authority of the universal in apodeictic judgments is established on the basis of the very constitution of the matter at hand. Normative judgments thematize the mediated or conceptual character of any given determination. The universal is no longer an abstract predicate external to the particular that it seeks to determine, but is rather concrete.

Note that Hegel has *not* argued that judgment implies a primordial unity that it seeks to restore. On the contrary, he has shown that an account of determinacy that takes concepts as the minimum unit belies the difference and hence division internal to concepts. The move from concept to judgment explains why universals are to be understood not only as determinate but also as concrete. Accordingly, concepts cannot be understood in isolation from forms of judgments. That is to say, concepts cannot be coherently accounted for divorced from the logic of division and combination distinctive of the activity of judging. By the same token, judgments cannot be understood apart from concrete universals, the content of which is what establishes not only the validity of judgments but also—and more importantly—the truth of judgments, the way in which subjects and predicates are actually combined. For this reason, I maintain that it is precisely the idea of a primordial unity that Hegel calls into question. *Pace* Longuenesse, negativity, division, and difference are irreducible to the different types of judgment. What remains to be examined, however, is the transition of judgment to the syllogism, which purportedly restores the originary unity of the concept out of the division of judgment.

THE SYLLOGISM AS DETERMINATE NEGATION

The discussion of the apodeictic judgment is itself the transition to the syllogism.[93] With the apodeictic judgment, Hegel argues, we have before us "the *determinate* and *accomplished* [*erfüllte*] copula which hitherto consisted in the abstract 'is' but has now further developed into *ground* in general. It first attaches to the subject as *immediate* determinateness, but it is equally the connection to the predicate—a predicate that has no other content than this correspondence itself, or the connection of the subject to the universality."[94] The copula—which establishes the relation between subject and predicate—can now be read as a function of identity. The subject and the predicate share the same content.[95] At this point, the form of the judgment "has perished."[96] The concept or universal is now the "ground" of judgment, since the identity of the subject and predicate is established by the content that they both share. Such a totality was already intimated by the disjunctive judgment, and will be crucial for the disjunctive syllogism, which, as we will see, transitions from Subjectivity to Objectivity later in the Doctrine of the Concept.[97] Earlier in the chapter, Hegel argued that the species-genus relation implies a complex *totality*—a genus can contain many species, it can also be the species of higher genera. This totality implied in any given determination leads to the disjunctive judgment—"Color is either violet, indigo, blue, green, yellow, orange or red."[98] The crucial point is that the subject and predicate cannot be considered as two "self-subsistents."[99] Subject and predicate are rather inseparable; they determine each other reciprocally.

The reciprocal determination of subject and predicate announces that the truth of judgment is the syllogism. The syllogism, Hegel maintains, has the totality of the concept as middle term.[100] The relation between subject and predicate on the model of the syllogism is one of inferential patterns that fix determinacy within a system of relations. Accordingly, determinacy is a result of *inferences* or *patterns of rationality* rather than ways of unifying subjects and predicates. In implying a totality, the syllogism is the "form of reason" and not merely the form of limited cognition, of *Verstand*. Indeed, Hegel argues that the syllogism is "the rational."[101] The syllogism establishes that determinacy is dependent on a totality of relations implicit in the unity of any given matter at hand. Determinacy depends on inferential processes of *exclusion*—of negation—that fix identity on the basis of inferential relations that extend far beyond the particular matter at hand, but that are implied in the particular matter at hand. As Hegel puts it, "in reason the *determinate* concepts are posited in their *totality* and *unity*."[102] The truth of the division implied by judgment as combination is thus the totality of the concept. For this reason, Hegel argues that inferential patterns determine in relation to a totality of *actual* rather than possible relations, which will be crucial to understanding *objectivity*. The point is that inferential moves depend on the very constitution of the matter at hand.[103]

Generally speaking, a syllogism is comprised by three successive judgments. For Hegel, however, they are "determinations of form."[104] The significance of the shift from judgment to the syllogism resides in the fact that, according to Hegel, syllogisms are inferences on the basis of content. Syllogisms are determinations of absolute form, since they are determinations of form together with rather than external to content. The types of universality, particularity, and individuality that distinguish the types of judgment that we have examined are the basis for Hegel's typology of syllogisms.[105] The syllogism of existence (*der Schluß des Daseins*) relates qualitative judgments, where abstract universality predicates judgments of inherence; the syllogism of reflection (*der Schluß der Reflexion*) links quantitative judgments, where universality and particularity are united on the basis of class membership; and the syllogism of necessity (*der Schluß der Notwendigkeit*) links judgments of genus–species relations. Hegel examines three rather than four types of syllogisms. Crucially, what is missing is a syllogism of the concept. As we will see, the syllogism of necessity refers to sheer and thus *full* mediation. Complete mediation in effect *collapses* the syllogism. The collapse of the syllogism effectively expresses the self-mediation of the matter at hand—*objectivity*. Rather than a syllogism of the concept, then, the syllogism of necessity establishes the need to consider the mediation of things themselves. The disjunctive syllogism is the structure of complete mediation that itself expresses a form of immediacy—objectivity as the self-mediation of *die Sache*.

The most significant problem that the syllogisms of existence and reflection present and that the syllogism of necessity solves is the fact that the premises of a syllogism are simply *given*. An inference or inferential pattern may be valid, but it will be contingent on its given premises. Reliance on given premises implies an appeal to an unjustified principle or instance, thus expressing a form of foundationalism. It also belies that the premises themselves are conclusions, which is to say, the outcome of other syllogisms or patterns of inference. The reliance on premises that are merely given is overcome, however, if the syllogism is effectively understood as sheer mediation. The syllogism of necessity is more truthful, then, because it makes explicit that all elements of a syllogism are products of mediation, of judgments and, more importantly, patterns of inferences comprised of multiple judgments. For this reason, Hegel argues that "[t]he essential element of the syllogism is the *unity* of the extremes, the *middle term* that unites them and the *ground* that supports them."[106]

In the chapter on *der Schluß*, Hegel also moves in the form of a *reductio*. He begins with the syllogism of existence in which the terms are simply given—"immediate and abstract." For this reason, the relation between the terms can only be an external connection. The syllogism of *Dasein* is thus, Hegel argues, a formal syllogism.[107] Within the syllogisms of existence, universal, particular, and individual are aspects whose mediating capacity is determined by the position in which they are located, namely, as extremes or as middle term. Hegel discusses four figures of the syllogism of existence. For example, the first figure, I-P-U, has individuality and universality as its extremes and particularity as the middle term. Accordingly, the particular inheres in the individual and the universal in the particular; therefore, the universal also inheres in the individual.[108] "With respect to the side of the universal," Hegel writes, "the particular is the subject; with respect to that of the individual, it is predicate; or as against the one it is individual, as against the other it is universal. Since both these determinations are united in it, by virtue of this unity of determinations the extremes are joined together."[109] Hegel's exposition of the four forms of qualitative syllogisms explores the way in which all three elements of the syllogism (universal, particular, individual) can occupy different positions (extremes as well as the middle). The radical substitutability of positions establishes that each element will refer to an increasing number of possible combinations. This problem is compounded by the fact that, as we saw above in the discussion of the judgment of existence, predication is based on merely accidental relations. As Winfield explains, if all positions can be equally substituted, the very forms of universality, particularity, and individuality have been rendered meaningless.[110] Universality, particularity, and individuality can no longer be distinguished by the role they play. This is why the last syllogism of quality is the figure of U-U-U. What we encounter are infinite possibilities. But this means that mediation itself, determinacy itself, cannot be accounted for adequately. What is generated is a bad infinity that can only impose determinacy externally.[111] The inference is "subjective," and in fact, Hegel says, we are here speaking of *Verstandesschlüsse*.

The failure of the syllogism of *Dasein* reveals that in fact each term "contains in it the reference connecting it to others, and the determination of the middle term is not just a determinateness opposed to the determinations of the extremes but contains these extremes *posited* in it."[112] Each term essentially "shows in or is reflected into the other."[113] The truth of the syllogism of *Dasein* is thus the syllogism of reflection. We begin to see that mediation is revealed to be irreducibly concrete. The term reflects its identity through the other, as Winfield puts it. The syllogism of reflection pertains to class membership. A class is mediated by its members and members are mediated by being grouped into a class. Accordingly, inferences are drawn on the basis of relations of one, some, or all members of a class as determined by the judgments that comprise the syllogism. Particularity in class membership is therefore necessarily concrete, not abstract, since it "relates all members to one another as well as to the universal."[114] The figures of the syllogism of reflection mediate on the basis of the features that individuals share. The features that individuals share are what connect the extremes. For example, in the syllogism of allness, "Silver, copper, and iron are metals. Silver, copper, and iron conduct electricity. All metals conduct electricity." The syllogism of allness groups together particulars in a class or universal. The inference is drawn on the basis of induction. It is thus the logic of induction that is being tracked in this discussion.

Now, Hegel argues, induction implies analogy: establishing similarities that will allow such a grouping. In the syllogism of analogy, "The Earth is a heavenly body and it is inhabited. The Moon is a heavenly body. Therefore, the Moon is inhabited." While the syllogism of analogy is thus the truth of the syllogism of allness, since similarities are implied in collecting particulars into a group and such a collection is what establishes the group itself as a group, as a universal the syllogism of analogy itself implies the genus-species relation. The syllogism of analogy already expresses, in other words, that such an inference can be drawn if the shared feature is *in fact* shared. The point here, however, is that the logic of induction presupposes genus-species relations that will make possible determinacy of that which is taken as available for collection into a class. For this reason, Hegel argues that while the syllogism of reflection elaborates inferential patterns on the basis of class membership in which universals, particulars, and individuals are linked to the others, the syllogism implies necessary relations between its elements. We have before us the syllogism of necessity.

In the third syllogism, the syllogism of necessity, "the mediating element is the objective nature of *die Sache*."[115] Because the middle term is not an "alien, immediate content," it is a syllogism of *necessity*.[116] The extremes of the concept are "also totalities." Thus, Hegel argues, the syllogism "has attained the correspondence of its concept, or the middle term, and its existence, or the difference of the extremes; that is, it has attained its truth—and with that it has stepped forth out of subjectivity into *objectivity*."[117] This syllogism is accordingly "*full of content*."[118] We have seen that the syllogism of existence implies reference to a content, to a concrete identity, and that the syllogism of reflection implies reference to the essential relations between universal, particular, and individual that make possible a logic of induction and, by extension, a logic of substitutability in the first place. Like the chapter on judgment, the chapter on the syllogism also moves to higher levels of formality that establish richer concreteness. A formal analysis of inference leads to an account of the implicit appeal to content that makes such inferences possible in the first place.

Under the heading of the syllogism of necessity, Hegel examines categorical, hypothetical, and disjunctive syllogisms. As we will see, with his discussion of the syllogism of necessity, and in particular the transition from the hypothetical to the disjunctive syllogism, Hegel addresses the problem of the givenness of the premises. The categorical syllogism asserts the unity of an individual by appealing to its determination as a species within a genus. "Gold is a metal. Metals are elements. Gold is an element."[119] While the species–genus relation establishes a unity that is appropriate to the matter at hand, rather than merely subjectively imposed, the problem resides in the extremes of the syllogism. Hegel argues that "under the same genus are also an *indeterminate number of many* other individuals; it is therefore *contingent* that only *this* individual is posited as subsumed under it."[120] The extremes themselves have "objective universality" or "self-subsistent nature." Although both extremes have a relation to the middle term, they nonetheless appear as "immediate actualities."[121] "The genus may be inherently differentiated into its species," Winfield explains, "but the nature of the genus does not provide the identity distinguishing each individual from any other of the same kind."[122] The inference is thus still external and subjective, performed by a subject that makes an inferential move on the basis of genus–species relations that are found. The problem of givenness is not overcome but is rather made explicit. Indeed, what is made explicit is that the premises of a syllogism, its judgments, are in fact given or found by a subject rather than internally related by the matter at hand. At this point, however, we have the hypothetical syllogism before us.

In the hypothetical syllogism, "If A is, then B is; But A is; Therefore B is," we move up one level of formality.[123] The hypothetical syllogism expresses the "necessary *connection* without the immediacy of the connected terms," Hegel explains.[124] The necessity of the inference is now contingent upon the first premise rather than on genus–species relations. The inference merely expresses in a different way what the hypothesis stated.[125] For this reason, the premise remains a given—"as found existing in the subject." The problem with the hypothetical syllogism, therefore, is like the problem of the necessity of causality. The necessity of causality resides in the law-like relation between cause and effect "completely indifferent to what it governs." It does not involve concrete universality, particularity, and individuality.[126] It establishes abstract necessity, a mere law. It is mere form to be applied to content.[127] For this reason, Hegel argues that the hypothetical syllogism is a "formal syllogism."[128]

Nonetheless, there is a crucial shift made with the hypothetical syllogism. It announces that mediation between the terms is irreducible, and—more importantly—that such mediation is the consequence of the negativity of form. The unity of the elements of the hypothetical syllogism is a negative unity, Hegel argues. The necessary relation between the terms of a hypothetical syllogism is the "*form-activity* of translating the conditioning actuality into the conditioned."[129] Such an activity represents the unity of positing and posited, ground and grounded, cause and effect that we saw in part 2 of this book. The terms correctly appear as mediated, posited, in the syllogism. "[T]he being of A is also not its own being," Hegel writes, "but that of B and *vice versa*, and in general the being of the one is the being of the other, and, as determined in the conclusion, their immediate being or indifferent determinateness is a mediated one."[130] In being mediated such that the determinacy of A is tied to the determinacy of B and vice versa, form is understood as dependent on content. "The mediation of the syllogism," Hegel writes, "has hereby determined itself as *individuality*, *immediacy*, and *self-related negativity*, or as a differentiating identity that retrieves itself into itself out of this differentiation—as absolute form, and for that very reason as objective universality, self-identical existent *content*."[131] At this point we are speaking no longer of the hypothetical syllogism but rather of the disjunctive syllogism, in which form is explicitly understood in terms of relations of exclusion or negation and therefore as explicitly depending on content.

In the disjunctive syllogism "A is either B or C or D; But A is B; Therefore A is neither C nor D or again: A is either B or C or D; But A is neither C nor D; Therefore A is B."[132] Given his critique of the hypothetical syllogism, one would think that Hegel argues that what occurs in the disjunctive syllogism is a union-with-self of the concept. What is in fact happening in the disjunctive syllogism, however, is the *collapse* of the syllogism: "What is posited in the disjunctive syllogism is thus the truth of the hypothetical syllogism, the unity of the mediator and the mediated, and for that reason the disjunctive syllogism is no longer *a syllogism at all*. For the middle term which is posited is in it as the totality of the concept itself contains the two extremes in their complete determinateness."[133] As disjunctive, the syllogism effectively collapses because no mediation—*understood as the connection between two independent terms*—is occurring. The disjunctive syllogism makes explicit that mediation cannot be consistently thought as the work of a medium of two extremes. Mediation must rather be thought of as the inseparability of the extremes. The middle term, Hegel argues, "has determined itself as a *totality*, as developed objective universality."[134] When considering the disjunctive form, then, we are speaking of a system of relations within which determinations are specified. This does not mean that Hegel is proposing the full presence of nonmediation, of the concept that has caught up with itself in a static totality. While the disjunctive syllogism is a collapsed syllogism, mediation itself is not canceled. It is redescribed as *determinate negation*. Elements in a syllogism are related to each other by way of relations of exclusion via *negation*. Hegel argues that in the disjunctive syllogism, "the middle term is a *universality replete with form*."[135] The middle term, Hegel argues, is constituted by negativity—by "form-activity" (*Formtätigkeit*). The totality is not comprised of relations between fixed determinations, but is rather an inferential process of exclusion.[136] Negation specifies determinacy of an individual via inferential moves that coextensively institute the totality of relations involved in the inference itself. The middle term is for this reason "complete determinateness." It is the totality of the concept. The concept can be understood as a totality, since form and content are grasped as inseparable albeit distinguishable.[137]

Hegel follows Kant in his account of the syllogism and does not include a syllogism of the concept. As we have seen, with the syllogism of necessity—in particular, the disjunctive syllogism—the syllogism collapses into the full mediation of the matter at hand. Recall that in the assertoric judgment the subjectivity of an individual is dependent on its own constitution yet in accordance with its concept. This establishes the judgment of the concept as a normative judgment, since there exists a gap between the constitution of an individual and its concept. A house can be good or bad according to its own constitution, yet only in light of its own concept. With the disjunctive syllogism, however, such a gap has collapsed. This collapse does not establish a logical-ontological adequation. On the contrary, it represents a turn to modes of account-giving that follow a logic of content rather than form. As such, they pertain to the logic of objective processes rather than a logic of the form of intelligibility. The collapse of the syllogism, Hegel writes, signals that "the concept in general has been realized; more precisely, it has obtained the kind of reality that is *objectivity*."[138] With the collapse of the syllogism, we are now speaking of the full mediation—which is to say, the *self-mediation*—of matters themselves.[139] At this point we are no longer speaking of the self-determination of the concept as a mere question of form. We are now speaking of form in terms of the self-determination of matters themselves. By making explicit the role of negativity in mediation and hence the necessary dependence on content of any concrete form of rationality, the *self-determination* of objective processes can also be made explicit. When we abandon models of judgment and inference and, moreover, practices of judging and inferring parasitic on a notion of mediation as a bridging of two extremes, speaking of the self-determination of things themselves is warranted. The transition from subjectivity to objectivity, then, allows us to speak not only of the determinacy of the concept as self-determination but of the determinacy of the 'other' of the concept in terms of *self-determination*. An account of full mediation is thus an account of the *self-determination* of the matter at hand, of *die Sache*.[140]

Pace Longuenesse, rather than an account of the concept that has coincided with itself, the Subjective Logic establishes that division is irreducible. As I have argued, the opening chapters of the Doctrine of the Concept rethink unity in light an irreducible negativity. Unity is subject to the strictures set by negativity. With this, we can reread the passage on love with which I began. The universal is free power, yet it does not do violence to the other—it does not subsume the other with blind might. The power of the concept is like the power of love, since it is only powerful when it is authoritative. The concept is like love, since it depends on its authority for the determinacy of an individual. The freedom of the concept is powerful in inspiring authority rather than in exerting sheer might. The universal must thus inspire reciprocity. In inspiring reciprocity, the freedom of the concept can also be called *free* love, boundless blessedness. It bears itself towards its other as towards its own self—it returns to itself, it relates to itself, it can establish its own actuality only on the basis of its relation to the other. It is only with and not merely through the other that the concept can be said to be actual. Yet a love that recognizes the irreducible division between self and other, that recognizes that it is only as powerful as it is authoritative, is a love that must negotiate its own actuality.

CHAPTER 7

Idea

In the chapters on Subjectivity, as we have seen, Hegel develops a notion of the concept as the normative structure of matters themselves. The subjectivity of *die Sache* is a matter of relations of exclusion that in instituting distinctions articulate the concept—the rationality, the subjectivity—of matters themselves. The theory of normativity that Hegel begins to develop in the section on Subjectivity is fully elaborated in terms of a theory of normative authority in the chapter on the absolute idea. The absolute idea rewrites Kant's account of cognition by developing the unity of the concept and objectivity as a matter of the unity of the theoretical and the practical. "Now it must certainly be admitted that the concept *as such* is not yet complete," Hegel indeed writes; "it must be raised to the *idea* which alone is the unity of the concept and reality."[1] He later clarifies that the idea is not merely the unity of concept and reality, but more precisely is the unity of the "subjective concept and objectivity."[2] Moving from an account of the structure of normativity to an account of normative authority means moving to an account of the strictures of intelligibility. The absolute idea elaborates the necessary historicity of intelligibility by arguing that intelligibility is a matter of *bindingness*.

I have argued that Hegel's idealism is a post-Kantian philosophy of *Geist*. Rationality must accordingly be understood as a concrete form of rationality—a historically specific understanding of the nature of nature, self, and society. A concrete form of rationality is based on distinctions that articulate what counts as nature rather than *Geist*, for instance, within a specific society in a given moment in time. The fact that normative distinctions are historically variable is due to their *bindingness*. Bindingness refers to the *authority* of understandings of nature, self, or society that comprise a specific form of life. Any such understanding is authoritative, in other words, when it is a structuring commitment within a shape of *Geist*. A form of rationality, then, is made possible by existent conditions yet actual by gaining authority. In his discussion of the absolute idea, Hegel proposes to think of the idea as "free subjective concept that exists for itself and therefore has personality [*Persönlichkeit*]."[3] The notion of personality is not a reference to the first-person standpoint of epistemic or moral subjectivity. The authority of a given conception of nature, self, society is not established by the activity of a single epistemic or moral subject. It is a matter of a process of actualization that exceeds the individual. Currency or bindingness is a matter of the development of a practice or institution that expresses a form of rationality.

The *Logic* comes to an end with a discussion of the absolute idea as absolute method. Method is the "*absolute self-knowing concept* [*sich selbst wissende*] *Notion*."[4] As a form of self-knowing, method elaborates the strictures of the theory of normative authority elaborated under the banner of the idea. These strictures respond to the irreducibility of negativity. Straightforwardly, method clarifies the mode of advance of speculative logic by thematizing its two features: beginning (*Anfang*) and dialectics.[5] Hegel discusses beginning and dialectics through what he calls the syllogism of method. Following his discussion of the syllogism in the earlier parts of the Subjective Logic, the syllogism of method effectively *collapses* the dualism between form and content present in Kant's account of cognition. This collapse does not establish the sovereignty of reason but rather emphasizes the negativity of form and the necessity of content. Form is nothing but negation, according to Hegel. Negation, however, requires content in order to be negation. Negativity is nothing but the self-negating character of content. Content refers to concrete—read: always already mediated—conditions that sustain or debunk a specific form of rationality. The negativity of form and the necessity of content, as we will see, specify the status of bindingness in ways radically beyond Kant. Their inseparability establishes the necessary precariousness and ambivalence of any historically specific form of rationality.

In establishing the inseparability of form and content, Hegel argues, the concept has "proved itself to be the absolute foundation [*Grundlage*]."[6] The concept as foundation refers to the necessity of moving from a philosophical account of intelligibility to a thinking of nature and eventually of *Geist* in a *Realphilosophie*. Method is the philosophical perspective that gives an account of the account of intelligibility given in a science of logic. It thereby provides a critical perspective on concrete forms of understanding the nature of nature and *Geist* further along in the system. Hegel's discussion of method thus allows us to clarify the normative function of the very idea of a science of logic. Rather than *a* norm, Hegel's logic establishes a philosophical perspective for a philosophical thinking of historically specific conceptions of nature and *Geist*. It provides a *critical* perspective, since it makes possible assessing a normative commitment, practice, or institution in light of the fact that any commitment, practice, or institution is necessarily precarious and ambivalent.

ABSOLUTE IDEA, PERSONALITY, NORMATIVE AUTHORITY

It is instructive to begin examining Hegel's notion of the idea by recalling his account of the absolute idea as the identity of the theoretical idea and the practical idea.[7] The absolute idea designates the collapse of the dualism present in Kant's account of theoretical and practical reason. In the chapters on Subjectivity and Objectivity, Hegel argues that both the concept and objectivity can be understood in terms of self-determination.[8] Self-determination is Hegel's answer to the failure of a logic of essence, in particular, the dualism at the heart of philosophies of reflection that we saw in part 2 of this book. To recall, in assuming that essence and reality, form and matter, cause and effect are different ontological orders, a logic of essence cannot make sense of reflexivity. It cannot account for the reciprocal determination of ground and grounded, cause and effect. A logic of the concept acknowledges this reciprocity but also recognizes that the relation between ground and grounded, cause and effect is not a blind reciprocity. Reciprocity involves normative distinctions that are not merely given but can be said to express the form of rationality of the matter at hand as *authoritative*. It is therefore necessary to establish the connection between self-determination and normative authority.

In the chapter on the idea of cognition, Hegel argues that any account of intelligibility that places theory and practice in separate spheres is mired in inconsistency. When understood in light of Kant's transcendental idealism, both theoretical reason and practical reason generate a problematic teleology. Recall the central claim of Kant's transcendental idealism: finite cognition can only know appearances rather than things in themselves. Recall as well the central claim of Kant's practical philosophy: morality is a matter of reason's privileging duty over inclination. Hegel glosses Kant's central claims as maintaining that theoretical and practical reason strive for but can never reach knowledge beyond experience or a good beyond being. In the chapter on the idea of cognition, Hegel traces Kant's problematic teleology to what he sees as an untenable distinction between the theoretical and the practical. Hegel sets out to show that the bad infinity of the idea of cognition is the result of the unrecognized inseparability of the theoretical and the practical. For Hegel, this inseparability establishes that determinacy is a matter of normative authority. Action is necessary for cognition, since any epistemic or moral determination requires taking as—authorizing—the determination as 'true' or 'good.' Yet self-awareness is necessary for action, since any such authorization can only be understood as critical when understood as a distinction of reason rather than a matter of givenness.

The problem that Hegel tracks in his discussion of the theoretical idea (read: Kant's critical epistemology) is that the concept stands over against an empirical reality that is beyond epistemic reach.[9] Kant sets out to give an account of the objectivity of epistemic conditions to be applied to what is given in sensation, to an other that appears as a "given" (*eines Gegebenen*), as Hegel repeatedly says.[10] The project of a transcendental deduction, then, is one of bridging the gap between two independent orders by overcoming "the idea's mere subjectivity," that is, by establishing the objectivity of cognition. However, on this model, knowledge remains knowledge of the activity of "reflective positing," of transcendental conditions, and therefore it does not extend to the thing itself—to "reality" or "determinateness."[11] The contradiction here, Hegel argues, is that theoretical cognition strives to know a truth that it itself has named unknowable. The unknowable, Hegel concludes, is considered the true. As we saw in part 1 of this book, for this reason the young Hegel argued in *Faith and Knowledge* that Kant's critical epistemology is a philosophy of faith rather than knowledge.

Establishing the objectivity of subjectivity requires action (*Handeln*).[12] In order to establish that epistemic conditions are objective, have purchase on reality rather than on mere appearances, Kant must take stock of action. Hegel's appeal to action introduces the thought that Kant's signature problem of objectivity is in effect a problem of normative authority. Objectivity is a question of the grip of subjectivity on reality, of the authority of transcendental conditions over reality. In the context of the *Logic*, an appeal to action does not mean that an account of cognition must be grounded in the sociality of reason. At this formal register, showing the objectivity of subjectivity means showing that the source of the authority of the relation between subjectivity and objectivity is reason itself. That determinacy depends on the authority of reason means here that only reason can establish the adequacy of the relation between subjectivity and objectivity, of a form of rationality and the existent conditions that express it. This insight establishes that determinacy is never a simple given, but a product of reason. And for this reason, it requires action. It requires the activity of establishing the adequacy of a form of rationality in light of the actual conditions that it purports to express.

With the practical idea, Hegel argues, we encounter the inverse problem than the one we encountered with the theoretical idea. Practical cognition (read: Kantian morality) attempts to bridge the gap between the idea and reality by overcoming the objectivity of the idea. It does so by establishing the subjectivity of willing. Yet the idea of the good that drives the will to its actualization is not in itself realizable, since it is itself an "absolute end" confronted with a world that it takes to be a fundamental limitation.[13] The good that the will is driven to realize is in itself "the objective," Hegel says, and reality must receive its true being "through the ends of the good."[14] The contradiction here is the following: willing is said to be the source of objectivity—of authority—in seeking to realize itself in the world. Yet it is equally fully limited by reality, because it can never bring about its end—the good—in full. The postulates of practical reason make morality impossible to actualize since they establish conditions for the highest good (freedom, immortality, God) beyond experience. The authority of morality must thus be established in volition rather than a good beyond being. "[W]hat still *limits* the objective concept," Hegel explains, "is its own *view* of itself, and this view vanishes in the reflection on what its realization is *in itself*. By this view the concept only stands in its own way, and all that it has to do about it is to turn, not against an external actuality, but against itself."[15]

This turning against itself is neither a renunciation of the possibility of its actualization nor the debunking of the idea of the good. It is rather the realization that reason is the source of authority of some 'good' and therefore of the attempt to actualize that good. If such good is sustained by reasons, however, internal to it is its own possible contestation. For Hegel, practical cognition ends up losing sight of the fact that the actualization of morality is the result of the reciprocal determination of willing and reality. Hegel notes that on a basic level willing is a form of authorizing, since testing whether any action is universalizable necessarily depends on maxims that themselves refer to inclinations.[16] In being authorized by reason, however, willing can be contested, revised, or denied in light of new reasons. Reality, then, cannot be reduced to the sheer determination of a will that endows it with actuality in the good that it seeks. The good is not fully objective but is rather subjective in being revocable. For these reasons, Hegel argues that "what is still lacking in the practical idea is the moment of consciousness proper itself" and that "this lack can also be regarded in this way, namely that the *practical* idea still lacks the moment of the *theoretical* idea."[17]

Kant's failure to acknowledge the inseparability of the theoretical and the practical, then, leads him to deep inconsistency. Theoretical cognition can only establish the objectivity of any given determination by recognizing its irreducible practical dimension. Practical cognition can only establish the subjectivity of any given determination by thematizing its revisability. Hegel calls the unity of the theoretical and the practical the "absolute idea." The theoretical and practical idea by themselves are "one-sided, possess[ing] the idea only as a sought-for beyond and unattained goal; each is therefore a *synthesis of striving*, each possessing as well as *not* possessing the idea within it."[18] As "rational notion," as "absolute," the idea is "free subjective concept that is for itself and therefore possesses personality [*Persönlichkeit*]."[19] Although Hegel's characterization of the absolute idea has personality is strange and puzzling, it is not mystifying. In describing the absolute idea as personality, Hegel inherits and radically transforms the structure of bindingness of Kantian autonomy. This transformation further specifies the role of authority that we have seen is central to the theoretical and the practical.

The crucial feature of Hegel's transformation of Kant's understanding of bindingness is moving away from the first-person perspective of critical philosophy toward a philosophy of *Geist*. The objectivity (to keep with the discussion of cognition) or actuality (to refer to Hegel's overall discussion) of concrete forms of rationality is not a matter of the limits of finite cognition. Normative authority is a matter of the development of practices and institutions of rendering intelligible. It is helpful to consider Brandom's reading of Hegel at this point. He also argues that the distinctive feature of Hegel's transformation of Kant is his rewriting of Kantian autonomy as a theory of *Geist*. Indeed, Brandom maintains that Hegel transforms Kant's account of the normative character of mind, meaning, and rationality such that normative statuses are social statuses. As we will see, although Brandom helps specify the notion of bindingness at the heart of Hegel's concept of the absolute idea, he does not fully develop the radicality of Hegel's transformation of Kantian autonomy.

In part 1 of this book, we saw that Kantian self-legislation is central to Fichte and Hegel's understanding of reason. Brandom deepens this connection by tracing the structure of autonomy to Kant's theory of judgment. According to Brandom, Kantian judgment involves commitments. Judging, as well as acting, is a type of endorsement, which entails an exercise of authority.[20] To judge is for this reason to make oneself liable to normative assessment. Judging is thus a kind of responsibility. "[O]ne is responsible for having *reasons* for one's endorsements," Brandom writes, "using the contents one endorses *as* reasons for and against the endorsement of other contents, and taking into account possible *countervailing* reasons."[21] For Kant, Brandom argues, the transcendental unity of apperception is the locus of responsibility. The "I think" *must* accompany all my representations, since I must integrate present and future endorsements with previous ones. "What one makes oneself responsible *for* and what one makes oneself responsible *to*, by judging," Brandom writes, "is also to be explained in terms of the original synthetic activity of integrating one's commitments according to their rational relations to one another."[22] Judging is thus a form of *binding*.[23] The concept involved in judgment binds us to what it entails. One is bound by the norm that one institutes and at the same time authorizes. One is constrained by it, since one is liable to normative assessment according to it. One *binds* oneself and binds *oneself*, as Brandom puts it.

Unlike Kant, Brandom maintains, Hegel argues that such a logic of authority and responsibility is a matter of recognition (*Annerkennung*).[24] The authority of any application of a concept or norm depends on the recognition of others who "administer" the application. Such administration assumes a "realm of the normative."[25] *Geist*, according to Brandom, is the "realm of conceptually articulated norms, of authority and responsibility, commitment and entitlement." It is "the recognitive community of all those who have such normative statuses, and all their normatively significant activities." Negotiating the claims of reciprocally conditioning authorities, Brandom accordingly argues, entails administering conceptual norms by applying them in actual cases. He takes common law to be the best model for understanding Hegel's point. All there is to instituting a conceptual norm—to specifying the commitment undertaken when a concept is applied—are other applications of the concept. Tradition thus has authority over concept-use.[26] This means that present concept-users defer to tradition while at the same time petitioning vindication from future users. Future concept-users have the responsibility to redeem past determinations of the concept whether by consolidation or revision.[27] An intersubjective logic of authority-responsibility, then, accounts for the historical revisability of norms and explains their bindingness within a given shape of *Geist*. The question of authority is thus a question of authorization over time by negotiating subjects.

Although Brandom's account is insightful, he conceives of normative authority as the progressive negotiation of content by individuals within a stable normative realm. He thereby still emphasizes the first-person perspective, since he anchors authority in revisions made by individuals within a specific set of institutions at a specific moment in time. Furthermore, he assumes the stability of *Geist* and the unambiguously progressive character of conceptual change. Hegel's insistence on describing the absolute idea as personality, however, represents a deeper transformation of Kantian bindingness than Brandom's reading allows. Normative authority is a matter of the actualization of commitments, practices, and institutions. This is not to exclude individual agency. It is rather to recognize strictures that apply to both individuals and the normative orders within which they act. Normative authority exceeds an individual's ability to appeal to tradition or her being liable to normative assessment by those that might seek to inherit said tradition, since she cannot secure the stability of her use of a concept within a "slice of Spirit," as Brandom puts it. Conversely, practices and institutions cannot fully determine the content of a normative commitment within a slice of spirit, since even individuals seeking to act *within* the parameters set by them may nevertheless transgress them.[28] While Brandom accounts for historical revision, then, he does not account for normative reversal. Indeed, the progressive revision of a stable normative order through relations of recognition does not fully capture Hegel's insistence on a logic of actualization that emphasizes negativity. In order to clarify the impact of negativity on the theory of normative authority developed under the banner of the idea, however, we must turn to Hegel's discussion of the idea as method.

METHOD, PRECARIOUSNESS, AMBIVALENCE

Hegel's discussion of method specifies strictures that make clear the radicality of his transformation of Kantian bindingness. I argued above that as the unity of the theoretical and the practical, the absolute idea articulates that the objectivity—the actuality—of a form of rationality is a matter of normative authority. In establishing that the truth of a matter is a matter of normative authority, rather than a given, reason refers only to itself. Now, in establishing the inseparability of the theoretical and the practical, the absolute idea does not represent a reduction of the theoretical to the practical or vice versa. Hegel is clear that the absolute idea does not eliminate the "opposition" between reality and ideality encountered in theoretical and practical cognition. The absolute idea in fact "harbours the most extreme opposition within."[29] It contains the highest degree of opposition since it *recognizes* the gap between cognition and the given that we have seen both theory and practice struggle with when their inseparability goes unacknowledged. The absolute idea thematizes that such gap is always already negotiated theoretically *and* practically. It thematizes the role of reason in epistemic and moral determination. It recognizes the fact that any such gap is understood and negotiated *as a gap* by reason itself—by practices of rendering intelligible that articulate a concrete form of rationality. The absolute idea is thus the standpoint of reason that knows itself as reason. In this sense, it is a form of absolute knowing—what Hegel calls "absolute method."[30]

"[M]ethod," Hegel writes, "has resulted as the *absolutely self-knowing concept*, as the *concept that has* the absolute, both as subjective and objective, *as its subject matter*."[31] As a form of absolute knowing, method clarifies crucial features of the structure of authorization that the idea designates. What Hegel describes as the syllogism of method takes stock of the advance of a science of logic and of its results, thereby thematizing its insights and allowing us to articulate its implications. Key here is Hegel's discussion of the work of dialectics, which thematizes the irreducibility of negativity and therefore the necessity of content. This final discussion of the unity of form and content allows us to draw the implications of such a unity for the theory of normative authority elaborated under the banner of the idea. These consequences, as we will see in the conclusion to this book, have a bearing on a philosophical thinking of nature and *Geist* further along in the system.

Hegel introduces the syllogism of method in the chapter on the absolute idea by repeating the challenge to the modern notion of method that he most famously launches in the Introduction to the *Phenomenology of Spirit*. "In cognition as *enquiry* [*suchenden Erkennen*]," Hegel reiterates in the *Logic*, method is an "*instrument* . . . a means that stands on the side of the subject, connecting it with the object."[32] Accounts of determinacy that attempt to clarify their own mode of proceeding and standards for accuracy before beginning their inquiry assume that form and content are of different orders. They assume that their norms of assessment can be settled in abstraction from such content. For Hegel, there is no way to establish the forms to be applied independently of their application or to determine the study of a subject matter without already appealing to assumptions about its content.

In the *Logic*, Hegel pursues his critique by modeling the method of cognition of inquiry and absolute method on the hypothetical and the disjunctive syllogisms respectively. With respect to the cognition of inquiry, method is the middle term that mediates between the subject and the object, which occupy the two extremes of the syllogism. So understood, method generates a set of problems akin to those generated by the hypothetical syllogism.[33] To recall, in the hypothetical syllogism the subject does not "*unite with itself*."[34] Because the necessity of the inference is contingent upon the first premise, the subject is merely reasserted; the inference merely expresses in a different way what the hypothesis stated. The premise remains a given. The problem with the hypothetical syllogism, as we have seen, is like the problem of the necessity of causality—it resides in the law-like relation between cause and effect, not in existent conditions. Therefore, it establishes abstract necessity, a mere law. It is mere form to be applied to content. For this reason, Hegel argued that the hypothetical syllogism is a formal syllogism. Similarly, method unites the subject with the conclusion, but it does so as an application of form onto content that does not take into account content but merely asserts what is already contained in form. Method is here mere instrument—external form.

Unlike in the cognition of inquiry, in true cognition (*wahrhaften Erkennen*), method is "absolute." In absolute method "the concept is the middle term only because it equally has the significance of the objective; in the conclusion, therefore, the objective does not attain only an external determinateness by virtue of the method, but is posited rather in its identity with the subjective concept."[35] Absolute method posits the identity of the objective and subjective. What does this mean? It is helpful to recall Hegel's discussion of the disjunctive syllogism.[36] As we saw, the disjunctive syllogism collapses any remaining gap in the structure of the syllogism. It is a notion of full mediation. The disjunctive syllogism makes explicit that mediation cannot be understood on the model of bridging. It must rather be thought of as the reciprocal determination of the extremes within a system of relations. As I argued above, in being a 'collapsed' syllogism, the disjunctive syllogism redescribes mediation as determinate negation. Inferential patterns comprised of relations of negation coextensively institute the totality of relations involved in the inference itself. As "complete determinateness," the middle term is not the medium that unites two extremes, but the totality of the concept.

The collapse of the hypothetical syllogism is a dissolution of the inadequate distinction between cognition and reality. Recall that the collapse of the syllogism earlier in the Subjective Logic warrants a move to speaking of reality as positedness, and hence "*eine Sache* . . . that is in and for itself—objectivity."[37] The dissolution of the distinction between subjectivity and objectivity allows us to speak of the determinacy of the other of the concept as self-determination. By making explicit the role of positing, the role of objective determination can thus also be made explicit. The crucial point that I noted above is that this is possible when we abandon models of judgment and inference parasitic on a notion of mediation between two extremes that require bridging. Absolute method, accordingly, does not follow the logic of mediation qua medium. Method thematizes the unity of form and content as what has been implicit throughout the *Logic*. Like the collapse of the syllogism that allows for the transition from subjectivity to objectivity, method allows for an understanding of the determinacy of the 'other' of the concept as self-determination—an understanding that amounts to the passage from logic to the *Naturphilosophie*. I will come back to this transition.

Hegel speaks of logic as "the science of *absolute form*," and he calls both the disjunctive syllogism and absolute method "absolute form" (*absolute Form*).[38] As the universal aspect of the idea, method exists "wholly as form."[39] As absolute form, however, method does not reinstate a distinction between form and content. Absolute method contains the notion of form that makes possible giving an account of the relation between concept and reality without affirming a notion of form over against reality. Indeed, absolute form is the notion of form that Hegel develops in order to account for the relation between concept and reality formally—*philosophically*. Idealism must work from the side of form.[40] Form is absolute when it articulates the inseparability of concept and reality, form and content. In being nothing but negativity, form requires reality. In being nothing but existent conditions, reality/sensuousness admits of a distinctive form of rationality. Ideality *and* reality always already express concrete forms of rationality. They always already contain aspects of each other. Conceptions of reality are *conceptions*—articulations by and within historically specific practices, discourses, and institutions of sense-making (science, art, philosophy, etc.). Conceptions of ideality are expressions of *real commitments*—notions of truth, beauty, the good elaborated in historically specific contexts. Absolute form, then, takes stock of the unity of the concept and reality expressed by a concrete form of rationality.

To say that method exists wholly as form is to say that it is wholly dependent on content. It is a philosophical perspective that is nothing but an expression of content. To state the point concretely, method is the self-authorizing activity of reason at work in a science of logic. It is an expression of content, since such self-authorizing activity expresses a specific conception of reason—a post-Kantian conception of the autonomy of reason. Now, it is crucial to note that while the inseparability of form and content establishes the historicity of the conception of reason at work in the *Logic*, for Hegel it also establishes that this conception of reason reveals the *truth* of intelligibility. Method thematizes the one nonrevisable, ahistorical principle that establishes the necessary historicity of intelligibility: the negativity of form and the necessity of content. Notice, however, that in so doing method thematizes that any historically specific form of intelligibility is necessarily precarious and ambivalent. Method clarifies that irreducible negativity introduces a structural precariousness and ambivalence to any form of intelligibility. As I mentioned above and will explicate in detail below, this helps us elaborate the critical function of Hegel's notion of method. Method is a critical philosophical perspective that does not depend on a final, fully stable norm of assessment.

Method thematizes the two features of the advance of a science of logic: beginning and dialectics.[41] These two features are elaborated via a discussion of the coextensively analytic and synthetic movement of the concept.[42] Hegel speaks of the syllogism of method as containing analysis and synthesis as its premises.[43] I suggest reading Hegel's discussion of method as the analytic–synthetic movement of the concept in light of the inseparability of form and content. The movement of the concept is both analytic and synthetic insofar as, in being nothing but negativity, the concept depends on content. Hegel's characterization of method as analytic–synthetic recalls his critique of Kant's distinction between analysis and synthesis laid out most prominently in the chapter on the idea of cognition. There, Hegel is mostly interested in Kant's distinction as a matter of explication (*Entwicklung*), as a question of the extension of knowledge in synthetic judgment.[44] Once again, Hegel frames the problem, on the one hand, as the inconsistency of subjective idealism, which represents analysis as a 'positing' that leaves the thing-in-itself beyond it, and, on the other hand, as the inconsistency of realism, which characterizes determinacy as simply apprehended.[45] These two positions express but fail to realize that determinacy is "a positing that no less immediately determines itself to be equally a presupposing," that determinacy is already something "completed" as well as "a product . . . of a merely subjective activity."[46] Because positing and presupposing are reciprocally related, analysis is at the same time synthesis. What does this mean?

Let me first recall that Hegel's extension of Kant does not attempt finally to bridge the gap between mind and world by performing a deduction of the existence of objects of thought or the rationality of being in itself. It aims at making explicit the authority of reason in the self-determination of the concept *and* its other. Along these lines, Pippin suggests that we bear in mind that Hegel's extension of Kant's idealism is based on the claim that a transcendental deduction fails to give an account of a possible object of thought. In aiming at giving an account of the conditions of possibility of experience, Kant only provides an analysis of the notion of an apperceptive subject. However, the account of apperceptive judging presupposes a "nonanalytic claim about the proper way to understand the relation between spontaneous human thought and objectivity."[47] The very notion of the *a priori*, Hegel argues, presupposes that pure concepts are appropriate to providing determinacy to an object of experience, and hence to the 'other' of thought. Analysis of the concept is also its synthetic extension, since specifying what is contained in a concept that is assumed to be able to provide the determinacy of objects of thought is also an explication of the way in which it provides such determinacy to the 'other' of thought. For Hegel, then, the fact that the analysis of the concept turns out to *extend* our understanding of it calls into question a strict distinction between the analytic and the synthetic. The determinateness of what is merely found and is to be analyzed, whether sheer positing or apprehended determinacy, suggests that it is already related to the other.[48] The explication of the concept is, therefore, also its extension; its extension is but an explication of what is contained in it or—more precisely—presupposed by it. An account of determinacy thus entails an account of both reflective positing *and* "reality" or "determinateness."

In the discussion of absolute method, analysis is the "immediate relationship to its other" (beginning), and synthesis "the relation of the differentiated term as such to the term from which it is differentiated" (dialectics). The point of discussing beginning once more at the end of the *Logic* is to examine how the advance of logic got underway, and what was necessary for such an advance to be carried forward in the first place.[49] In order to *arrive* at the account of determinacy the *Logic* offers immanently—without appeal to a first principle or given—the beginning must have been "deficient."[50] Giving an account of intelligibility is possible because the purported immediacy of the beginning turned out to be already in relation to an other, hence not immediate at all.[51] Rather than taking the deficiency of the beginning as a sign of arbitrariness, absolute method knows the incompleteness of the beginning to be necessary because "truth is but the coming-to-oneself through the negativity of immediacy."[52] The crucial point here is that absolute method thematizes this negativity as irreducible. Negativity shows that the movement of the concept requires content; its relation to its other is precisely what maintains it.[53] In being "infected" with negativity, the concept itself *requires* content.[54] The advance of the logic depends on more than the movement generated by negativity; it depends on the content through which negativity finds traction as a *relation* of qualitative or quantitative opposition (in the logic of being) or retrospective determination of cause and effect (in the logic of essence). Analysis is, therefore, described as the negative, and synthesis as the negative of the negative, which represents a return to "determinateness." In thematizing the negativity of form, the necessity of content has been demonstrated throughout the *Logic*: "Its [the concept's] determinateness as content is no longer something merely taken up but is deduced and proved."[55]

While in the *Logic* the necessity of content is specified philosophically, this necessity compels the movement from a philosophical account of determinacy and intelligibility to an exposition of the intelligibility of nature and, further along in the system, *Geist*. "On the new foundation that the result has now constituted as the subject matter," Hegel writes, "the method remains the same as in the preceding subject matter. The difference concerns solely the status of the foundation as such."[56] It is this relationship that is crucial. It indicates that, at this point in the text, method, the self-knowing of the idea, is not only a retrospective recapitulation of the advance of a science of logic. Method is also prospective. It allows the *passage* from the philosophical account of intelligibility to a "real" exposition of nature, self, or society—a philosophy of nature, a philosophical psychology, or a political philosophy.[57] The necessity of content refers us to concrete conceptions of nature and *Geist* that are the subject matter of the real sciences (*Realphilosophien*). Philosophy can only speak of nature, for example, by referring to actual scientific discourses. In Hegel's obscure formulation, the *Logic* therefore ends with the idea externalizing itself into nature. Negativity, then, establishes that the intelligibility of nature and spirit must refer to the concrete content of the real sciences. The prospective movement of method, however, is a way of thinking nature and *Geist* that contains the central insight of a science of logic. Rather than *a* method and hence stable norm for assessing concrete conceptions of nature and *Geist*, method is a mode of self-knowing that makes explicit the precariousness and ambivalence of concrete forms of rationality.

The transition between the *Logic* and the *Naturphilosophie* is, in fact, not a transition per se, not an *Übergang*, but rather a "free release" (*frei entläßt*) of the idea. Qua logical, the idea is "enclosed within pure thought."[58] In order to examine something other than itself—that is, other than reason—the idea requires an "unclosing" that Hegel characterizes in terms of *freedom*. The idea "*freely releases* itself" and "on account of this freedom, the *form of its determinateness* is just as absolutely free: the *externality of space and time* absolutely existing for itself without subjectivity."[59] How should we understand the free release of the idea? Many commentators have argued that, as a free act, the release should be understood as a decision, an *Entschluß*. The status of decision, however, has been widely disputed. Hegel has been read (perhaps most famously by Marx) as proposing that speculative logic is in some way the creator of nature. In this vein, the free act of decision has been cited by critics of Hegel as evidence for his theological and ontotheological commitments. It has also been read as the logical grounding of nature, insofar as the presuppositionless exposition of determinacy shows that being is nothing less than nature in its rational unfolding (Houlgate). Along this line, the return to a discussion of the idea at the end of the *Logic* establishes the rationality of being itself. As we will see in detail in a moment, it has been argued that the decision refers to the choice of finite thinkers to think according to reason (Nuzzo). Finally, it has also been suggested that the transition to the *Naturphilosophie* represents a normative distinction rather than an ontological divide (Pippin).

The transition from nature to spirit does not amount to an ontological grounding of nature, but rather to normative distinctions that articulate ontological *commitments* along philosophical, natural, and eventually historical lines. The free release of the idea thus refers back to the authority of reason. The transition signals a distinction between a specific conception of reason and a concrete conception of nature draw by reason itself. However, this transition is not a full determination of the other of the concept—nature—by reason. I suggest that Hegel speaks of the passage as a "free release" in order to avoid suggesting such full determination.[60] As the comprehension of the inseparability of form and content, method is the determinate moment of the *Logic* that spells out the consequences of irreducible negativity. It shows that specific determinations of nature (ways of accounting for phenomena as natural) or spirit (ways of accounting for historically specific commitments, practices, institutions) are sustained by reason itself rather than by an appeal to a given. It also shows that a concrete articulation of nature or *Geist* can never be fully fixed or authorized.

Angelica Nuzzo has provided a systematic interpretation of absolute method helpful for clarifying the status of absolute idea as method.[61] Nuzzo argues that the task of the final movement of the *Logic* is to develop a notion of philosophical knowledge that includes both the knowing that has been at work in the *Logic* and the knowledge of the real sciences.[62] Method provides a norm for philosophical thinking along epistemic and ontological lines, which provides a normative perspective from which to engage the real sciences. As the universal aspect of the idea, Nuzzo argues, method is both the ontological modality of being and the epistemological modality of cognition. As a modality of knowing, "method is the way in which all subjective knowledge works insofar as it implies a self-knowing of reason," and as a modality of being, "it expresses the substantiality of things, their objective, immanent and rational structure."[63]

Thinking in terms of the strictures of method, Nuzzo maintains, is "thinking and living in the dimension of truth and freedom."[64] To live in the dimension of truth and freedom is to be an embodied, finite thinker that can approach knowledge of nature and spirit from a *Vernunftig* rather than *Verständlich* perspective.[65] It is to submit finite knowing and acting to the "infinite power" of reason—to consider finite knowing and acting as moments of the process of the "final unity of reason." This type of assessment can only take place from the philosophical perspective laid out in the *Logic*, where logical determinations have been clarified. Method, in this way, "describes the *form* in which the self-knowing *idea itself is in our thinking*." Nuzzo highlights the opposition that for Hegel is contained within the absolute idea. To engage in philosophical knowing is to overcome the resistance of the finite that is intrinsic to the infinite unfolding of reason.[66]

The opposition between the finite and the infinite power of reason allows not only for an anti-teleological account of reason but also for an anti-deterministic one.[67] While finite knowing and acting find their truth in recognizing that they are a moment within the unity of reason, rational assessment by finite thinkers is not an "automatic" necessity. The standpoint of method, of reason, is not immediately given: the "finite must relate to reason through the method in order to be true."[68] Thinking in terms of method, therefore, represents a *decision* of finite thinkers to take on the project of philosophical knowing that can, in turn, guide a critical investigation of nature and spirit. Relating to reason, Nuzzo argues, is thus to be understood as a free *choice* that not only must be taken in order to begin philosophical inquiry but must also be continuously renewed.[69] This free choice, furthermore, represents an "obligation." To decide to undertake a commitment is to follow the imperative that such a commitment entails. Whoever is committed to truth must be responsible for following the strictures of method, for following the imperative to think in terms of the necessity of reason rather than the contingency of an isolated moment of reason.

Method is, therefore, not a set of rules that facilitate the achievement of a given goal. It is the "imperative that prescribes at every new level of the process how to set a new goal and invent the means to reach it."[70] Indeed, the commitment to the dialectical method must be continuously renewed, since at any point finite thinkers have the choice to give up the attempt to think and live according to reason. The lesson of method is, accordingly, "not *that* reason will necessarily be victorious over its otherness, but that *if* reason wants to succeed in the task of knowledge of the world and action in it, it *must* follow the prescriptions of the method."[71] Absolute method is thus the norm *for* what knowledge can become when finite thinkers engage in speculative philosophy. It is a demand to think and live according to the strictures of method, which is to say, to think and live within reason.[72]

My reading inverts the roles that Nuzzo allocates to the absolute idea and absolute method. Rather than providing a norm *for* thinking nature and spirit, method makes explicit strictures *of* the intelligibility of nature and *Geist*. To be sure, Nuzzo does not argue that method represents *a* norm, but rather the demand to assess the finite in light of its position within the unity of reason. However, there are several reasons why it is the absolute idea that should be understood as designating the authority of reason, while method should be understood as making explicit the strictures of the process of authorization or actualization. Method thematizes constraints that the inseparability of form and content places on the authority of any form of rationality. It is crucial here to stress again that the absolute idea does not refer to the single finite thinker thinking in light of reason. As I have argued, the absolute idea refers to the authority of a form of rationality distinctive of a shape of *Geist*. It is thus helpful to return to Brandom's reading of Hegel at this point and further elaborate what this means.

Above I argued that, although modeled on recognition, Brandom's account of normative authority retains focus on the first-person perspective. Like Nuzzo, Brandom emphasizes the first-person perspective by arguing that conceptual change is the result of progressive revisions made by individuals within a stable normative order. In contrast, I argued that normative authority refers to the grip or currency of a commitment, practice, or institution that exceeds the individual. This is not to exclude individual agency, but to recognize strictures that apply both to individuals and to the normative orders within which they act. The point is that negativity impacts the way that normative authority should be understood. Although he does not develop negativity as normative revision *and* reversal, Brandom's account already suggests the deeper significance that I attribute to negativity. Recall Brandom's insistence that normative authority is a matter of authorization over time within a shape of *Geist*. We refer to past specification of a normative commitment but reformulate its content in light of new cases. Only future judges, however, could determine whether the present specification is authoritative given their vantage point. Temporality and intersubjectivity already suggest that *Geist* cannot be understood as a stable normative order the progressive development of which is the result of individuals revising conceptual content. The temporal and intersubjective logic of authority–responsibility points to the fact that content is inherently divided, establishing that a commitment cannot have full authority in a given "slice of spirit." Even when enjoying authority, a present commitment, practice, institution is precarious and ambivalent given the authority of past-use and the responsibility of future-use. This division and hence instability cannot be reduced to a progressive revision by appealing to self-conscious applications of a concept within a stable normative context.

Precariousness and ambivalence, for Hegel, are not the unfortunate effects of the temporal or social character of intelligibility. Method establishes negativity as an irreducible feature of intelligibility, which introduces a structural precariousness and ambivalence to any form of rationality. Precariousness and ambivalence are features of the actuality of any form of rationality. Hegel's commitment to understanding the unity of form and content as the unity of the positive and negative is key here. In the words of the *Phenomenology*, "the negative belongs to the content itself, and is the positive" or, in the words of the *Logic*, "the positive aspect is nothing else but the inner negativity of the determinations."[73] When considered from the perspective of the necessity of content, the negativity of form follows the logic of historically specific commitments, practices, institutions. Negativity is the inner determination of the way in which intelligibility is articulated within discursive formations that Hegel calls the real sciences or institutions such as modern ethical life. When considered from the perspective of the necessity of form, negativity calls into question the assumption that the content of concepts retain stability when 'playing roles' in a historically specific form of intelligibility. Negativity establishes that concrete forms of rationality are precarious, since they are commitments that have or cease to have grip within a given shape of *Geist*. They are also ambivalent, given that they accommodate opposite valences even when enjoying normative authority. They are subject not only to reversals of meanings and effects, but also to coextensive positive and negative meanings and effects.

Logic and *Geist* are thus mutually constraining. Logic establishes normative precariousness and ambivalence, while the content of historical commitments, practices, institutions establishes concretely the form of revision or reversal a commitment could take. However, this should not be understood as a normative relation, if by that we mean that logic shows how one ought to act or how a society ought to be structured. Method cannot provide a norm *for* thinking nature and spirit. It rather explains *that* normative commitments can lose their grip. Indeed, it explains that such a grip cannot be fully secured in the first place. Precisely for this reason, a concrete understanding of nature or *Geist* requires the authorization of reason—a consideration of the actuality of a given commitment, practice, institution in light of its own concrete conditions. Any assessment of given forms of intelligibility must accordingly refer to its content, to the concrete conditions that sustain it or call it into question. Method thus informs a *critical* thinking of nature and eventually spirit, since it makes explicit the historicity and ambivalence of intelligibility. It cannot provide a norm or demand to live according to reason, as Nuzzo suggests, because any given assessment must refer to concrete forms of rationality distinctive of a historically specific mode of intelligibility. The relation of the new subject matter (nature) and subsequent subject matters (*Geist*) to the foundation, to method, is thus one that takes into account the consequences of negativity. The *Logic* thereby provides a critical perspective, but one that must go beyond philosophy itself. It must assess concrete ways of understanding the nature of nature and *Geist,* taking into account the lack of finality and stability of any form of rationality.

CONCLUSION

Philosophy's Work

Hegel's idealism is in the first and last instance a philosophy of *Geist*. Hegel's system of science—comprised of a logic, a philosophy of nature, and a philosophy of *Geist*—begins and ends with *Geist*. It begins with logic, which I have argued gives a philosophical account of determinacy necessary for clarifying the strictures of intelligibility, and it ends with philosophy, which is a form of absolute *Geist* in which *Geist* knows itself as the idea.[1] As we have seen, logic shows that intelligibility is the result of the authority of normative commitments within practices of rendering intelligible in a given moment in time. Logic thereby provides an account of intelligibility as the result of the ongoing work of distinction-making and remaking—between what is understood as nature rather than history, for instance. Hegel's emphasis on negativity, however, establishes not only the historicity of reason but also the precariousness and ambivalence of concrete forms of rationality. Specific conceptions of nature and *Geist* are based on normative distinctions that are historically variable precisely because they are precarious and ambivalent. This insight provides a rubric for understanding conceptions of nature and *Geist* further along in the system.

IDEALITY RECONSIDERED

In the opening paragraphs of the chapter on the absolute idea, Hegel argues that the concept as idea "is the sole subject matter and content of philosophy."[2] "Nature and spirit," he continues, "are in general different modes of presenting *its* [the idea's] *existence* [*ihre Dasein darzustellen*], art and religion its different modes of apprehending itself and giving itself adequate existence [*sich zu erfasen und ein sich angemessenes Dasein zu geben*]." The absolute idea, as we have seen, establishes that the intelligibility of nature and *Geist* are concrete articulations or *conceptions* of nature, self, history. Concrete conceptions of nature and spirit are "ideal presentations" of material reality, life, self, social life, so on. They are articulations of nature and *Geist* in light of scientific discourses, the history of metaphysics, and as a result of implicit normative commitments that express a cultural, political, and religious legacy.[3] Art and religion, on the other hand, are modes of collective self-understanding. They are modes of what Hegel calls absolute *Geist*. They articulate the orienting commitments of a society in a given moment in time through artistic and religious practice. They have been, are, or have the potential to be authoritative practices for a community's self-understanding. "Philosophy has the same content and the same purpose as art and religion," Hegel goes on to argue, "but it is the highest mode of apprehending the absolute idea, because its mode, that of the concept, is the highest mode. Hence it seizes those shapes of real and ideal finitude as well as infinity and holiness, and comprehends them and itself."[4] Clarifying the necessary historicity and structural ambivalence of intelligibility is itself a practice of self-understanding. Philosophy is the highest form of comprehension, then, since it articulates the status of all practices of rendering intelligible—including itself.

PRESENTATION, APPREHENSION, COMPREHENSION

The difference between presentation (*Darstellung*), apprehension (*Fassung*) and comprehension (*Begriefen*) is key.[5] Presentation is the activity of articulating a distinction between nature, self, and society that grounds intelligibility within a specific shape of *Geist*. Nature and spirit are different modes of presenting the idea's existence by instituting the grounding distinction between what is understood as either natural or *geistige*.[6] Consider how Hegel understands *Geist* also as an achievement.[7] From the perspective of subjective *Geist* (of an anthropology and a psychology), *Geist* is a mode of comportment that natural beings with a certain level of complexity reach. As Pippin has argued, by reaching such a level of complexity, a solely naturalistic account of their deeds becomes inappropriate.[8] "Such creatures," Pippin writes, "do not, say, just register threatening stimuli; they experience what is taken to be a threat, take the threat 'in a way,' fearfully, feelingly."[9] This "taking" reveals a comportment that is no longer a simple self-relation, i.e., mere registering the threat as threat. Registering the threat *fearfully* is a mode of comportment, one that is irreducibly bound to the body, yet no longer describable in terms of a mere bodily registering. Hegel thus argues that the more complex this way of taking up the world is, the more such creatures have "left nature behind." Drawing the line between nature and *Geist* is therefore a matter of ways in which we account for and understand the activity of a creature that negotiates its surroundings in highly complex ways—through a history, oriented by moral or religious beliefs, with complex technologies. Such negotiations are not reducible to their 'natural' existence.[10]

Apprehension is a matter of grasping (*Fassung*). It is a collective mode of self-understanding that articulates the authoritative commitments for a society in a given moment in time *consciously* yet not self-consciously. Art and religion, according to Hegel, are practices of collective self-understanding that do not offer a commentary on themselves as practices of collective self-understanding. In the lectures on fine art, for example, Hegel claims that art is "the sensible appearance of the idea."[11] The lectures deny that aesthetics is concerned with the experience of the beauty of nature or the universality of aesthetic experience, as it was for Kant.[12] The idea "steps forward into reality," it externalizes itself, by being concretely and consciously elaborated in and through artistic practices and by modes of artistic representation. Aesthetics, in other words, is a matter of the history of art. It is concerned with historically specific artistic practices and works of art that articulate the structuring commitments of a culture and society at a specific point in time. The lectures thus move through particular forms of art—the Symbolic, the Classical, and the Romantic—that express the main normative commitment of a given society. The artistic articulation of the ideal of freedom, Hegel argues for example, involves the advent of a representation of inwardness. Inwardness is initially inadequately represented in Greek sculpture, only to be more appropriately elaborated in Romantic tragedy and comedy.

Although art and religion are practices of apprehension, they lack comprehension (*Begreifen*). They do not give an account of themselves as being practices of articulation that concretely settle and unsettle intelligibility. As a *philosophy* of art, Hegel's lectures offer such commentary. They aim to understand the role of art in modernity.[13] Art is a thing of the past in modernity, he famously argues, since it is no longer *authoritative* as the main practice of collective self-articulation, as it was (according to Hegel) in ancient Greece. Unlike art, philosophy is a mode of *comprehension* (*begreifen*) that is coextensively the work of articulation or grasping and self-awareness. Artistic or religious apprehension is not aware of its own activity of articulation. Philosophical comprehension, in contrast, articulates the most general commitments of a society in a given moment in time as well as its own work and normative assumptions. Philosophy, Hegel argues, is the "self-thinking idea," "truth aware of itself."[14]

SYLLOGISMS OF PHILOSOPHY

The distinction between presentation, apprehension, and comprehension provides a rubric for understanding the three syllogisms of philosophy with which Hegel brings his sketch of a system to a close.[15] The meaning and status of the three syllogisms are central puzzles within Hegel's dense and difficult corpus.[16] The syllogisms, however, are a crucial clue for specifying the work of philosophy. They are three distinct combinations of logic, nature, and *Geist*. The syllogisms are philosophical perspectives for treating the relation between logic, nature, and *Geist*. They establish perspectives from which to consider the relation between a *logische*, *naturalphilosophische*, and *geistige* account of intelligibility. The perspectives are carved out by the positions that logic, nature, and *Geist* occupy within a syllogism: starting point (*Ausgangspunkt*) and presupposition (*Voraussetzung*), middle term (*Mitte*), and form of gathering (*Zusammenschluß*). Each syllogism represents a perspective carved out by the mediating aspect. The syllogisms can be abbreviated as follows:

Logic—Nature—*Geist*
Nature—*Geist*—Logic
Geist—Logic—Nature

The first syllogism has logic (*das logische*) as its starting point, nature as its middle term, and *Geist* as the form of gathering. Logic is the starting point for thinking about nature. A conception of nature provides a link between logic and spirit by "sundering itself"—by being a historically specific conception of nature the metaphysical ("logical") assumptions of which can be specified. But the determinate relation of logic and nature are finally established or gathered together by *Geist*. Nature is hence "defined as a transition point, and negative factor, and as implicitly idea." Nature mediates logic and *Geist*. It thus appears as necessity and *Geist* as recollection.[17] Nature is *geistlos*; it lacks the freedom of *Geist*, since it is not an activity of conscious or self-conscious positing. Logic transitions to nature, since the intelligibility of nature is specified within specific shapes of *Geist*. Logic gives an account of the relation between the non-normative status of nature—itself a specific conception of nature—and gives a formal account of the determination of nature, of specific conceptions of nature, by *Geist*.

In the second syllogism, *Geist* is the mediating element, thus it "presupposes" (*voraussetzt*) nature. Both spirit and nature are gathered together by logic.[18] Spirit presupposes nature, since the self-determining activity of *Geist* depends on material reality, on nature. The second syllogism itself is the standpoint of *Geist*, which presupposes nature and reflects on itself as idea. Here "philosophy appears as a subjective cognition, of which freedom is the aim, and which is itself the way to produce it." Philosophy appears as subjective cognition, insofar as it is dependent on nature and at the same time free from it. Subjectivity or rationality is here narrowly construed, as a matter of epistemic or moral subjectivity, rather than as a general theory of intelligibility. The logical distinctions established by *Geist* are nevertheless thematized by a logical account of determinacy, by philosophy as an individual's practice. Philosophy here is accordingly not yet a form of absolute knowing, of *Geist* that knows itself as *Geist*, of a society that knows itself in its historicity.

In the third syllogism, logic is the middle term, which Hegel here glosses as "self-knowing reason" (*die sich wissende Vernunft*), the "absolute universal" (*das Absolut-Allgemeine*). Logic, in the third syllogism, *divides itself* (*entzweit*) into *Geist* and nature. *Geist* is thus made into the "presupposition, the process of the idea's subjective activity," and nature into the "universal extreme, as process of the objectively and implicitly existing idea."[19] Logic is both the practice of articulating the most general assumptions involved in a historically specific conception of intelligibility and the acknowledgment that these assumptions themselves express the commitments of a concrete shape of *Geist*. Logic must externalize itself, however, it must refer to nature, to material reality, if its critical assessment of intelligibility is to be a concrete articulation of what is. This move to nature is eventually also a move back to *Geist*.

By reconstructing the intersection between logic, nature, and *Geist*, the syllogisms of philosophy clarify the work of philosophy. Philosophy can account for intelligibility on the basis of three different grounds: reason in general, nature and material constrains in particular, and historically individuated normative commitments in their singularity. These perspectives, however, make possible the critical assessment of the combinations in light of the theory of determinacy elaborated in the *Logic*. A philosophical account of nature or *Geist* from any one of these perspectives must incorporate the consequences of the theory of normative authority that makes them possible in the first place. I have argued that Hegel's insistence on negativity has consequences for the theory of normative authority elaborated under the banner of the absolute idea. Normative distinctions—distinctions between conceptions of nature and *Geist*—are precarious and ambivalent. They are for this reason a matter of concrete articulation. Philosophy, then, provides occasion for the critical history of normative commitments, of concrete conceptions of nature and *Geist*. A critical history is one that makes explicit the norm at work in practices of articulation and delivers it for the purposes of assessment and critique. It clarifies the commitment that the norm expresses together with the insurmountable risk internal to the commitment in question: that it is an institution to be maintained and can be debunked, that it can sustain precisely the opposite of what it purports to represent.

NOTES

INTRODUCTION

1. For discussions of the genesis of Hegel's idea of freedom in the economic, political, and religious shifts in eighteenth- and nineteenth-century Germany, see Laurence Dickey's classic study, *Hegel: Religion, Economics, and the Politics of Spirit, 1770–1807* (Cambridge: Cambridge University Press, 1989). See also Georg Lukács's *The Young Hegel: Studies in the Relation Between Dialectics and Economics*, trans. Rodney Livingston (Cambridge, Mass.: MIT Press, 1977); Raymond Plant, "Economic and Social Integration in Hegel's Political Philosophy," in *Selected Essays on G. W.F Hegel*, ed. Lawrence Stepelvich (New Jersey: Humanities Press, 1993); Terry Pinkard, *Hegel: A Biography* (Cambridge: Cambridge University Press, 2001); and H. S. Harris, *Hegel's Development*, vols. 1 and 2 (Oxford: Clarendon Press, 1972 and 1983).

2. I am here following Terry Pinkard, *German Philosophy, 1760–1860: The Legacy of Idealism* (Cambridge: Cambridge University Press, 2002) and Robert Pippin, esp. *Hegel's Practical Philosophy* (Cambridge: Cambridge University Press, 2008).

3. See Jerome Schneewind's *The Invention of Autonomy* (Cambridge: Cambridge University Press, 1998) for an account of the development of notion of autonomy in seventeenth- and eighteenth-century Europe. Schneewind argues that it is a mistake to trace the development of the notion of autonomy to the *Aufklärung* or *Lumière* intellectuals (see, e.g., p. 8). Cf. Pinkard, *German Philosophy*.

4. Rousseau first made the connection between freedom, self-governance, and lawfulness in *The Social Contract* when he argued that "obedience to the law one has prescribed to oneself is freedom" (*The Social Contract* in *The Social Contract and Other Later Political Wrings*, ed. Victor Gourevitch [Cambridge: Cambridge University Press, 1997], bk. 1, chap. 8, p. 54). It was Kant, however, who sought to establish the connection between lawfulness and freedom in the notion of autonomy. We are self-governing *because* we are autonomous, Kant argued, because of the legislative character of willing itself. See Schneewind, *The Invention of Autonomy*.

5. Plant, "Economic and Social Integration," p. 92.

6. See Plant, "Economic and Social Integration," p. 97.

7. G.W.F. Hegel, *Lectures on the Philosophy of Spirit, 1805–6*, in *Hegel and the Human Spirit*, trans. Leo Rauch (Detroit: Wayne State University Press, 1983), p. 140.

8. PR 244.

9. See Merold Westphal, "Hegel and the Reformation," in *Hegel, Freedom, Modernity* (Albany: SUNY Press, 1992).

10. Hegel, *Lectures on the History of Philosophy,* vol. 3: *Medieval and Modern Philosophy* (Lincoln: University of Nebraska Press), pp. 217–18.

11. Ibid., vol. 3, p. 114.

12. Hegel, *Philosophy of History,* p. 243.

13. SL 9/WL 5:43.

14. The phrase "rendering intelligible" is Pippin's. See *Hegel's Practical Philosophy.*

15. See EG 572ff.

16. See Allan Wood, *Hegel's Ethical Thought* (Cambridge: Cambridge University Press, 1990), which argues that a defense of Hegel's social theory requires an outright rejection of Hegel's speculative logic. See Gillian Rose's *Hegel Contra Sociology* (London: The Athlone Press, 1981) and Pippin's *Hegel's Practical Philosophy* for the opposite claim, which this book also defends. For a very good account of these debates and a systematic reading of the *Philosophy of Right*, see Thom Brooks, *Hegel's Political Philosophy* (Edinburgh: Edinburgh University Press, 2012).

17. See Robert Pippin, *Idealism as Modernism: Hegelian Variations* (Cambridge: Cambridge University Press, 1997); *Modernism as a Philosophical Problem* (Oxford: Blackwell, 1999); and *Hegel's Practical Philosophy.* See also Pippin, *Hegel's Idealism: The Satisfactions of Self-Consciousness* (Cambridge: Cambridge University Press, 1989). To be fair, it was Jürgen Habermas who first argued that "Hegel is not the first philosopher to belong to the modern age, but he is the first for whom modernity becomes a problem." See *The Philosophical Discourse of Modernity,* trans. Frederick Lawrence (Cambridge, Mass.: MIT Press, 1990), p. 43. For a powerful rejoinder of Habermas's critique of Hegel, see Pippin's, "Hegel, Modernity, and Habermas," *Monist* 74, no. 3 (1991).

18. Kant's decisive formulation of autonomy in the *Groundwork* reads as follows: "[The will is] not merely subject to the law but subject to it in such a way that it must be viewed as also giving the law to itself and just because of this as first subject to the law (of which it can regard itself as the author [*Urheber*])" (G 4:431). See my "Kant's Hyperbolic Formalism," *Idealistic Studies* 42, no. 1 (2013) for a reading of Kantian *Moralität* as a theory of normative authority.

19. See CPR A126.

20. See Pippin's differentiation between Cartesian and Kantian modernism in "Hegel, Modernity, Habermas," p. 14. While the former is a matter of the "self's apprehension of the indubitable, the incorrigibly given contents of its own consciousness, and to proceed 'outwards' by methodologically rigorous means," the latter "establishes 'the autonomy of reason,' the demand that reason determine for itself what it shall accept as evidence about the nature of things, and that it determine for itself the rule under which it shall evaluate actions. Reason thus emerges as the supreme self legislator, in Kant's crucial, anti-metaphysical phrase, 'occupied with nothing but itself,' 'commanding' and 'legislating' to nature, 'framing for itself with perfect spontaneity an order of its own according to ideas, to which it adapts the empirical conditions.'"

21. For Hegel, in Pippin's words, what is required is "a historical account of why we have come to regard some set of rules or a practice as authoritative or even indispensable." See "Hegel, Modernity, Habermas," p. 21.

22. My gloss on modernism as the self-consciousness of modernity follows Jay Bernstein, "Arendt's Political Modernism," *Graduate Faculty Philosophy Journal* 28, no. 1 (2007).

23. For helpful discussions of *die Sache*, see Béatrice Longuenesse, *Hegel's Critique of Metaphysics* (Cambridge: Cambridge University Press, 2007), pp. 106ff.; Terry Pinkard, *Hegel's Phenomenology: The Sociality of Reason* (Cambridge: Cambridge University Press, 1994), pp. 122–24; and especially Brady Bowman, *Hegel and the Metaphysics of Absolute Negativity* (Cambridge: Cambridge University Press, 2013), chap. 6. I discuss "*die Sache Selbst*" in parts 2 and 3 below, in the context of an assessment of the notion of ground and the notions of universality, particularity, and individuality.

24. See Bowman's *Hegel's Metaphysics of Absolute Negativity*, esp. pp. 39, 54, for an account of negativity as a logical operation. See also William Torrey Harris, *Hegel's Logic: A Book on the Genesis of the Categories of Mind* (Chicago: S.C. Griggs, 1980), quoted in Bowman, *Hegel's Metaphysics of Absolute Negativity*, 53 n. 38.

25. For overviews of the reception of Hegel within analytic philosophy, see Paul Redding, *Analytic Philosophy and the Return of Hegelian Thought* (Cambridge: Cambridge University Press, 2007); Tom Rockmore, *Hegel, Idealism, and Analytic Philosophy* (New Haven: Yale University Press, 2005); and Angelica Nuzzo, *Hegel and the Analytic Tradition* (London: Continuum, 2010). Notwithstanding significant differences, the following are important contemporary continental readings of Hegel: Rebecca Comay, *Mourning Sickness: Hegel and the French Revolution* (Stanford: Stanford University Press, 2010); Angelica Nuzzo, *Memory, History, Justice in Hegel* (London: Palgrave, 2012); Karin de Boer, *On Hegel: The Sway of the Negative* (London: Palgrave, 2010); Jean Lucy-Nancy, *Hegel: The Restlessness of the Negative*, trans. J. Smith and S. Miller (Minneapolis: University of Minnesota Press, 2002) and *The Speculative Remark (One of Hegel's Bon Mots)*, trans. Céline Surprenant (Stanford: Stanford University Press, 2001); and Slavoj Žižek, *Tarrying with the Negative* (Durham: Duke University Press, 1996), *A Parallax View* (Cambridge, Mass.: MIT Press, 2006), and *Less than Nothing* (London: Verso, 2012).

26. See Pippin, *Hegel's Idealism* and *Hegel's Practical Philosophy*. See Robert Brandom, "Some Pragmatist Themes in Hegel's Idealism" and "Holism and Idealism in Hegel's Phenomenology," in *Tales of the Mighty Dead: Historical Essays on the Metaphysics of Intentionality* (Cambridge, Mass.: Harvard University Press, 1991), "Sketch of a Program for a Critical Reading of Hegel: Comparing Empirical and Logical Concepts," *Internationales Jahrbuch des Deutschen Idealismus* 3 (2005), and *Reason in Philosophy: Animating Ideas* (Cambridge, Mass.: Harvard University Press, 2009).

27. See de Boer, *On Hegel*, and "Différance as Negativity: The Hegelian Remains of Derrida's Philosophy," in *A Companion to Hegel*, ed. Michael Baur and Stephen Houlgate (London: Blackwell, 2011); Comay, *Mourning Sickness*; and Catherine Malabou, *The Future of Hegel: Plasticity, Temporality, Dialectics*, trans. Lisabeth During (London: Routledge, 2004), and "Deconstructive and/or Plastic Readings of Hegel," *Bulletin of the Hegel Society of Great Britain* 41–42 (2007).

28. For an account of Hegel's philosophy centered on the notion of *Versöhnung*, see Michael Hardimon's *Hegel Social Philosophy: The Project of Reconciliation* (Cambridge: Cambridge University Press, 1994).

29. Jacques Derrida, *Positions*, trans. Alan Bass (Chicago: University of Chicago Press, 1981), p. 44.

30. Klaus Hartmann's "Hegel: A Non-Metaphysical View," in *Hegel: A Collection of Critical Essays,* ed. Alasdair MacIntyre (Notre Dame, Ind.: University of Notre Dame Press, 1977) arguably initiated this interpretive trend by proposing that a "non-metaphysical" reading of Hegel depends on establishing Hegel's indebtedness to Kant. Nevertheless, *Hegel's Idealism* set the parameters of the debate about the status of Hegel's idealism. See Stephen Houlgate, *The Opening of Hegel's* Logic: *From Being to Infinity* (West Lafayette, Ind.: Purdue University Press, 2005) and Robert Stern, *Hegelian Metaphysics* (Oxford: Oxford University Press, 2009) for readings of Hegel as offering a post-Kantian ontology. See Hans Friedrich Fulda, "Ontologie nach Kant und Hegel," in *Metaphysik nach Kant?,* ed. Dieter Henrich and R.-P. Horstmann (Stuttgart: Klett-Cotta, 1987), and Brady Bowman, *Hegel's Metaphysics of Absolute Negativity* (Cambridge: Cambridge University Press, 2013) for readings of Hegel's metaphysics as a critique and overcoming of traditional ontology. For helpful summaries of the debate, see James Kreines, "Hegel's Metaphysics: Changing the Debate," *Philosophy Compass* 1, no. 5 (2006); Simon Lumsden, "The Rise of the Non-metaphysical Hegel," *Philosophical Compass* 3, no. 1 (2008); and also Rolf Peter Horstmann, "What is Hegel's Legacy and What Should We Do With It?" *European Journal of Philosophy* 7, no. 2 (1999).

31. Pippin, *Hegel's Idealism*, pp. 6, 18.

32. Pippin, *Hegel's Practical Philosophy,* p. 101.

33. Ibid., p. 102.

34. Ibid., p. 19.

35. Ibid., p. 103.

36. Ibid., p. 130.

37. Ibid., p. 238.

38. Brandom, *Reason in Philosophy*, p. 38.

39. See ibid., pp. 64ff.

40. Ibid., pp. 36ff.

41. Derrida, *Positions*, p. 44.

42. Derrida, "The Ends of Man," in *Margins of Philosophy,* p. 74.

43. Jacques Derrida, "*Différance,*" in *Margins of Philosophy*, trans. Alan Bass (Chicago: University of Chicago Press, 1982), p. 11.

44. See Martin Hägglund, *Radical Atheism: Derrida and the Time of Life* (Stanford: Stanford University Press, 2008).

45. De Boer, *On Hegel*, p. 2.

46. Ibid., p. 3.

47. See Bowman's account of absolute negativity and his reply to de Boer in *Hegel and the Metaphysics of Absolute Negativity*, p. 49 n. 35.

48. De Boer, *On Hegel*, p. 3.

49. Ibid., p. 4.

50. Ibid., p. 37.

51. Ibid., pp. 54, 71.

52. Ibid., p. 100.

PART 1

1. SL 60/WL 5:83.

2. See Rosen, *The Idea of Hegel's* Science of Logic, pp. 47ff.

3. See, for example, Sonsgsuk Susan Hahn, *Contradiction in Motion: Hegel's Concept of Life and Value* (Ithaca: Cornell University Press, 2007); Angelica Nuzzo, "Dialectic as a Logic of Transformative Processes," in *Hegel: New Directions*, ed. Katerina Deligiorgi (Montreal: McGill Queen's University Press, 2006); and de Boer's *On Hegel*.

4. For treatments of the problem of synthesis, see Robert Stern, *Kant, Hegel, and the Unity of the Object* (London: Routledge, 1990), and Béatrice Longuenesse, *Kant and the Capacity to Judge: Sensibility and Discursivity in the Transcendental Analytic* (Princeton: Princeton University Press, 2001).

5. CPR B103/A77.

6. To be sure, as Henry Allison stresses in *Kant's Transcendental Idealism* (New Haven: Yale University Press, 2004), to be manifold is already to be a certain kind of unity—singular, whole, immediate. Synthesis proper, as we will see, is a matter of a synthetic unity—combination of the manifold in one cognition.

7. This also holds for Hegel's critique of Kantian morality. For Hegel, Kant's emphasis on a moral subject monologically determining her action by referring to an abstractly universal moral law misconstrues the determinacy of an action or moral worth.

8. For his account of positivity during the Frankfurt period, see esp. "The Spirit of Christianity and its Fate" and "The Positivity of the Christian Religion" in G.W.F. Hegel, *Early Theological Writings*, trans. T. M. Knox (Philadelphia: University of Pennsylvania Press, 1971). For classic discussions of the problem of positivity in Hegel, see Lukács, *The Young Hegel*, and Dickey, *Hegel: Religion, Economics, and the Politics of Spirit*. More recent engagements with the topic include Alice Ormiston, *Love and Politics: Reinterpreting Hegel* (Albany: SUNY Press, 2004).

9. See Hegel's general Introduction to the SL, and the introduction to the Subjective Logic. See also the Preface to the PG. Finally, see the *Vorbegriff* to the EL.

10. See, e.g., SL 35, 741/WL 5:43, 6:556.

11. PS 30–31/PG 36.

12. SL 507/WL 6:243.

13. See esp. Pippin's discussion of PG in *Hegel's Idealism*.

14. SL 33/WL 5:16. See Bowman's engagement with Lawrence Horn in chapter 7 of *Hegel's Metaphysics of Absolute Negativity*. In *A Natural History of Negation* (Chicago: University of Chicago Press, 1989), Horn provides a history of negation and assesses this history in terms of what he calls symmetricalism and asymmetricalism, the latter being the position that negation presupposes and may thus be reducible to true affirmative propositions—a position that Horn attributes to Hegel. Bowman argues that Horn fails to grasp that Hegel is a "negative asymmetricalist" insofar as for Hegel affirmation presupposes and is reducible to negation (see pp. 24,

247–49). Hegel's key insight, then, is that such unity is itself the product of negation, establishing mediation as ongoing.

15. Bowman's discussion of Dieter Henrich's influential account of negation as "autonomous negation" is helpful here. Hegel "autonomizes negation," Henrich argues, by arguing that it is the logical operation from which all others derive. Negation negates something. It applies to itself, however. The self-referential application of negation has an affirmative result. The identity of negation with itself establishes relation to an other as a feature of relation to self. The point is that negation, for Hegel, is a matter of *self*-negation, not the operation over against something deemed other. As Henrich sums it up: "The absolute is at one with itself only in its being other" (quoted in Bowman, *Hegel's Metaphysics of Absolute Negativity*, p. 53). As we will see, negation is not an operation over against content or matter. As will become clear in parts 2 and 3, negation is the self-negation and hence self-relation of matters themselves.

16. I am here disagreeing with Spinozist readings of Hegel, one of which (Stephen Houlgate's) I will discuss at length in part 2 below.

17. See, e.g., Graham Priest, *Beyond the Limits of Thought* (Oxford: Oxford University Press, 1995); Paul Redding, *Analytic Philosophy and the Return to Hegelian Thought*; and Robert Brandom "Holism and Idealism in Hegel's *Phenomenology*" for discussions about Hegel's treatment of the principle of noncontradiction.

18. For example, in the Doctrine of Essence, Hegel explains that positedness is not the merely the "determinateness that exists quiescent, one which would be related to an other in such a way that the related term and its relation would be different, each something existing in itself, each a something that excludes its other and its relation to this other from itself" (SL 353/WL 6:35; trans. mod.).

CHAPTER 1

1. CPR A50/B74.

2. CPR B75/A51.

3. CPR B75/A51.

4. In *Kant and the Capacity to Judge*, p. 28, Longuenesse writes: "If the solution proposed is to be at all possible, something *in the nature of appearances themselves* must make them agree with the forms of the logical use of the understanding and, if the categories are originally nothing but the logical functions according to these forms, with the categories. It must therefore be shown that these functions are not only conditions of the subordination of the concepts according to logical use, but conditions *of the very presentation of the appearances in sensible intuition*, a presentation that generates for these appearances objects reflected under concepts."

5. I will bracket the claim that we can only know appearances and not things in themselves, and consider division and unity in Kant as features of his exposition of the problem of representation and self-consciousness. I will come to the doctrine of transcendental idealism below, in my discussions of Fichte and Hegel.

6. See Henry Allison, *Kant's Transcendental Idealism*, pp. 138ff., for an account of discursivity that is informing my discussion. See also Robert Pippin, *Kant's Theory of Form: An Essay on the Critique of Pure Reason* (New Haven: Yale University Press, 1982).

7. For recent debates about conceptualism and nonconceptualism relevant to this point, see Hannah Ginsborg, "Was Kant a Nonconceptualist?" *Philosophical Studies* 137 (2008); Lucy Allias, "Kant, Non-Conceptual Content and the Representation of Space," *Journal of the History of Philosophy* 47, no. 3 (2009); Robert Hannah, "Kantian Nonconceptualism," *Philosophical Studies* 137 (2008) and "Kant, Hegel, and the Fate of Non-Conceptual Content," *Hegel Bulletin* 34, no. 1 (2013); and Colin McLear, "Two Kinds of Unity in the Critique of Pure Reason," forthcoming in *Journal of the History of Philosophy*, and "Kant on Perceptual Content," forthcoming in *Mind.* Cf. John McDowell, *Mind and World* (Cambridge, Mass.: Harvard University Press, 1996) and *Having the World in View* (Cambridge, Mass.: Harvard University Press, 2009); Stephen Engstrom "Understanding and Sensibility," *Inquiry* 49, no. 1 (2006); and Sebastian Rödl, *Self-Consciousness* (Cambridge, Mass.: Harvard University Press, 2007).

8. There are two major problems that I will not go into here but that are relevant to the point that I am making. First, the Aesthetic is important for Hegel insofar as it establishes that givenness itself requires a constraint, for otherwise we cannot account for the fact that we are sensibly affected. Second, for Hegel, Kant's claim in B160n that space and time are pure intuitions represents an admission that spontaneity is already at work in receptivity. See Sally Sedgwick's discussion in *Hegel's Critique of Kant: From Dichotomy to Identity* (Oxford: Oxford University Press, 2012), pp. 34ff. and 113ff.

9. I am here following Sedgwick.

10. I discuss the notions of intuitive understanding (*intuitiver Verstand*) and intellectual intuition (*intellektuelle Anschauung*) below.

11. CPR A21–22/B36.

12. See, e.g., A92–93/B125, and esp. A89/B121–22. See also Longuenesse, *Kant and the Capacity to Judge*, e.g., p. 24.

13. See Angelica Nuzzo, *Ideal Embodiment: Kant's Theory of Sensibility* (Bloomington: Indiana University Press, 2008), which argues that as the transcendental site of sensibility, the body displays a formal, ideal dimension essential to our experience as human beings (see pp. 9–10). Cf. for example Marcus Willaschek, "Der transzendentale Idealismus und die Idealität von Raum und Zeit," *Zeitschrift für philosophische Forschung* 51, no. 4 (1997).

14. See, e.g., CPR A320/B 377.

15. Longuenesse glosses Kant's understanding of a concept as a function of unity, as a rule for bringing a manifold to unity, in a helpful way when she writes that "every concept is a *rule* insofar as its explication (e.g., a body is extended, limited in space and impenetrable) can function as a major premise in a syllogism whose conclusion would be the attribution of the marks belonging to this concept to an object of sensible intuition" (*Kant and the Capacity to Judge*, p. 50).

16. "All judgments," Kant writes, "are functions of unity among our representations, since instead of an immediate representation a higher one, which comprehends this and other representations under itself, is used for the cognition of the object, and many possible cognitions are thereby drawn together into one" (CPR A69/B94).

17. Kant writes: "Thus a difficulty is revealed here that we did not encounter in the field of sensibility, namely, how *subjective conditions of thinking* should have *objective validity*; i.e., yield conditions of the possibility of all cognition of objects, for appearances can be given in intuition without the functions of the understanding" (CPR A89–90/B122). An exposition of the capacity

for synthesis and of the activity of synthesizing is the centerpiece of a transcendental deduction, of the attempt to establish the objectivity of cognition by showing the applicability of pure *a priori* concepts to a sensible given.

18. Hegel was perhaps the first to dismiss the metaphysical deduction as Kant's illegitimate move from general logic to transcendental logic, from an analysis of logical validity to an account of transcendental synthesis in judgment. In merely borrowing the forms of judgment from logic books of his day, Hegel argued, Kant's deduction is "inconsequential." See Hegel, SL 541/WL 6:288. In addition to the problem of unexamined presuppositions, Hegel and others have called into question Kant's emphasis on the completeness of the table of categories. For helpful discussions of these two issues, see Allison, *Kant's Transcendental Idealism*; P. F. Strawson, *The Bounds of Sense* (London: Methuen & Co. Ltd, 1966); Michael Wolff, *Die Vollständigkeit der kantischen Urteilstafel* (Frankfurt am Main: Klostennarm, 1995); and Longuenesse, *Kant and the Capacity to Judge*. See also Allison's discussion of the problem of circularity between the metaphysical and transcendental deduction in *Kant's Transcendental Idealism*, p. 152.

19. Allison borrows "form follows function" from Frank Lloyd Wright. See *Kant's Transcendental Idealism*, p. 148.

20. This is a paraphrase of Allison, *Kant's Transcendental Idealism,* p. 149.

21. See ibid., pp. 147, 148.

22. Ibid. p. 151.

23. Unlike general logic, which deals with matters of validity abstracting from the content of cognition, "[t]ranscendental logic . . . teaches how to bring under concepts not the representations but the **pure synthesis** of representations" (CPR A78/B104). This establishes, Kant maintains, an isomorphism between the forms of judgment and the specific functions of unity, and hence between the table of judgments and the table of categories. The rule implicit in the form of judgment shows the correspondence between the two catalogues. What is crucial here, however, is Kant's claim that "[t]he same function that gives unity to the different representations **in a judgment** also gives unity to the mere synthesis of different representations **in an intuition**, which, expressed generally, is called the pure concepts of the understanding" (A79/B105).

24. "We can trace all actions of the understanding back to judgments," Kant writes in CPR A69/B94, "so that the **understanding** in general can be represented as a faculty of judging."

25. CPR A78–79/B104. In the A deduction, Kant elaborates his account of synthesis as a threefold synthesis as a matter of apprehension in intuition, reproduction in imagination, and recognition in a concept. These are ways in which an indeterminate manifold is synthesized from the given in sensation, the representation of the sensible in imagination, and the universal representation under a rule. See Longuenesse's *Kant and the Capacity to Judge* for a two-directional account of the deduction, one that follows a discursive-reflective model of logic, and the other that follows an intuitive-constructive model of mathematics. Consider also Rudolph Makkreel, *Imagination and Interpretation in Kant: The Hermeneutical Import of the* Critique of Judgment (Chicago: University of Chicago Press, 1995), who argues against Norman Kemp Smith and others that "it is possible to maintain the cumulative thesis by regarding the synthesis of apprehension as a gathering, imaginative reproduction as an associative synthesis, and the synthesis of recognition as a connecting or unifying synthesis" (p. 27). Cf. H. J. Paton, *Kant's*

Metaphysic of Experience (London: Macmillan, 1936); and Norman Kemp Smith, *A Commentary to Kant's* Critique of Pure Reason (London: Macmillan, 1918).

26. "[S]ynthesis alone," Kant also writes, "is that which properly collects the elements for cognitions and unifies them into a certain content" (A77–78/B13).

27. CPR A77/B102.

28. CPR A78/B103.

29. The role of the imagination, in its transcendental sense, is combining the manifold in a way that it can be subjected to a rule, but it also provides the condition for iterability—the repetition of the application of a rule in different cases. The imagination synthesizes according to a rule (A100).

30. "[T]o bring this synthesis [of the imagination—RZ] **to concepts**," Kant reiterates in A78/B103, "is a function that pertains to the understanding, and by means of which it first provides cognition in the proper sense."

31. The upshot of the deduction is the claim that cognition a priori makes possible "prescribing the law to nature and even making the latter possible" (B161; see also B164–65), which is perhaps Kant's strongest statement. See also Kant's famous footnote of B160 and Pippin, *Hegel's Idealism,* for an account of the impact of this claim on the development of Fichte and Hegel's idealism. I will come back to this below.

32. CPR B151.

33. CPR B138.

34. See CPR B130.

35. CPR B135.

36. "The *transcendental unity* of apperception is that unity though which all of the manifold given in an intuition is united in a concept of the object" (CPR B139).

37. In fact, Kant argues that "[c]ombination is the representation of the synthetic unity of the manifold" (CPR B130).

38. CPR B132.

39. For Kant's gloss on the transcendental unity of apperception as "original unity," see, e.g., CPR B135 and B157. For a stronger version of this claim, see CPR A107: "Now no cognitions can occur in us, no connection and unity among them, without that unity of consciousness that precedes all data of the intuitions, and in relation to which all representations of objects is alone possible. This pure, original, unchanging consciousness I will now name transcendental apperception."

40. See SL 516/WL 6:256.

41. See SL 520/WL 6:260.

CHAPTER 2

1. See Pippin, *Hegel's Idealism,* chap. 2.

2. While there is a growing literature reconsidering Hegel's relation to Fichte, the most common interpretive line still maintains that Hegel's own brand of idealism is closer to Schelling's. See Frederick C. Beiser, *Hegel* (London: Routledge, 2004), *German Idealism: The Struggle*

Against Subjectivism, 1781–1801 (Cambridge, Mass.: Harvard University Press, 2008), and *The Fate of Reason: German Philosophy From Kant to Fichte* (Cambridge, Mass.: Harvard University Press, 1993); see also Markus Gabriel, "The Mythological Being of Reflection: An Essay on Hegel, Schelling, and the Contingency of Necessity," in *Mythology, Madness, and Laughter: Subjectivity in German Idealism,* by Markus Gabriel and Slavoj Žižek (New York: Continuum, 2009), and "Contingency or Necessity? Schelling versus Hegel," in *Transcendental Ontology: Essays in German Idealism* (New York: Continuum, 2011).

3. In addition to Pippin's *Hegel's Idealism*, his "Fichte's Alleged Subjective, Psychological, One-Sided Idealism," in *The Reception of Kant's Critical Philosophy: Fichte, Schelling, Hegel*, ed. Sally Sedgwick (Cambridge: Cambridge University Press, 2000), and Pinkard's *German Philosophy*, see Frederick Neuhouser, *Fichte's Theory of Subjectivity* (Cambridge: Cambridge University Press, 1990); Wayne Martin, *Idealism and Objectivity: Understanding Fichte's Jena Project* (Stanford: Stanford University Press, 1997), and Daniel Breazeale, "Check or Checkmate? On the Finitude of the Fichtean Self," in *The Modern Subject*: *Conceptions of the Self in Classical German Philosophy,* ed. Karl Ameriks and Dieter Sturma (Albany: SUNY Press, 2005).

4. See Wayne Martin, "From Kant to Fichte," forthcoming in *Cambridge Companion to Fichte* (Cambridge: Cambridge University Press) and available at http://privatewww.essex.ac.uk/~wmartin/, and "Fichte's Legacy in Logic," in *Fichte and the Phenomenological Tradition,* ed. Violetta L. Maria Waibel et al. (Berlin: de Gruyter, 2010). See also Nectarios G. Limnatis, *German Idealism and the Problem of Knowledge* (New York: Springer, 2008), and Dean Moyar, *Hegel's Conscience* (Oxford: Oxford University Press, 2011).

5. Fichte, First Introduction to the *Science of Knowledge (Wissenschaftslehre)*, ed. and trans. Peter Heath and John Lachs (New York: Appleton-Century-Crofts, 1970), p. 4. He also writes that it is "Kantianism properly understood," p. 43.

6. Ibid.

7. In the Second Introduction to the *Wissenschaftslehre*, Fichte writes: "since nothing exists for him that is not consciousness, while everything else therein is conditioned by this very act, and so cannot again condition it in the same respect, he will grasp it, moreover, as *for him* a wholly unconditioned and thus absolute act. He will then, we trust, realize accordingly that the *presupposition in question*, and the *though of the self as originally posited by itself*, are again perfectly identical; and that transcendental idealism, if it is to go to work systematically, cannot possibly proceed in any other way than it does in the *Science of Knowledge*" (pp. 37–38).

8. See esp. the discussion in the 1797 Introduction to the *Wissenschaftslehre*, pp. 58ff.

9. In the Second Introduction to the *Wissenschaftslehre*, Fichte writes: "though the self may exist only for itself, there necessarily arises for it at once an existence external to it; the ground of the latter lies in the former, and it is conditioned thereby: self-consciousness and consciousness of something that is to be—not ourselves—are necessarily connected, but the first is to be regarded as a conditioning factor and the second as the conditioned" (p. 33).

10. Fichte, First Introduction to the *Wissenschaftslehre,* p. 69.

11. Fichte, Second Introduction to the *Wissenschaftslehre*, p. 34. The German reads: "Erst durch diesen Akt und lediglich durch ihn, durch ein Handeln auf ein Handeln selbst, welchen bestimmten Handeln kein Handeln überhaupt vorhergeht, wird das Ich *ursprünglich* für sich selbst" (I, 39). See also: "the self and the self-reverting act are perfectly identical concepts."

12. Ibid., p. 37.

13. See Fichte's discussion in ibid., pp. 47 and esp. 48.

14. This is Pippin's metaphor throughout his work.

15. Fichte discusses the problem of a regress addressed by the priority of action in the Second Introduction to the *Wissenschaftslehre*, p. 49. See Henrich, "Fichte's Original Insight," trans. David Lachterman, in *Contemporary German Philosophy*, vol. 1, ed. Darrel E. Christensen (University Park: Pennsylvania State University Press, 1982); and Pippin's discussion of it in *Hegel's Idealism*.

16. Fichte, Second Introduction to the *Wissenschaftslehre,* p. 35.

17. Ibid., p. 42.

18. Cf. Brazeale's gloss in "Fichte's *Aenesidemus Review* and the Transformation of German Idealism," *The Review of Metaphysics* 34, no. 3 (1981).

19. Fichte, Second Introduction to the *Wissenschaftslehre,* p. 72.

20. Ibid., p. 41.

21. CPR B145, and B151. See Eckart Förster, *Twenty-Five Years of Philosophy: A Systematic Reconstruction* (Cambridge, Mass.: Harvard University Press, 2012), and "The Significance of §§76 and 77 of the *Critique of Judgment* for the Development of Post-Kantian Philosophy (Parts 1 and 2)," trans. Karen Ng and Matthew Congdon, *Graduate Faculty Philosophy Journal* 30, no. 2 and 31, no. 2 (2009–10); cf. Longuenesse, *Hegel's Critique of Metaphysics*. See also Sedgwick, *Hegel's Critique of Kant*.

22. In all three *Critiques*, Kant develops a contrast concept crucial for establishing the strictures of finite cognition and action. Because the understanding and sensibility are two stems of cognition independent of one another, we must distinguish between possibility and actuality (otherwise we would have intellectual intuition); because we are both sensible and rational beings, the moral law appears to us as what ought to be, not as what is (otherwise we would have a holy will); because our understanding is discursive, the power of judgment judges organisms inevitably as natural purposes (otherwise we would have intuitive understanding). See Forster, *Twenty-Five Years of Philosophy*.

23. Pippin, Seminar on Post-Kantian Idealism, sponsored by *Journal of the History of Philosophy*, University of Chicago, Summer 2012.

24. Fichte, Second Introduction to the *Wissenschaftslehre,* p. 46.

25. Pinkard, *German Philosophy*, chap. 5, and Pippin, *Hegel's Idealism*, esp. pp. 54ff.

26. See, e.g., Second Introduction to the *Wissenschaftslehre*, pp. 40–41, where Fichte writes: "This comes about solely by exhibition of the moral law in us, wherein the self is presented as a thing sublime beyond all original modifications effected by that law; is credited with an absolute activity founded only in itself and in nothing else whatever; and is thus characterized as an absolute agency. The consciousness of this law, which itself is doubtless an immediate consciousness derived from no other, forms the basis for the intuition of self-activity and freedom; I am given to myself by myself, as something that is to be active in a certain fashion; I have life within me, and draw it from myself. Only through this medium of the moral law do I behold *myself*; and in thus seeing myself, I necessarily see myself as self-active; and thereby arises for me the wholly alien factor of my self's real efficacy, in a consciousness that would otherwise be merely that of succession among my representations." And also, "philosophy is . . . a product of *practical*

necessity. I *can* go no further from this standpoint. . . . I *ought* in my thinking set out from the pure self, and to think of the latter as absolutely self-active; not as determined by things, but as determining them" (p. 41). For a full account of Fichte's theory of normativity, see Pinkard, *German Philosophy*.

27. See my "Kant's Hyperbolic Formalism" for a full account of this gloss.

28. "Everyone, to be sure," Fichte for example writes, "can be shown, in his own admitted experience, that this intellectual intuition occurs at every moment of consciousness. I cannot take a step, move hand or foot, without an intellectual intuition of my consciousness in these acts; only so do I know that *I* do it, and only so do I distinguish my action, and myself therein, from the object of action before me. Whoever ascribes an activity to himself, appeals to this intuition" (Second Introduction to the *Wissenschaftslehre*, p. 38).

29. Ibid., p. 49. The German reads: "das Ich in ihm ist lediglich durch sich selbst bestimmt, und ist absolut bestimmt," p. 57.

30. G 4:448.

31. G 4:452. Reason is involved in instituting the distinction between the two standpoints from which agency should be understood and which serve an orienting role for the justification and assessment of agency (G 4:452). Precisely because rational creatures distinguish the intelligible and sensible aspects of themselves, they consider themselves as participants in the "world of the understanding"—as participants in a normative order rather than subject to given nature. The concept of action, Fichte also argues, is "only possible though this intellectual intuition of the self-active self," making possible an account of the objective unity of the sensible and the intelligible (Fichte, Second Introduction to the *Wissenschaftslehre*, p. 41).

32. Fichte, Second Introduction to the *Wissenschaftslehre,* p. 59.

33. Ibid., p. 61. This limitation is an "originary feeling," which ought not be confused with an original feeling of limitation. Forgetfulness of this feeling, Fichte notes, leads to an "extravagant form of transcendental idealism." The absolute determination of the self institutes a normative distinction whereby what is felt limits the self's determination of the not-self. This is a feature of rather than a challenge to Fichte's understanding of the free activity of the self. Indeed, this experience of limitation is precisely what brings into being the concept of the Thou: "That which posits itself in the act in question, not in general, but *as a self*, is myself; and that which is posited not *by itself*, is you" (ibid., p. 72).

34. Fichte, *Wissenschaftslehre*, p. 93.

35. Pippin, *Hegel's Idealism*, pp. 52–53.

36. Fichte, *Wissenschaftslehre*, p. 99.

37. Ibid., p. 94.

38. Ibid., p. 95.

39. Pippin glosses this relation in terms the "*possibility* of identification itself, considered independently of the metaphysics of identity" (*Hegel's Idealism*, p. 53).

40. Fichte adds: "what is *absolutely posited*, and *founded on itself*, is the ground of *one particular* activity . . . of the human mind, and thus of its pure character" (*Wissenschaftslehre*, p. 97).

41. Ibid., pp. 95–96. He arrives at this conclusion by arguing that "[b]y means of X, . . . *A* exists absolutely for the judging self, and . . . simply in virtue of its being posited in the self

as such; which is to say, it is asserted that within the self—whether it be specifically positing, or judging, or whatever it may be—there is something that is permanently uniform, forever one and the same; and hence the X that is absolutely posited can also be expressed as I=I; I am I." See also Fichte's note, which reads: "i.e., in plain language: I, who posits A in the predicate position, necessarily know, because the same was posited in the subject position, about my positing of the subject, and hence know myself, again contemplate myself, am the same with myself."

42. "[T]he possibility of differentiation," Pippin explains, "depends on the self's ability to distinguish itself and *its* 'determinations' from the not-self and its limits on my determinations'" (*Hegel's Idealism*, p. 55).

43. Fichte, *Wissenschaftslehre*, p. 104.

44. Ibid., p. 103.

45. Fichte adds: "Opposition is possible only on the assumption of a unity of consciousness between the self that posits and the self that opposes. For if consciousness of the first act were not connected with that of the second, the latter would be, not a *counter*positing, but an absolute positing. It is only in relation to a positing that it becomes a counterpositing" (ibid., p. 104).

46. Ibid., p. 105.

47. See CPR B125.

48. Fichte, *Wissenschaftslehre*, p. 108.

49. See ibid., p. 106.

50. Pippin, *Hegel's Idealism*, p. 56.

51. Fichte, *Wissenschaftslehre*, p. 108.

52. Ibid.

53. "[T]he primordial act it [the third principle] expresses, that of combining opposites in a third thing, was impossible without the act of counterpositing; and that this also was impossible was impossible without the act of combination; so that both are in practice inseparably united, and can be distinguished only in reflection" (ibid., p. 112).

54. Ibid., p. 110. The principle, as Pippin explains, works in both ways: "Either the self posits the not-self as limited by the self . . . , or the self posits itself as limited by the not-self" (*Hegel's Idealism*, p. 57). While the first direction develops the structure of practical intending, the latter articulates the structure of theoretical intending. The first possibility describes the practical shaping of the world, and hence the material limiting action of the self upon the world. The second possibility describes the constraints that material reality present for the absolute activity of positing.

55. Fichte, *Wissenschaftslehre*, p. 112.

56. "*Both the self and the not-self*," Fichte argues, "*are posited as divisible*; for the act Y cannot *succeed* the act of counterpositing, cannot, that is, be considered as if it was only this latter act that made it possible; for by the foregoing argument, mere opposition alone destroys itself and thus becomes impossible. But the act Y cannot *precede* either; for it is undertaken simply to make opposition possible, and divisibility is nothing without something to divide. Hence it occurs immediately, within and alongside the act of opposition; both are one and the same, and are distinguished only in reflection" (ibid., p. 108).

57. Ibid., p. 109.

CHAPTER 3

1. SL 673/WL 6:465.

2. FK 68/GW 302.

3. "Because the essence of the Kantian philosophy consists in its being critical idealism," Hegel writes, "it plainly confesses that its principle is subjectivism and formal thinking" (FK 67/GW 300).

4. FK 68/GW 302.

5. SL 389/ WL 6:13. Angelica Nuzzo has provided a compelling rubric for understanding the status of "absolute" in Hegel. She points out that the most significant uses of the term "absolute" in Hegel are adjectival rather than nominative—absolute knowing, absolute spirit, the absolute idea. The " 'absolute' is [accordingly] not the highest ens of an ontology, but rather the term that designates the way in which the structures of thinking, cognition, and knowing function once they are grounded in the speculative method" ("The Idea of 'Method' in Hegel's Science of Logic—a Method for Finite Thinking and Absolute Reason," *Bulletin of the Hegel Society of Great Britain* 39–40 [1999], p. 14). See also Markus Gabriel, "The Dialectic of the Absolute: Hegel's Critique of Transcendent Metaphysics," in *Dimensions of Hegel's Dialectic,* ed. Nectario Limnatis (London: Continuum, 2012). See also Pippin, *Hegel's Practical Philosophy,* for a forceful gloss on the absolute as result.

6. FK 69/GW 303.

7. FK 69/GW 303.

8. FK 70/GW 304. See Sally Sedgwick's discussion of this passage in *Hegel's Critique of Kant: From Dichotomy to Unity*.

9. CPR B152.

10. CPR B152; my emphasis.

11. See CPR A138/B177, where Kant defines schema as "pure, that is, void of all empirical content, and yet at the same time, while it must be in one respect *intellectual*, it must be in another sense *sensible*." In his *Imagination and Interpretation in Kant*, Makkreel writes: "The imagination schematizes by translating the rules implicit in the categories into a temporally ordered set of instructions for constructing an objectively determinate nature" (p. 30). The categories apply to appearances if the norm that each represents can be made concrete according to a time determination.

12. FK 70/GW 304.

13. FK 73/GW 307.

14. FK 70/GW 304.

15. Hegel writes: "The productive imagination is a truly speculative idea both in the form of sensuous intuition and in that of experience which is the comprehending of the intuition. For the expression 'synthetic unity' might make identity look as if it presupposes antithesis and needs the manifold of the antithesis as something independent and existing for itself; the identity might look as if it was by nature posterior to the opposition. But in Kant the synthetic unity is undeniably the absolute and original identity of self-consciousness, which of itself posits judgment absolutely and a priori" (FK 71/GW 305).

16. FK 72/GW 306.

17. FK 73/GW 307.

18. According to Hegel, Fichte conceives of such a check in terms of absolute exteriority, which Hegel will show time and again is an incoherent thought. Something can function as a check if it is already implicated in the logic of boundary that Hegel will maintain is the basis for determination. I will say more about this in part 2 below.

19. FK 172/ GW 404–5. He continues: "Just as for knowledge true identity and eternity are in a beyond that is faith, so in the practical sphere, the sphere of reality, they are in a beyond that is infinite progress."

20. FK 171/GW 405.

21. FK 190/GW 430. See also FK 194/GW 431.

22. FK 73/GW 307.

23. FK 72/GW 306.

24. SL 520 /WL 6:260; my emphasis.

25. SL 520/WL 6:260

26. SL 508/WL 6:244: "Ob nun wohl der Begriff nicht nur als eine subjektive Voraussetzung, sondern als absolute Grundlage anzusehen ist, so kann er dies doch nicht sein, als insofern er sich zur Grundlage gemacht hat."

27. Traditionally, debates about the relation between a phenomenology and philosophy proper center around the relation between the *Phenomenology* and the *Logic*. For a recent and insightful overview of debates, see Ardis B. Collins, *Hegel's* Phenomenology*: The Dialectical Justification of Philosophy's First Principles* (Montreal: McGill Queens University Press, 2013), chap. 2; and Rosen, *The Idea of Hegel's* Science of Logic, chap. 3. See also H. S. Harris *Hegel: Phenomenology and System* (Indianapolis: Hackett, 1995), chap. 10.

28. PS 20/PG 23.

29. PS 22/PG 24: "daß die Vernunft das zweckmäßige Tun ist." See Alfredo Ferrarin, *Hegel and Aristotle* (Cambridge: Cambridge University Press, 2007) for an understanding of Hegelian subjectivity as Aristotelian *energeia*.

30. Hegel continues: "The result is the same as the beginning because the beginning is purpose—that is, the actual is the same as its concept only because the immediate, as purpose, has the self, that is, pure actuality, within itself" (PS 22/PG 24).

31. Second emphasis is mine.

32. PS 18/PG 22.

33. PS 22/PG 23.

34. PS 22/PG 23.

35. PS 25/PG 27–28; see also 802/PG 584. Substance is subject, Hegel reiterates in the *Logic*, in being "absolute power or self-referring negativity" (SL 509/WL 6:246).

36. PS 37/PG 38. Hegel writes that "[t]he spiritual alone is the actual."

37. PS 20/PG 23.

38. Hegel writes: "the living substance is the being that is in truth *subject*, or, what amounts to the same thing, it is in truth actual only insofar as it is the movement of self-positing, that is, that it is the mediation of itself and its becoming-other-to-itself" (PS 20/PG 23).

39. PS 25/PG 27.

40. See Taylor, *Hegel*, and Houlgate, *The Opening of the* Science of Logic.

41. See Robert Brandom, manuscript of *A Spirit of Trust: A Systematic Reading of Hegel's* Phenomenology, http://www.pitt.edu/~brandom/spirit_of_trust_2014.html.

42. While the phenomenological moments of the text assess freedom as the main normative commitment structuring modernity, the metaphenomenological moments of the text give a philosophical account of the role that the norm of freedom plays in the reconstruction that the book undertakes.

43. Recall my account of Hegel's modernism in the Introduction to this book.

44. PS 25/PG 29.

45. "der sich als Geist wissende Geist" (PG 509; see also PS 808/PG 590).

46. PS 808/PG 590; PS 803/PG 585.

47. PS 808/PG 589: "der an die Zeit entäußerte Geist."

48. For Hegel, "[n]egativity thus posited for itself is time." See PN 257. See also Hegel's discussion of time in the Jena Logic of 1804–5, and Stephen Houlgate's "Time for Hegel," *Bulletin of the Hegel Society of Great Britain* 53–54 (2006).

49. "*Geist* necessarily appears in time," Hegel argues, "as long as it does not grasp its pure concept, which is to say, as long as it does not annual time" (PS 801/PG 583).

50. PS 808/PG 589.

51. PS 808/PG 589; trans. mod.

52. PS 797/PG 580; see also 808/PG 589.

53. Cf. Angelica Nuzzo's "History and Memory in Hegel's *Phenomenology*" and "Memory, History, and Justice in Hegel's System" in *Graduate Faculty Philosophy Journal* 29, no. 1 (2008) and 31, no. 2 (2010) respectively, and also published in *Memory, History, Justice*. Nuzzo develops what she calls individual, ethical, and logical memory in Hegel's system, and clarifies Hegel's understanding of *Weltgeschichte* as *Weltgericht.*

54. See Habermas, "Hegel's Theory of Modernity"; Pippin, *Idealism as Modernism*; and Pinkard, *German Philosophy*.

55. "For themselves, those moments are individual, and it is their spiritual unity alone which constitutes the force of this reconciliation" (PS 793/PG 577).

56. PS 808/PG 589.

57. See PS 788–93/PG 574–78.

58. For an important account of Hegel's treatment of conscience, see Dean Moyar, *Hegel's Conscience* (Oxford: Oxford University Press, 2011).

59. PS 666/PG 488–89.

60. PS 667/489–90.

61. For a reconstruction of Hegel's critique of sovereign subjectivity, see Frederick Neuhouser, "Desire, Recognition, and the Relation between Bondsman and Lord," in *The Blackwell Companion to Hegel's Phenomenology of Spirit,* ed. Kenneth Westphal (London: Blackwell, 2008).

62. PS 670/PG 491–92.

63. PS 669, 670/PG 491–92.

64. PS 670/PG 491.

65. PS 669/PG 491.

66. Bernstein, lectures NSSR, 4.25.2007. (http://www.bernsteintapes.com).

67. PS 796/PG 579–80.

68. For insightful accounts that do argue that Hegel's notion of history is modeled on a logic of forgiveness, see J. M. Bernstein's "Conscience and Transgression: The Exemplarity of Tragic Action," in *Hegel's Phenomenology of Spirit: A Reappraisal,* ed. Gary K. Browning (Dordrecht: Kluwer Academic Publishers, 1997), and refer to his lectures on the *Phenomenology* at the New School for Social Research (http://www.bernsteintapes.com). Additionally, see Comay's *Mourning Sickness*; María del Rosario Acosta's "Hegel and Derrida on Forgiveness: The Impossible at the Core of the Political," *Derrida Today* 5 (2012); and Brandom's *A Spirit of Trust.*

69. Cf. Hegel's notion of *Erfahrung* in the Preface and Introduction to the *Phenomenology,* esp. as reconstructed by Pippin, "The 'Logic of Experience' as 'Absolute Knowledge' in Hegel's *Phenomenology of Spirit,* in *Hegel's Phenomenology of Spirit: A Critical Guide,* ed. Dean Moyar and Michael Quante (Cambridge: Cambridge University Press, 2008).

70. PS 803/PG 585.

71. PS 25/PG 27–28; see also 802/PG 584.

72. PS 802/PG 584.

73. Hegel writes: "What in religion was content, that is, the form of representing an other, is here the self's own activity" (PS 797/PG 581). Hegel adds that "the content of religion expresses what spirit is earlier in time than science does, but it is science alone which is spirit's true knowledge of itself" (PS 802/PG 584). See also the *Encyclopedia of the Philosophical Sciences,* where Hegel argues that the Protestant conscience is "free Geist learning to see itself in its reasonableness and truth" (§552; quoted in Westphal, *Hegel, Freedom, History,* p. 155).

74. See, e.g., J. M. Bernstein, " 'the celestial Antigone, the most resplendent figure ever to have appeared on earth': Hegel's Feminism," and Fanny Söderbäck, "Impossible Mourning: Sophocles Reversed," in *Feminist Interpretations of Antigone*, ed. Fanny Söderbäck (Albany: SUNY Press, 2010) for insightful readings of Hegel's reading of the *Antigone.*

75. See, e.g., Comay's *Mourning Sickness* for a full account of the centrality of the French Revolution in Hegel's *Phenomenology.*

PART 2

1. To be sure, Fichte is the first among the post-Kantians to argue for the necessity of intersubjectivity—see his *Foundations of Natural Right.* However, for Hegel, it is history, not intersubjectivity, that is the minimum unit of analysis for an account of intelligibility.

2. "The fixed principle of this system of culture," Hegel writes, "is that the finite is in and for itself, that it is absolute, and is the sole reality" (FK 60/GW 287).

3. See FK 64/GW 292.

4. FK 62/GW 293.

5. This is Hegel's transformation of Kant's claim that reason is involved in its own criticism. See the Prefaces (especially to the A edition) of CPR.

6. Cf. Bowman on his translation of *die Sache* as reality in *Hegel and the Metaphysics of Absolute Negativity,* p. 18. Cf. as well Yeoman's discussion of *die Sache* in *Freedom and Reflection,* p. 110, as the "point of expression" between ground and condition.

7. I will use the term "reflexive" rather than "reflective" to stress the self-determination of matters themselves, hence in line with Hegel's' critique of external reflection. I am here following Stephen Houlgate's "Essence, Reflection, and Immediacy in Hegel's *Logic*," in *Blackwell Companion to Hegel*, ed. Stephen Houlgate and Michael Baur (London: Blackwell, 2011), since he argues that "reflexive" captures the self-relation of *die Sache Selbst* that is distorted by external reflection. Cf. Christopher Yoeman's *Freedom and Reflection*, who argues that "reflection" takes the place of "reflexion," since the latter refers to the notion of self-relation through self-negation distinctive of the Doctrine of Being. Reflection, according to Yeoman, articulates Hegel's point that the "ground-relation internalizes the relation to another" rather than simple relation to self. Now, although I agree with Houlgate's terminological preference, against Houlgate I argue that the reflexive or self-articulating character of actuality developed in the Doctrine of Essence is rewritten in normative rather than ontological terms. Against Yeoman, I argue that the notion of actuality as reciprocity develops a nondualist notion of reflection as the articulation of matters themselves. Key here is understanding the necessity of contingent conditions that are understood as the ground of matters, or, better stated, that is *die Sache*. The chapters that follow spell out the details my argument.

8. See Kant's critique of dogmatism in the Prefaces to the first *Critique* as well as the Canon of Reason also in the first *Critique*. See Fichte's critique of dogmatism in the Introductions to the *Wissenschaftslehre*.

9. SL 42/WL 5:60.

10. SL 42/WL 5:60.

11. SL 64/WL 5:61; trans. mod.

CHAPTER 4

1. For a Fichtean response to Hegel, see Wayne Martin, "In Defense of Bad Infinity: A Fichtean Response to Hegel's *Differenzschrift*," *Bulletin of the Hegel Society of Great Britain* 55–56 (2007).

2. For an insightful discussion of this classical problem as it relates to deconstruction, see Rodolphe Gasché, "Structural Infinity," in *Inventions of Difference: On Jacques Derrida* (Cambridge, Mass.: Harvard University Press, 1994).

3. SL 119/WL 5:164. "If the absolute were *put together* out of the finite and the infinite," Hegel writes in *Faith and Knowledge*, "abstracting from the finite would indeed be a loss. In the Idea, however, finite and infinite are one, and hence finitude as such, i.e., as something that was supposed to have truth and reality in and for itself, has vanished. Yet what was negated was only the negative in the finitude; and thus the true affirmation was posited" (FK 66/GW 300). As we will see, the dialectic of the finite and the infinite in the Doctrine of Being within the *Science of Logic* follows the spirit of Hegel's 1802 statement.

4. Houlgate, *The Opening of Hegel's* Logic, p. 440.

5. See Houlgate, *The Opening of Hegel's* Logic; Winfield, *Overcoming Foundations: Studies in Systematic Philosophy* (New York: Columbia University Press); and William Maker, *Philosophy Without Foundations: Rethinking Hegel* (Albany: SUNY Press, 1994).

6. Ibid., pp. 115, 135, and also 9: In providing "an analysis of the basic categories of thought," Houlgate maintains, Hegel's *Logic* "presents being itself in its immanent logical self-determination."

7. Houlgate, *The Opening of Hegel's* Logic, p. 438. "Finitude is what every something itself proves to be," Houlgate also maintains, "and infinity is what finite being itself turns out to constitute" (436).

8. Although Houlgate insightfully analyzes what he calls Hegel's critique of categorial purity, he suppresses the thought of categorial impurity, arguing that the constitutive impurity of logical categories *establishes* the rationality of being in itself. See Houlgate, *The Opening of Hegel's* Logic, pp. 285ff., esp. 302–3.

9. Ibid., p. 425.

10. Ibid.

11. This first dialectic has been the subject of great debate within Hegel scholarship. See Dieter Henrich's "Anfang und Methode der Logik," in *Hegel im Kontext* (Frankfurt am Main: Suhrkamp, 1971). See also, for example, the discussion in Ernst Tugendhat, "Das Sein und Das Nichts," in *Durchblicke: Martin Heidegger zum 80. Geburtstag* (Frankfurt am Main: Suhrkamp, 1976), and Michael Rosen's engagement with it in *Hegel's Dialectics and Its Criticism* (Cambridge: Cambridge University Press, 1982); see also Peter Rohs, "Das Problem der vermittelten Unmittelbarkeit in der Hegelschen Logik," *Philosophisches Jahrbuch* 81 (1974) and John McCumber's engagement with it in *The Company of Words: Hegel, Language and Systematic Philosophy* (Evanston: Northwestern University Press, 1993); K. L. Michelet, *Das System der Philosophie als exacter Wissenschaft* (Berlin: Nicolaischer Verlag, 1876) and the discussion of his position in Rinaldi, *A History of Interpretation of the Logic of Hegel*, p. 181; see also Hans-Georg Gadamer, *Hegel's Dialectics*: *Five Hermeneutical Studies*, trans. P. Christopher Smith (New Haven: Yale University Press 1982).

12. SL 59/WL 5:81.

13. SL 59/WL 5:81.

14. SL 60/WL 5:82.

15. SL 80/WL 5:85.

16. Pippin, *Hegel's Idealism*, p. 189.

17. See, e.g., Houlgate, *The Opening of Hegel's* Logic, p. 428. Houlgate's gloss is closer to Spinoza's substance, whose modes are positive particularizations, and which Hegel rejects in the Doctrines of Essence and Concept precisely on the grounds that it lacked subjectivity, i.e., negativity (see SL 472/WL 6:194; and 580ff./6:48ff.).

18. Cf. Angelica Nuzzo, "Thinking Being: Method in Hegel's Logic of Being," in *A Companion to Hegel*, ed. Stephen Houlgate and Michael Baur (Oxford: Blackwell, 2011).

19. Houlgate, *The Opening of Hegel's* Logic, p. 395.

20. SL 114/WL 5:56.

21. In the Preface to the Second Edition of the *Logic*, Hegel writes: "The forms of thought are first set out and stored in human *language*" (SL 12/WL 5:20). He clarifies, however, that in a science of logic the "forms of thought have been freed from the material in which they are submerged" (SL 13/WL 5:21). A science of logic leaves language behind and examines categories, subjective and objective principles (from the principle of noncontradiction to mechanism

as a principle of objectivity), the activity of judging and inferring, the structure of normativity, and the strictures of normative authority. These are distinguishable from particular languages on the basis of their universality. For accounts of the dialectic of the said and the meant as part of Hegel's *philosophical strategy* in the *Logic*, indeed as part of Hegel's commitment to immanent critique, see Richard J. Bernstein, *The New Constellation: The Ethical/Political Horizon of Modernity/Post-Modernity* (Cambridge: Polity Press, 1992), p. 188, and Chong Fuk Lau, "Language and Metaphysics: The Dialectics of Hegel's Speculative Proposition," in *Hegel and Language*, ed. Jere Surber (Albany: SUNY Press, 2006), n. 16. Cf. Houlgate's discussion of language in *The Opening of Hegel's* Logic, chap. 4. Cf. also Di Giovanni, Introduction, SL.

22. Cf. Hegel's discussion of sense-certainty in the *Phenomenology of Spirit*. In both texts Hegel shows that immediacy is untenable. Immediacy is the result of mediation and may or may not be actual given conditions that sustain it or, as we will see, call it into question.

23. SL 101/WL 5:138.

24. SL 102/WL 5:139.

25. SL 102/WL 5:139.

26. SL 102/WL 5:139.

27. SL 103/WL 5:141.

28. SL 102/WL 5:140.

29. SL 103/WL 5:140–41.

30. See Gillian Rose, *Hegel Contra Sociology* (London: The Athlone Press, 1981), chap. 6.

31. Houlgate, *The Opening of Hegel's* Logic, pp. 395ff.

32. See Charles Taylor, *Hegel* (Cambridge: Cambridge University Press, 1977); quoted in Houlgate, *The Opening of Hegel's* Logic, p. 394.

33. See Houlgate, *The Opening of Hegel's* Logic, p. 196.

34. In the *Encyclopedia Logic*, Hegel writes: "something becomes an other; this other is itself something therefore it likewise becomes an other, and so on ad infinitum" (EL 93).

35. Strictly speaking, this gives rise to the first version of the bad infinite as progress to infinity, namely, qua endless series (SL 113f./WL 5:154f.). The second version, endless striving, is a consequence of this first version of the bad infinite, since the endless series leads to a qualitatively different notion of being.

36. SL 102/WL 5:140.

37. SL 109/WL 5:150.

38. SL 110/WL 5:151.

39. SL 111/WL 5:151.

40. SL 113/WL 5:154.

41. SL 114/WL 5:157.

42. SL 112/WL 5:153.

43. Ibid. "In each," Hegel also writes, "there is the *determinateness of the other*" (SL 114/WL 5:156).

44. SL 114/WL 5:156.

45. Ibid. "In *saying* what the infinite is, namely the negation of the *finite*," Hegel writes, "the finite itself is said also; it cannot be avoided in the determination of the infinite. One need only *know what is being said* in order to find the determination of the finite in the infinite."

46. Houlgate, *The Opening of Hegel's* Logic, p. 428.

47. SL 119/WL 5:165.

48. SL 120/WL 5:165.

49. SL 116/WL 5:159.

50. SL 117/WL 5:161.

51. SL 119/WL 5:163.

52. SL 119/WL 5:163–64.

53. SL 119/WL 5:164.

54. Houlgate, *The Opening of Hegel's* Logic, p. 426.

55. SL 154/WL 5:170.

56. Ibid.

57. Accounts of Hegel's philosophy of action to which I am indebted include: Pippin, *Hegel's Practical Philosophy*; J. M. Bernstein, "Confession and Forgiveness: Hegel's Poetics of Action," in *Beyond Representation and Poetic Imagination*, ed. Richard Eldridge (Cambridge: Cambridge University Press, 1996), and "Conscience and Transgression: The Exemplarity of Tragic Action," *Hegel's* Phenomenology of Spirit: *A Reappraisal*, ed. Gary Browning (Dordrecht: Kluwer Academic Publishers, 1997); Allen Speight, *Hegel, Literature, and the Problem of Agency* (Cambridge: Cambridge University Press, 2001); and the essays contained in Arto Laitinen and Constantines Sandis, eds., *Hegel on Action* (London: Palgrave, 2008).

58. PS 200/PG 249.

59. Notice the significance of the dialectic of the said and the meant in these sections. Again, it is central to Hegel's strategy of showing what is implicit in a given concept or position on the basis of its own commitments.

60. PS 199–200/PG 248–49.

61. PS 185ff./PG 322ff. See Michael Quante, "'Reason . . . apprehended irrationally': Hegel's Critique of Observing Reason," in *Hegel's* Phenomenology of Spirit*: A Critical Guide*, ed. Dean Moyar and Michael Quante (Cambridge: Cambridge University Press, 2008); and Alasdair MacIntyre, "Hegel on Faces and Skulls," in *Hegel: A Collection of Critical Essays*, ed. Alasdair MacIntyre (Notre Dame, Ind.: University of Notre Dame Press, 1976).

62. See Hegel's famous reference to Shakespeare's Hamlet: "A variety of ideas may well occur to us in connection with a skull, like those of Hamlet over Yorick's skull" (PS 201/PG 250). The infinity of a life is called forth when Hamlet sees Yorick's skull.

63. PS 193–95/PG 241–42.

64. See Pippin, *Hegel's Practical Philosophy*, esp. pp. 265ff.

65. Bernstein, "'the celestial Antigone.'"

66. For assessments of debates concerning Hegel's critical targets in these sections (the Romantics, *Sturm und Drang*, Rousseau, Fichte, Goethe), see H. S. Harris, *Hegel's Ladder*, vol. 2 (Indianapolis: Hackett Publishing, 1997), esp. pp. 460ff.; and Frederick Beiser, "'Morality' in Hegel's *Phenomenology of Spirit*," in *Blackwell Guide to Hegel's* Phenomenology of Spirit, ed. Merold Westphal (London: Blackwell, 2009). See also Pinkard, *Hegel's* Phenomenology.

67. PS 387/PG 468.

68. PS 397/PG 480.

69. See Beiser, "'Morality,'" p. 221.

70. Ibid.

71. See, e.g., Donald Verene, *Hegel's Absolute: An Introduction to Reading the* Phenomenology of Spirit (Albany: SUNY Press, 2007), p. 89.

72. PS 390/PG 471–72.

73. PS 405/PG 489.

74. PS 407/PG 490.

75. Beiser, "'Morality,'" p. 222.

76. See Pippin, *Hegel's Practical Philosophy.*

77. Houlgate, *The Opening of Hegel's* Logic, p. 431.

78. Ibid.

79. Ibid., p. 425.

80. Furthermore, becoming aware of the infinity of reason is crucial, Houlgate argues, since we should seek to become "willing agents of infinite self-determining reason" (ibid., p. 426).

81. See Houlgate's "Essence, Reflection, and Immediacy in Hegel's *Logic*" for an account of the transition from being to essence as a matter of a transition from immediacy to mediation. However, given the methodological commitments elaborated in *The Opening of Hegel's* Logic, he argues that reflexivity is what is shown to be implicit in being and only a moment of the idea. The structure of reflexivity, accordingly, is as a matter of self-negation and self-relation that gives way to the idea understood as reason implicit in being. As will become clear in part 3 below, Hegel understands the structure of reflexivity in a decidedly post-Kantian vein: first in the chapters on subjectivity, where he establishes that determinacy is a matter of normativity, second in the chapters on the idea, where he establishes that intelligibility is a matter of normative authority.

CHAPTER 5

1. SL 350/WL 6:30.

2. I will come back to this problem when I discuss the syllogism (*der Schluß*) in the third part below.

3. Especially a logic of being but also a logic of essence, as we will see in part 3 of this book, cannot appropriately account for the consequences of self-negation, which have to do with normative ambivalence rather than sheer instability.

4. SL 352/WL 6:33: "Negation as quality is *existent negation;* being constitutes its ground and element. The determination of reflection, on the contrary, has for this ground immanent reflectedness. Positedness gets fixed in determination precisely because reflection is self-equality in its negatedness; the latter is therefore itself reflection into itself. Determination persists here, not by virtue of being but because of its self-equality."

5. SL 353/WL 6:34; trans. mod. This passage is the transition to the important chapter of essentialities of determinations of reflection, yet it captures succinctly the difference between being and essence, and the character of negation according to each model of determinacy.

6. The determinations of reflection, Hegel argues, are conceived as "universal laws of thought" and therefore are considered "opposed to each other; they contradict each other and mutually sublate each other" (SL 356/WL 6:35). Hegel challenges the integrity of these rules of thought and shows that each presupposes the other.

7. SL 340/WL 6:18.

8. SL 342/WL 6:19.

9. See the section on Force and the Understanding in the *Phenomenology of Spirit*.

10. "In the sphere of being," Hegel writes, "external reflection was the infinite; the finite stands as the first, as the real from which the beginning is made as from a foundation that abides, whereas the infinite is the reflection into itself standing over against it" (SL 349/WL 6:28).

11. SL 347/WL 6:26; trans. mod.

12. "Because it is thus immediacy as a turning back, the coinciding of the negative with itself, it is equally the negation of the negative as negative. And so it is presupposing. Or immediacy is as a turning back only the negative of itself, just this, not to be immediacy; but reflection is the sublating of the negative of itself, coincidence with itself; it therefore sublates its positing, and inasmuch as it is in its positing the sublating of positing, it is presupposing. In presupposing, reflection determines the turning back into itself as the negative of itself, as that of which essence is the sublating. It is its relating to itself, but to itself as to the negative of itself; only so is it negativity which abides with itself, self-related negativity" (SL 347/WL 6:25–26; trans. mod.).

13. Hegel writes: "The immediacy which reflection, as a process of sublating, presupposes for itself is simply and solely a positedness, something in itself sublated which is not diverse from reflection's turning back into itself but is itself only this turning back. But it is at the same time determined as a negative, as immediately in opposition to something, and hence to an other. And so is reflection determined. According to this determinateness, because reflection has a presupposition and takes its start from the immediate as its other, it is external reflection" (SL 348/WL 6:27).

14. Although Fichte's "infinite obstacle" (*Anstoß*) as the immediate nonbeing of the I is also Hegel's critical target, Hegel's critique of Kant is especially important here.

15. In the first introduction to the *Critique of Judgment*, Kant writes: "Judgment in general is the ability to think the particular as contained under the universal. If the universal (the rule, the principle, the law) is given, then judgment, which subsumes the particular under it, is determinate. . . . But if only the particular is given and judgment has to find the universal for it, then this power is merely reflective" (pp. 179–80).

16. SL 349/WL 6:27–28. See also the first formulation of this retrospective logic in the section on *Schein*, SL 342ff./WL 6:18ff.

17. Reflection is a movement of "turning back; that is to say, there is not an other beforehand, one either from which or to which it would turn back; it is therefore, only as a turning back or as the negative of itself" (SL 347/WL 6:25–26).

18. Ng, "The Life of the Concept: Freedom and Form in Hegel's *Logic*" (Ph.D. diss., New York: The New School for Social Research, 2012), p. 104.

19. SL 387/WL 6:80. See Longuenesse's study of the Logic of Essence, *Hegel's Critique of Metaphysics*, for a compelling account of the significance of ground.

20. SL 388ff./WL 6:82ff.

21. The concept has a teleological structure, which establishes determination on the basis of internal purposiveness. It is crucial to stress that the teleological structure of the concept refers to the normative structure of determinacy, as we will see in part 3 below. The self-determination of the concept is a matter of *actual conditions* rather than possible relations, and thus is a matter

of a norm that is internal to existent conditions. It is based on the matter at hand, the thing, *die Sache,* rather than a metaphysical law or formal epistemic faculty.

22. SL 394/WL 6:87–88.

23. "*The activity of form* by which matter is determined consists, therefore, in a negative relating of the form to itself. But, conversely, form thereby negatively relates itself to matter also; the movement, however, by which matter becomes determined is just as much the form's own movement. Form is free of matter, but sublates its self-subsistence; but this, its self-subsistence, is matter itself, for it is in this matter that it has its essential identity" (SL 394/WL 6:87–88).

24. Cf. Aristotle's notion of ὕλη, as mere possibility, as indeterminate. Hegel's point is that this is a conception of matter tied to a metaphysical perspective, hence not given but articulated on the basis of a set of assumptions.

25. Neither a conception of form nor matter can be consistently maintained without the other. Cf. Bowman, *Hegel's Metaphysics of Absolute Negativity*, chap. 6, which argues for the priority of content. My full argument concerning the inseparability of form and content is laid out in part 3.

26. SL 416/WL 6:121: "Wenn alle Bedingungen einer Sache vorhanden sind, so tritt sie in die Existenz. Die Sache ist, ehe sie existiert."

27. For example, Hegel writes: "If, therefore, all the conditions of the fact are at hand, that is, if the totality of the fact is posited as a groundless immediate, then this scattered manifold internally recollects itself" (Wenn also alle Bedingungen der Sache vorhanden sind, d. h. wenn die Totalität der Sache als grundloses Unmittelbares gesetzt ist, so *erinnert* sich diese zerstreute Mannigfaltigkeit an ihr selbst) (SL 416/WL 6:121).

28. Thus Hegel moves on to a consideration of existence and appearance and argues against the Kantian thing-in-itself. For Hegel, Kant does not give an account of the relation implied by the very doctrine of transcendental idealism, a problem that comes to the fore in the nebulous doctrine of affection mentioned in part 1. What is more, the notion of appearance reduces the existent to the unessential, which in any event does not recognize that the very distinction between appearance and thing in itself is one of "essential relation." See SL 420ff./WL 6:163ff.

29. Readings of these sections that emphasize the relation to Spinoza include: Pierre Machery, *Hegel or Spinoza*, trans. Susan M. Ruddick (Minneapolis: University of Minnesota Press, 2011); Paul Franks, *All or Nothing: Systematicity, Transcendental Arguments, and Skepticism in German Idealism* (Cambridge, Mass.: Harvard University Press, 2005); Ng, "The Life of the Concept." See also Angelica Nuzzo, "As if Truth Were a Coin," and especially, "Spinozas Amor dei intellectualis und Hegels methodologische Umdeutung des Liebesbegriffs," *Affekte ohne Norm: Spinozas Affektenlehre im historischen und aktuellen Kontext*, ed. A. Engstler and R. Schnepf (Hildesheim, Germany: Olms Verlag, 2002); Stephen Houlgate, "Substance, Causality, and the Question of Method in Hegel's *Science of Logic*," in *The Reception of Kant's Critical Philosophy*; and Yitzhak Y. Melamed, "Acosmism or Weak Individuals? Hegel, Spinoza, and the Reality of the Finite," *Journal of the History of Philosophy* 48, no. 1 (2010).

30. Rather than focusing on the section on the inner and outer in the chapter on the essential relation, I will discuss the dialectic of the inner and the outer in light of the significance of reciprocity. The section on the inner and the outer in the earlier chapter is significant for

understanding the critique of Kant's transcendental idealism, which Hegel argues cannot account for the work of form, of cognition, without establishing the significance of expression (*Äußerung*).

31. SL 462/WL 6:180; trans. mod.

32. Manifestation should be understood as a claim about a determination's dependence on a totality of conditions and hence on externality. There are at least three influential interpretations of Hegel's insistence on externality as Hegel's expressivism. First, in *Hegel* (Cambridge, Mass.: Cambridge University Press, 1975), Charles Taylor argued that Hegel's philosophy should be understood in the expressivist tradition of Rousseau, Herder, and the Romantics, given his commitment to anti-dualism, his interest on the modern problem of alienation, and his elaboration of freedom as self-realization. More recently, Robert Brandom has argued that Hegel's speculative logic is expressivist, since the forms of inferences that Hegel examines in the logic of the concept allow us to make explicit what is implicit in empirical and practical judgments and inferences. Accordingly, Hegelian speculative concepts make explicit implicit inferential commitments that articulate the content of empirical concepts. See Brandom's, "Some Pragmatist Themes in Hegel's Idealism," in *Tales of the Mighty Dead*, and "Sketch of a Program for a Critical Reading of Hegel." Pippin, on the other hand, has offered what is in my mind the most compelling way of understanding Hegel's expressivism. In *Hegel's Practical Philosophy*, Pippin elaborates Hegel's expressivism in terms of the identity of the inner and the outer. He reads Hegel's philosophy of action accordingly. Actions as well as intentions must be understood in light of the inseparability of the inner intention and the outer publicly performed deed. A subject's relation to her deeds should be understood not as a question of prior deliberation but as a question of comprehension and experiential understanding, hence as a matter of retrospective justification, which depends on temporal and spatial elements that the agent cannot control—elements of what was done that are *external* to her initial intention.

33. SL 477/WL 6:200.

34. CPR B265–66. For a lucid discussion of the postulates, see Guyer, *Kant* (London: Routledge, 2006), pp. 115ff.

35. My thanks to Brock Baines for this formulation.

36. CPR A227/B279.

37. SL 478ff./WL 6:200ff. See Longuenesse, *Hegel's Critique of Metaphysics*, esp. chap. 4, for the relation between modality and ground.

38. SL 478/WL 6:201: "Formeinheit des Ansichseins oder der Innerlichkeit und der Äußerlichkeit ist."

39. SL 479/WL 6:202.

40. For an account of Kantian morality, see my "Kant's Hyperbolic Formalism," *Idealistic Studies* 42, no. 1 (2012).

41. See Hegel's critique of Kant in "Reason as Testing Laws" in the PS and in "Morality" in the PR.

42. SL 481/WL 6:207.

43. "The contingent," Hegel argues, "is therefore necessary because the actual is determined as a possible; its immediacy is consequently sublated and is repelled into the *ground* or the

in-itself, and into the *grounded*, equally because its possibility, this *ground-grounded connection*, is simply sublated and posited as being. What is necessary *is*, and this existent is *itself the necessary*" (SL 481/WL 6:207). Because possibility is dependent on actuality, on a totality of conditions that set strictures for what is possible, the contingent is necessary, or, better stated, it becomes necessary after the fact, given the conditions that come into being in order for the possible to be possible at all. See Gabriel, "Contingency or Necessity? Schelling versus Hegel," in *Transcendental Ontology: Essays in German Idealism,* for an account of the necessity of contingency along ontological lines.

44. SL 482/WL 6:207–8. He continues: "Its relating to another is the manifestation of *itself*, and this manifestation is neither a transition (the immediate something *refers* to the other in this way) nor an appearing (in this way the thing only is i*n relation* to an other); it is a self-subsistent which has its immanent reflection, its determinate essentiality, in another self-subsistent."

45. SL 482/WL 6:209; trans mod.

46. SL 482/WL 6:209; trans. mod.

47. SL 483/WL 6:209.

48. SL 486/WL 6:211.

49. SL 487/WL 6:214.

50. SL 487/WL6:214.

51. SL 487/WL6:214.

52. SL 487/WL6:215–16.

53. Cf. *Hegel's Phenomenology,* where he glosses absolute knowing in terms of the process of actualization through externalization as "the self-assured spirit that acted" (PS 796/PG 580).

54. Cf. Yeoman, whose discussion of reciprocity is insightful in maintaining that Hegel wants to make "the very point about conditioning itself in terms of the reciprocity between ground and condition." Yeoman explains that "[t]he conditions do not transform themselves into material for the ground in order to submit themselves to it as to a dominating power, but rather because that is the only form in which they can express their own nature; they become what they are by submitting to processes of transformation that they only partially control" (*Freedom and Reflection*, p. 110). This establishes the necessity of conditions, displacing any dualism of inner or outer, internal and external conception of ground (see *Freedom and Reflection*, p. 11). I have glossed this collapse in terms of the necessity of contingent conditions, which now serve as ground and whose expression (in Yeoman's terms), action (in my terms), manifestation or exposition (Hegel's terms) are nothing but the "essence" of the thing itself (see also Yeoman, *Freedom and Reflection*, p. 113).

55. Cf. John McCumber, "Substance and Reciprocity in Hegel," *The Owl of Minerva* 35, nos. 1–2 (2010) for an alternative reading that also elaborates the relation between the *Logic* and the *Philosophy of Right,* albeit in fundamentally different ways than the reading I elaborate below.

56. SL 489, 490/WL 6:216–17.

57. SL 489/WL 6:217.

58. Hegel writes: "Substance is the *absolute*, the actual in-and-for-itself: *in itself*, because it is the simple identity of possibility and actuality; absolute, because it is the essence containing all actuality and possibility *within itself*; *for itself*, because it is this identity as absolute *power* or absolutely self-related *negativity*" (SL 509/WL 6:246; trans. mod.). Against Spinoza, Hegel

argues that the power of substance has to do with negativity or, as we will see, subjectivity. The crucial point is that the notion of causality at the heart of Spinoza's conception of substance does not account for the retrospective logic of condition and conditioned.

59. SL 492/WL 6:221.

60. SL 493/WL 6:222.

61. And indeed in the *Encyclopedia* Hegel speaks of *Geist* as a product of itself.

62. SL 500/WL 6:232.

63. SL 503/WL 6:236.

64. SL 503/WL 6:236.

65. SL 504/WL 6:237.

66. The effect, for Hegel, does not necessarily follow from the cause if the cause is not specified as implicit in the effect. Something is the effect of a cause, given the concrete conditions that sustain the development of the cause.

67. SL 505/WL 6:239.

68. "What is rational is actual; and what is actual is rational," Hegel famously writes in the preface to the *Philosophy of Right* (PR, p. 20). I will not consider the *Dopplesatz* itself but rather the overall role that Hegel's logical analysis of actuality and reciprocity plays in his assessment of modern institutional life. For a reading of the *Dopplesatz*, see Robert Stern, "Hegel's *Doppelsatz*: A Neutral Reading," *Journal of the History of Philosophy* 44, no. 2 (2006).

69. PR, p. 10.

70. The two books that make this connection in a compelling way are Rose, *Hegel Contra Sociology*, and Pippin, *Hegel's Practical Philosophy*. See also Michael Theunissen, *Sein und Schein: Die kritische Funktion der Hegelschen Logik* (Frankfurt: Suhrkamp, 1994).

71. In addition to Marx's classic critique of Hegel's notion of the idea especially in the postface of volume 1 of *Capital*, influential examples include Allen Wood, *Hegel's Ethical Thought* (Cambridge: Cambridge University Press, 1990); Dieter Henrich, "Logical Form and Real Totality: The Authentic Conceptual Form of Hegel's Concept of the State," in *Hegel on Ethics and Politics*, ed. Robert Pippin and Otfried Höffe (Cambridge: Cambridge University Press, 2004); K.-H. Ilting, "The Structure of Hegel's *Philosophy of Right*," in *Hegel's Political Philosophy: Problems and Prespectives*, ed. P. A. Pelczynski (Cambridge: Cambridge University Press, 1971); and Hardimon, *Hegel's Social Philosophy*.

72. See esp. part 2 of *Hegel: Myth and Legends*, ed. Jon Stewart (Evanston: Northwestern University Press, 1996) for rejoinders to this reading.

73. For an attempt at reviving a Hegelian notion of *Sittlichkeit* for an understanding of freedom, see Axel Honneth, *Das Recht der Freiheit: Grundriß einer demokratischen Sittlichkeit* (Frankfurt: Suhrkamp, 2011). Cf. Frank Ruda, *Hegel's Rabble: An Investigation into Hegel's Philosophy of Right* (London: Continuum, 2011), and Lydia Moland, *Hegel on Political Identity: Patriotism, Nationality, Cosmopolitanism* (Evanston: Northwestern University Press, 2011).

74. PR, p. 1.

75. PR, p. 20.

76. To be sure, Hegel is guilty of methodological bias in reconstructing the main normative commitments of Western modernity. He is not guilty, however, of making universal claims about what a society ought to be.

77. PR, p. 22.

78. "To recognize reason as the rose in the cross of the present," as Hegel famously adds, is accordingly to assess an institution or normative commitment in light of its concrete actualization. For alternative and diverging readings of this passage, see for example Michael Hardimon, *Hegel's Social Philosophy,* and Glen Alexander Magee, *Hegel and the Hermetic Tradition* (Ithaca: Cornell University Press 2008).

79. See PR, pp. 56, 72, 90, 94, 136, 138–40, 191, 197, 244.

80. In the introductory remarks on the section on Ethical Life, Hegel argues that ethical life is the embodiment of freedom.

81. PR, p. 3. In this way, the ideal can serve as a norm for assessing "determinations of right" that may or may not be "*grounded in* and *consistent with*" the commitment to self-determination. An institution or practice may be "contrary to right and irrational in and for itself."

82. See Honneth's *Suffering from Indeterminacy and Pathologies of Individual Freedom;* see also Neuhouser, *Foundations of Hegel's Social Theory;* Hardimon, *Hegel's Social Philosophy;* and Ormiston, *Love and Politics.*

83. See Pippin, *Hegel's Practical Philosophy,* for a full account of "institutional rationality."

84. PR, p. 23.

85. Ibid.

PART 3

1. PR, p. 31.

2. Cf. Klaus Düsing, *Das Problem der Subjektivität in Hegels* Logik (Bonn: Bouvier Verlag, 1976).

3. SL 518/WL 6:257.

4. SL 673/WL 6:466.

5. See e.g. SL 842/WL 6:570. Cf. Tom Rockmore's treatment of the problem of circularity in "Dialectic and Circularity: Is Hegelian Circularity a New Copernican Turn?" in Limnatis, ed., *Dimensions of Hegel's Dialectics.*

6. Further along in the system, Hegel specifies content as a matter of material conditions, social practices, historically specific institutions.

CHAPTER 6

1. SL 532/WL 6:276. See my "Logics of Power, Logics of Violence (According to Hegel)," in *Law and Violence*, ed. María del Rosario Acosta, *New Centennial Review* 14, no. 2 (2014) for an account of the relation between external reflection and violence in Hegel. See Theunissen's discussion of love in *Sein und Schein*, and Rose's discussion in *Hegel Contra Sociology*, p. 207.

2. See WL 5:23 and 6:428.

3. Hegel also provocatively writes that the universal "*continues* itself" though all its differences and is "endowed with the power of unalterable, undying self-preservation" (SL 531/WL 6:276).

4. SL 530/WL 6:273 and 582/6:250: "Im Begriffe hat sich daher das Reich der Freiheit eröffnet."

5. See esp. "The Spirit of Christianity and its Fate"; the 1797 or 1798 fragment on *Love* and "The Positivity of the Christian Religion," both in *Early Theological Writings*. Consider as well Hegel's earlier Bern discussion of positivity esp. in the 1795/6 "The Positivity of the Christian Religion," in *Early Theological Writings*, and the earlier "Tübingen Essay," "Berne Fragments" and "Life of Jesus," in *Three Essays, 1793–95: "Tübingen Essay," "Berne Fragments" and "Life of Jesus,"* ed. and trans. Peter Füss and John Dobbins (Notre Dame, Ind.: University of Notre Dame Press, 1984).

6. See Wilhelm Dilthey, *Die Jugendgeschichte Hegels, in Gesammelte Schriften,* vol. 4 (Leipzig and Berlin, 1925); H. S. Harris, *Hegel's Development: Toward the Sunlight 1770–1801* (Oxford: Clarendon Press, 1972); and Henrich, *Hegel im Kontext.* See also Pinkard, *Hegel*; Pippin, *Hegel's Practical Philosophy*; and Laura Werner, *"The Restless Love of Thinking": The Concept Liebe in G.W.F. Hegel's Philosophy* (Helsinki: Helsinki University Press, 2007).

7. See esp. PS 632/PG 463 for Hegel's critique of conscience and romantic irony, and PS 748/PG 544 for Hegel's critique of revealed religion. See also Pinkard, *Hegel's* Phenomenology, p. 214.

8. Houlgate, "Why Hegel's Concept is Not the Essence," in *Hegel's Theory of the Subject*, ed. David Carlson (New York: Palgrave Macmillan, 2005), p. 19.

9. Ibid., p. 26.

10. Pippin, *Hegel's Practical Philosophy,* p. 105.

11. Ibid., p. 36: To be with oneself in the other is, for Hegel, "but an achievement in practices wherein justificatory reasons can be successfully shared, wherein the basis of my justification of a course of action can be accepted by another as such a reason."

12. Pippin continues: "there is no 'self' to be legislated except by virtue of the constraint of what must be collective legislation." The free legislative power of the concept is not an arbitrary exercise of authority "upon a non-conceptual manifold or against other self-determining subjects."

13. See ibid. See also Redding's discussion of the inseparability of the concept and its other in his *Analytic Philosophy and the Return of Hegelian Thought.*

14. Cf. Houlgate, who argues that the *Logic* establishes that being is nothing less than nature esp. in *Freedom, Truth, and History: An Introduction to Hegel*, 2d ed. (Oxford: Blackwell, 2005).

15. See my "Hegel's Hyperbolic Formalism," p. 115.

16. See SL 524/WL 6:255.

17. See SL 528/WL 6:271.

18. Longuenesse, *Hegel's Critique of Metaphysics,* p. 217.

19. Longuenesse, *Hegel's Critique of Metaphysics,* chap. 5.

20. See Longuenesse, *Kant and the Capacity to Judge*, where she argues that the reflective role of judgment is crucial to Kant's first *Critique*, which in turn establishes a greater continuity between the first and the third *Critiques.*

21. CPR A68–69/B93–94; *Kant and the Capacity to Judge,* p. 85. See also *Kant and the Capacity to Judge,* p. 83.

22. See esp. SL 523–25/WL 6:264–65.

23. SL 552/WL 6:303. Hegel continues: "thus the word *Urteil* refers to what judgment is in and for itself" (WL 6:303).

24. "To restore again this *identity* of the concept, or rather to *posit* it—this is the goal of the *movement* of the judgment"(SL 556/WL 6:308).

25. See SL 556, 587, 588/WL 6:309, 350.

26. SL 556/WL 6:309.

27. WL 6:309.

28. SL 670/WL 6:461. Crucially, Hegel qualifies the quotation in the following way: "if anything has truth, it has by virtue of its idea, or *something has truth only in so far as it is idea*" (SL 670/WL 6:461). As we will see, the truth of determinacy is not only the concept, but also the authorization of the concept—the idea.

29. Longuenesse, *Hegel's Critique of Metaphysics*, p. 200. Although Schelling's influence in *Glauben und Wissen* is clear, Hölderlin's influence on Hegel should not to be overlooked. See Hölderlin, *Über Urtheil und Seyn (On Judgment and Being)*, in H. S. Harris, *Hegel's Development: Toward the Sunlight 1770–1801.* See Dieter Henrich, *Hegel im Kontext*; *The Course of Remembrance and Other Essays on Hölderlin*, ed. Eckart Forster (Stanford: Stanford University Press, 1997); and *Between Kant and Hegel: Lectures on German Idealism*, ed. David S. Pacini (Cambridge, Mass.: Harvard University Press, 2003). As I argued in part 1, Hegel abandoned this ontological model of unity in his mature thought.

30. Longuenesse, *Hegel's Critique of Metaphysics,* p. 203.

31. Longuenesse thus speaks of Hegel's account of judgment as "a mode of being itself rather than a mere psychological process or rather the latter is the manifestation of the former for a finite consciousness. Judgment is the self-division of being, first present to itself in the immediate and undifferentiated form that the *Phenomenology of Spirit* calls the 'this'" (Longuenesse, *Hegel's Critique of Metaphysics*, p. 203).

32. Ibid., p. 207.

33. Longuenesse, *Kant and the Capacity to Judge,* pp. 157–58.

34. Ibid., pp. 136–37.

35. SL 523/WL 6:264; see also SL 523/WL 6:266: "die Wissenschaft der absoluten Form, welche in sich Totalität ist und die reine Idee der Wahrheit selbst enthält. Diese absolute Form hat an ihr selbst ihren Inhalt oder Realität."

36. Cf. Brandom's, "Some Pragmatist Themes in Hegel's Idealism," and "Sketch of a Program for a Critical Reading of Hegel." See also Brandom, *Making It Explicit: Reasoning, Representing, and Discursive Commitment* (Cambridge, Mass.: Harvard University Press, 1994), esp. 104ff.

37. To begin with an account of content and thus with the material marks of concepts, or to seek to establish that material marks that comprise conceptual content are constitutive of logical form, would go far beyond the subject matter of a science of logic. Both of these tasks would require an epistemological account of concept formation or an account of specific socio-historical (inferential) practices of determination. Hegel addresses these questions via a phenomenology and philosophy of spirit, and brackets questions of genesis, empirical revisability, and application in the *Logic.* To be sure, Hegel argues that the Objective Logic is a "genetic exposition of

the concept" (SL 509/WL 6:244–45). The Objective Logic, however, is a genetic exposition insofar as it is a *critique* of the failures of the logic of being and the logic of essence that leads to the truth of the logic of the concept.

38. Robert Brandom, "Sketch of a Programme for a Critical Reading of Hegel," p. 140: for Hegel, "determinateness of content . . . is always a matter of exclusive [*ausschliessend*] contrast with, the ruling out of, other possibilities. These fundamental relations of material incompatibility, what he calls 'determinate negation,' in turn give rise to material inferential relations among the contents they articulate: what he calls 'mediation.' So for instance being a dog entails being a mammal in that everything incompatible with being a mammal is incompatible with being a dog. To be determinate or determinately contentful just is to stand in relations of material incompatibility and material inference to other such determinately contentful items." See also Brandom, *Making It Explicit*, p. 92.

39. Brandom, *Making It Explicit*, p. 92.

40. See Winfield's discussion in chapter 5 of *From Concept to Objectivity: Thinking Through Hegel's Subjective Logic* (London: Ashgate Publishing, 2006).

41. SL 530/WL 6:273. See also EL §163a.

42. In *From Concept to Objectivity*, Winfield makes an important clarification: "On the one hand, universality is presented as the point of departure, which then engenders particularity, which, for its part, develops into individuality. On the other hand, each term has its determination in relation to the other two and through this relation ends up taking on the character of each, thereby proving itself to be a totality of all three terms" (pp. 74–75).

43. See ibid., p. 80.

44. See ibid., 76ff. See also Stern, *Hegelian Metaphysics*, 156–57.

45. Now, to argue that judgment rather than concept is the minimum unit of determinacy is, to be sure, Kant's most influential move. As we will see, to argue that the syllogism rather than judgment is the basic unity of determinacy is Hegel's signature move. As Brandom explains: "The pre-Kantian tradition took it for granted that the proposed order of semantic explanation begins with a doctrine of *concepts* or *terms*, divided into singular and general, whose meaningfulness can be grasped independently of and prior to the meaningfulness of judgments. Appealing to this basic level of interpretation, a doctrine of *judgments* then explains the combination of concepts into judgments, and how the correctness of the resulting judgment depends on what is combined and how. Appealing to this derived interpretation of judgments a doctrine of *consequences* finally explains the combination of judgments into inferences, and how the correctness of inferences depends on what is combined and how" (*Making It Explicit*, p. 79).

46. Winfield, *From Concept to Objectivity,* p. 80.

47. See ibid., p. 72.

48. SL 534/WL 6:278.

49. SL 534/WL 6:278.

50. SL 548/WL 6:299.

51. SL 546/Wl 6:295.

52. SL 540/WL 6:288.

53. SL 547/ WL 6:297.

54. SL 547/ WL 6:297.

55. See Redding, *Analytic Philosophy and the Return of Hegelian Thought,* p. 181 n. 17.

56. SL 549/WL 6:300; trans mod.: "Als Einzelheit kehrt er in der Bestimmtheit in sich zurück; damit ist das Bestimmte selbst Totalität geworden. Seine Rückkehr in sich ist daher die absolute, ursprüngliche *Teilung seiner*, oder als Einzelheit ist er als *Urteil* gesetzt."

57. As Brandom succinctly explains the position that Hegel is here arguing against (although he is not engaging Hegel in this passage) when he writes "the tradition of formal semantics has been resolutely atomistic, in the sense that the assignments of a semantic interpretant to one element (say, a proper name) is taken to be intelligible independently of the assignment of semantic interpretants to any other elements (for instance, predicates or other proper names)" (*Articulating Reasons*, p. 15).

58. SL 550/WL 6:301–2.

59. SL 550/WL 6:301–2.

60. See CPR A70/B95ff.

61. As Longuenesse puts it, the four headings of judgment "no longer refer, as was the case with Kant, to different aspects according to which one and the same can be analyzed according to its form. Rather, what we now have under the different titles are different types of judgments characterized by their form *and their content*: they corresponds respectively to different moments in the progression towards the identity of predicate and subject in judgment and so to different contents for *both* predicate and subject" (*Hegel's Critique of Metaphysics*, p. 210).

62. See CPR A80; see Longuenesse, *Hegel's Critique of Metaphysics*, pp. 210ff., and "Kant on A Priori Concepts: the Metaphysical Deduction of the Categories," in *The Cambridge Companion to Kant and Modern Philosophy*, ed. Paul Guyer (Cambridge: Cambridge University Press, 2006). See also Winfield, *From Concept to Objectivity*, p. 92.

63. SL 557/WL 6:300.

64. Longuenesse, *Hegel's Critique Metaphysics,* p. 210.

65. Ibid.

66. Ibid., p. 214.

67. Winfield, *From Concept to Objectivity*, pp. 92–94. I am paraphrasing Winfield, although my gloss will take his reconstruction of Hegel's treatment of universality in judgments in a different direction.

68. SL 557/WL 6:300.

69. Winfield, *From Concept to Objectivity*, p. 95.

70. SL 567/WL 6:324.

71. SL 571/WL 6:330.

72. Winfield, *From Concept to Objectivity*, p. 98.

73. See ibid.

74. SL 576/WL 6:337.

75. Winfield, *From Concept to Objectivity*, p. 98.

76. The point is not that Hegel is here offering inferentialist semantics akin to Brandom's. It is rather that Hegel's discussion specifies the *status* of judgments of necessity vis-à-vis judgments of existence and reflection in order to establish that judgment itself involves inference—the syllogism.

77. SL 577/WL 6:338.

78. SL 578/WL 6:343.

79. As Winfield explains, individuality is effectively "left beyond the grasp of reason, together with those realities in which individuality is penetrated by universality, realities such as beauty and freedom" (*From Concept to Objectivity*, p. 93).

80. "To know how to form *judgments of existence,* such as 'the rose is red,' 'the snow is white,' etc., hardly counts as a sign of great power of judgment. The *judgments of reflection* are more in the nature of *propositions*; to be sure, in the judgment of necessity the subject matter is present in its objective universality, but it is only in the judgment now to be considered that *its connection with the concept is to be found.* The concept is at the basis of this judgment, and it is there with relation to the subject matter, as an *ought* to which reality may or may not conform" (SL 581–82/WL 6:343; trans. mod.).

81. Longuenesse, *Hegel's Critique of Metaphysics,* p. 213.

82. SL 582/WL 6:343.

83. See SL 582/WL 6:344.

84. SL 583/WL 6:345; trans. mod.

85. See SL 584; Longuenesse, *Hegel's Critique of Metaphysics*, p. 213.

86. SL 584/WL 6:346. Recall Hegel's transformation of modality in the Doctrine of Essence, especially Hegel's discussion of contingency (SL 474–78/WL 2:119–23), which I discussed in part 2. See also Karen Ng, "Hegel's Logic of Actuality," *The Review of Metaphysics* 63, no. 1 (2009), and Luis Guzmán, "El carácter contingente de la necesidad absoluta en la *Ciencia de la lógica* de Hegel," *Revista Colombiana de Filosofía* 131 (2006).

87. SL 585/WL 6:347; trans. modified.

88. SL 585/WL 6:348.

89. This is crucial for Hegel's rewriting of teleology and it responds to Hegel's critique of mechanism. See my "Logics of Power, Logics of Violence (According to Hegel)" for a full account.

90. SL 585/WL 6:348.

91. See Hegel's remark in his crucial final discussion of method, where he writes: "each step of the *advance* in the process of further determination, while getting further away from the indeterminate beginning is also *getting back nearer* to it; consequently, that what may at first appear to be different, the retrogressive grounding of the beginning, and the *progressive further determining* of it, run into one another and are the same" (SL 750/WL 6:569). I will come back to this in chapter 7.

92. Cf. Winfield, who writes: "That the concrete universal brings closure to the typology of universals is suggested by how it exhausts the conceptual gradations in predication—the universal determines either just the universal (quality or class), or itself and the particular (genus and species), or itself, the particular and the individual (concrete universal)" (*From Concept to Objectivity*, p. 94).

93. Some helpful discussions of Hegel's notion of *Schluß* include: Giocomo Rinaldi, *A History of Interpretation of the* Logic *of Hegel* (Lewiston, Me.: The Edwin Mellon Press, 1992); Richard Dien Winfield, *From Concept to Objectivity*; Robert Stern, *Kant and the Structure of the Object* (London: Routledge, 1990); John Burbidge, "Hegel's Logic," in *The Rise of Modern Logic: From Leibniz to Frege*, vol. 3 of *The Handbook of the History of Logic*, ed. Dov Gabbay

and John Woods (Amsterdam: Elsevier North Holland, 2004). See also Paul Redding's account of the relation between *Schluß* and *Anerkennung* in *Hegel's Hermeneutics* (Ithaca: Cornell University Press, 1996).

94. SL 586/WL 6:349.

95. SL 586/WL 6:350: "Indem Subjekt und Prädikat denselben Inhalt haben, so ist dagegen durch jene Bestimmtheit die Formbeziehung gesetzt, die Bestimmtheit als ein Allgemeines oder die Besonderheit."

96. SL 586/WL 6:350.

97. See SL 578–81, and 622–24/WL 6:339–44, 397–401. Indeed, Hegel writes: "[T]he concrete identity of the concept that was the *result* of the disjunctive judgment and constitutes the *inner* foundation of the judgment of the concept—the identity that was posited at first only in the predicate—is thus recovered in the whole" (SL 588/WL 6:349).

98. SL 581/WL 6:343.

99. SL 555, 589/WL 6:308, 6:352.

100. SL 589/WL 6:352.

101. SL 588/WL 6:351. Most provocatively, Hegel writes that "not only is the syllogism rational, but *everything rational is a syllogism*" (SL 588/WL 6:351).

102. SL 588/WL 6:351.

103. As Brandom suggests, "[t]hese relations are intrinsically modally robust: incompatibilities are impossibilities of co-instantiation, and the inferences they generate are counterfactual-supporting" ("Sketch of a Programme for a Critical Reading of Hegel," p. 140).

104. SL 595/WL 6:361–62.

105. Here again I am following Winfield's account in *From Concept to Objectivity*, pp. 108ff.

106. SL 589/WL 6:352.

107. SL 592/WL 6:353.

108. SL 592/WL 6:356.

109. SL 592/WL 6:356; trans. mod.

110. Winfield, *From Concept to Objectivity*, p. 115.

111. The premises are likewise to be presented as conclusions. "The two premises," Hegel writes, "therefore yield two further syllogisms. But these *two* new syllogisms together yield *four* premises that require *four* new syllogisms; these have *eight* premises whose *eight* conclusions yield in turn *sixteen* conclusions for their *sixteen* premises, and *so on* in a geometrical progression to *infinity*" (SL 596/WL 6:361). The problem of bad infinity and impotent ought to be that was at the heart of a *Seinslogik* reappears. The form of mediation of the figure I-P-U necessarily generates the problem of a progress to infinity, since the mediation between I-P and P-U is a mediation by predicates that have no essential relation to the subjects.

112. SL 589/WL 6:352.

113. SL 589/WL 6:352.

114. Winfield, *From Concept to Objectivity*, p. 118.

115. SL 590/WL 6:353.

116. SL 617/WL 6:390.

117. SL 590/WL 6:353.

118. SL 617/WL 6:390. Hegel says that this syllogism is "*full of content*, because the *abstract* middle term of the syllogism of existence has posited itself to be *determinate difference*, in the way it is as the middle term of the syllogism of reflection, but this difference has again reflected itself into simple identity" (SL 617/WL 6:390).

119. Example taken from Geoffrey Reginald Gilchrist Mure, *A Study of Hegel's Logic* (London: Clarendon Press, 1950).

120. SL 617/WL 6:393; trans. mod.

121. SL 620/WL 6:393.

122. Winfield, *From Concept to Objectivity*, p. 124.

123. SL 620/WL 6:394.

124. SL 620/WL 6:394.

125. See John Burbidge, "Hegel's Logic," in *The Rise of Modern Logic: From Leibniz to Frege*, p. 155.

126. Winfield, *From Concept to Objectivity*, p. 125.

127. See ibid., and Burbidge, "Hegel's Logic," p. 155.

128. SL 620/WL 6:394.

129. SL 622/WL 6:396.

130. SL 622/WL 6:397.

131. SL 622/WL 6:397; trans. mod.

132. SL 622–23/WL 6:398.

133. SL 623/WL 6:398.

134. SL 622/WL 6:398.

135. SL 622/WL 6:398.

136. For a discussion of the problem of strong versus weak holism in Hegel and Brandom, see Brandom, "Holisim and Idealism in Hegel's Phenomenology," and Pippin's reply in "Brandom's Hegel," in *European Journal of Philosophy* 13, no. 3 (2005). Cf. Stanley Rosen, *The Idea of Hegel's* Science of Logic (Chicago: University of Chicago Press, 2014), pp. 22–23.

137. For this reason, the disjunctive syllogism does not yield a blind infinity that fails to specify the determinacy of any individual because it attempts to account for an infinity of relations of exclusion (the problem encountered in the Doctrine of Being).

138. SL 624/WL 6:401.

139. "In the completion of the syllogism, where the objective universality is equally posited as the totality of the form determinations, the distinction of mediating and mediated has on the contrary fallen away. That which is mediated is itself an essential moment of what mediates it, and each moment is the totality of what is mediated" (SL 624/WL 6:399).

140. The chapters on Objectivity—Mechanism, Chemism, and Teleology—articulate *logics* of the self-determination of matters themselves. For a compelling account of these chapters, see James Kreines, "Hegel's Critique of Pure Mechanism and the Philosophical Appeal of the *Logic* Project," *European Journal of Philosophy* 12, no. 1 (2004) and "The Logic of Life: Hegel's Philosophical Defense of Teleological Explanation of Living Beings," in *The Cambridge Companion to Hegel and 19th Century Philosophy*, ed. Frederick C. Beiser (Cambridge: Cambridge University Press, 2008). See also my "Logics of Violence, Logics of Power (According to Hegel)."

CHAPTER 7

1. SL 518/WL 6:257.

2. SL 673/WL 6:465.

3. SL 735/WL 6:569.

4. SL 737/WL 6:550.

5. Cf. Angelica Nuzzo, who argues that method contains three not two features: beginning, advancement, end. See her *Memory, History, Justice in Hegel* (London: Palgrave Macmillan, 2013).

6. SL 737/WL 6:550.

7. SL 735/WL 6:547.

8. See Winfield, *From Concept to Objectivity*, for an alternative gloss on self-determination.

9. SL 729/WL 6:542.

10. See, e.g., SL 699/WL 6:500.

11. SL 728/WL 6:540.

12. SL 729/WL 6:540.

13. Thus, the world is thought of as "the evil or the indifferent, the merely determinable, whose worth does not reside in it" (SL 732/WL 6:545).

14. SL 733/WL 6:545.

15. SL 733/WL 6:546.

16. See my "Kant's Hyperbolic Formalism."

17. SL 731/WL 6:544.

18. SL 735/WL 6:548.

19. SL 735/WL 6:548. In "possessing *personality*," the concept is "the practical, objective concept determined in and for itself and is as person impenetrable atomic subjectivity—but which is not, just the same, exclusive individuality; it is rather explicitly *universality* and *cognition*, and in its other has *its own* objectivity for its subject matter" (SL 735/WL 6:548).

20. See Brandom, *Reason in Philosophy*, pp. 32ff.

21. Ibid., p. 38.

22. Ibid., p. 41. For Brandom, this is a critical, ampliative, and justificatory task (see pp. 36ff.).

23. See ibid., pp. 64ff.

24. Ibid., p. 68ff.

25. Ibid., p. 177.

26. Brandom writes: "The reciprocal recognitive structure within which Spirit as a whole comes to self-consciousness is *historical*. It is a relation between different time slices of Spirit, in which the present acknowledges the authority of the past, and exercises an authority over it in turn, with the negotiation of their conflicts administered by the future. This is the recognitive structure of *tradition*, which articulates the normative structure of the process of *development* by which concepts acquire their contents by being applied in experience" (ibid., p. 182).

27. Ibid., p. 179. This process is, according to Brandom, what Hegel calls experience (*Erfahrung*). "Experience," Brandom writes, "is at once the application and the institution of conceptual norms—is not merely a *temporal* process, but a *historical* one. [I]t exhibits a distinctive *recognitive* structure that is the product of the reciprocal authority exercised on the one

hand by past applications of concepts over future ones, and on the other hand by future applications of concepts over past ones."

28. See my discussion of action in parts 1 and 2 of this book.

29. SL 735/WL 6:548.

30. See the discussion of absolute knowing in part 1 above.

31. SL 737/WL 6:550.

32. SL 737/WL 6:551.

33. "If A is, then B is; But A is; Therefore B is" (SL 620/WL 6:394).

34. SL 737/WL 6:551.

35. SL 738/WL 6:551.

36. SL 622–23/WL 6:398.

37. SL 624/WL 6:400.

38. SL 592/WL 6:254; SL 622, 736, 749/WL 6:397, 550, 567.

39. SL 736/WL 6:550.

40. "The sense of any possible not-I, let us say, any objective content," as Robert Pippin puts it, "is inseparably linked to the structure of our asserting and inferring and justifying practices (our *Setzen*, let us say)" (*Hegel's Practical Philosophy*, p. 102).

41. Insightful discussions of the notion of *das Ende* in Hegel include: Stephen Houlgate, *Introduction to Hegel*; Winfield, *From Concept to Objectivity*; Rose, *Hegel Contra Sociology*; and Nuzzo, "The Idea of Method." Nuzzo rightly stresses the significance of *self-knowing* for an adequate understanding of the notion of an end of both phenomenological exposition (with the figure of absolute knowing in the *Phenomenology of Spirit*) and speculative exposition (with the figure of the absolute idea in the *Science of Logic*). As will become clear in what follows, I take Nuzzo's suggestion that the self-knowing of cognition is precisely what is at stake in 'ending' logical exposition in a different direction.

42. This introduces a crucial topic—the analytic–synthetic distinction. I shall address Hegel's engagement with this issue locally, only with respect to the discussion at hand. For helpful if eclectic discussions of the topic, see Pippin, *Hegel's Idealism*, pp. 250ff.; Longuenesse: *Hegel's Critique of Metaphysics*, pp. 183ff.; Winfield, *From Concept to Objectivity*, pp. 5ff., 24ff.; Stern, *Hegel, Kant and the Structure of the Object*, pp. 15ff.; Tom Rockmore, *Hegel, Idealism, and Analytic Philosophy* (New Haven: Yale University Press, 2005).

43. SL 741, 747/WL 6:556, 563. Method is analytic insofar as it "find[s] the further determination of its initial universal simply and solely in the universal" (SL 741/WL 6:556). "Equally so," Hegel adds, "is the method *synthetic*, for its subject matter, while immediately determined as the *simple universal*, through the determinateness which it has in its very immediacy and universality, proves to be an *other*."

44. The problem tackled by analytic and synthetic cognition is, in Hegel's words, the problem of "*explication of what is already in the object*, for the object itself is nothing but the totality of the concept" (SL 701/WL 6:502). See CPR, esp. A7/B11. For a helpful discussion of the distinction in the first *Critique*, see, e.g., Ian Proops, "Kant's Conception of Analytic Judgment," *Philosophy and Phenomenological Research* 20, no. 3 (2005).

45. SL 701/WL 6:502.

46. SL 701/WL 6:502.

47. Pippin, *Hegel's Idealism*, p. 252.

48. SL 708/WL 6:510.

49. Hegel argues that the "forthgoing" movement and the "further determination" of logic is "a withdrawing into itself, and the greater the *extension*, just as dense is the *intensity*" (SL 750/WL 6:569). He describes such intensity as "*pure personality* that, solely by virtue of the absolute dialectic which is its nature, equally embraces and holds *everything within itself*, for it makes itself into the supremely free—the simplicity which is the first immediacy and universality" (SL 740/WL 6:569). The movement of the concept is pure personality, highest intensity, insofar as it appeals only to itself, to reason, for its authority.

50. SL 740/WL 6:554.

51. See my discussion of the opening of the *Logic* in part 1 above.

52. SL 751/WL 6:569.

53. "The universal," Hegel writes, "first, considered in and for itself, proves to be the other of itself" (SL 744/WL 6:560).

54. SL 740/WL 6:554.

55. SL 748/WL 6:566: "ihre Bestimmtheit als Inhalt ist daher nicht mehr ein bloß Aufgenommenes, sondern Abgeleitetes und Erwiesenes" (WL 6:566).

56. SL 748/WL 6:566.

57. Further along in the system, the exposition is of space and time, matter and motion, the elements, geology, life, sentience, self-feeling, habit and so on, all the way to abstract right, morality, and ethical life.

58. SL 752–53/WL 6:571: "diese Idee noch logisch, sie ist in den reinen Gedanken eingeschlossen."

59. SL 753/WL 6:572; trans. mod.

60. Hegel writes: "the idea freely releases itself, absolutely discharges itself and internally at rest. On account of this freedom, the *form of its determinateness* is just as absolutely free: the *externality of space and time* absolutely existing for itself without subjectivity [daß die Idee sich selbst *frei entläßt,* ihrer absolut sicher und in sich ruhend]. By reason of this freedom, the form of determinateness is also utterly free—*the externality of space and time* exist on its own account without the moment of subjectivity [die absolut für sich selbst ohne Subjektivität seiende *Äußerlichkeit des Raums und der Zeit*]" (SL 753/WL 6:572; trans. mod.).

61. Nuzzo, "The Idea of Method." See also Andreas Arndt, "Wer Denkt Absolut? Die Absolute Idee in Hegels *Wissenschaft der Logik*," *Revista Electrónica de Estudios Hegelianos* 16, no. 1 (2012); Günther Maluschke, "Kritik und absolute Methode in Hegels Dialektik," *Hegel-Studien* 13 (1975); and Winfield, *From Concept to Objectivity*. Cf. Nuzzo's recent work on method in her *Memory, History, Justice in Hegel.*

62. Nuzzo, "The Idea of 'Method'," pp. 5–6.

63. Nuzzo, "The Idea of 'Method'," p. 7: "Method," Nuzzo argues along these lines, "is knowledge of things in their truth and the objective truth of things."

64. Ibid., p. 8.

65. Ibid., p. 3. Nuzzo argues that, in characterizing the absolute idea as the unity of life and cognition, Hegel's method of philosophical thinking refers to the "embodied finite knowledge that has run thoroughly through all the logical determinations as determinations of its own . . .

knowledge in order to eventually identify with the self-conscious form of the idea." Concerning the relation between *Vernunft* and *Verstand*, see also Nuzzo, "Dialectical Reason and Necessary Conflict: Understanding and the Nature of Terror," in *Cosmos and History* 3, no. 2–3 (2007).

66. See Nuzzo, "The Idea of 'Method'," p. 8. See Nuzzo's discussion of *Unterwerfung* also in ibid.

67. Ibid., pp. 8–9.

68. Ibid., p. 7.

69. Ibid., p. 9: "At every stage of its development reason has to renew its commitment to the dialectical method. At every point, in the process of its actualization through the absolute method, reason has the *freedom* of choosing whether to continue the struggle with its otherness or to give it up."

70. Ibid., p. 8.

71. Ibid., p. 9.

72. To be sure, Nuzzo reads method as providing a critical perspective given that it makes possible thinking actuality in its transformative character. Cf. her "Dialectic as a Logic of Transformative Processes" and *Memory, Justice, History in Hegel.*

73. PS 59/PG 56; SL 35/WL 5:51.

CONCLUSION

1. In the *Logic*, Hegel writes: "Spirit recognizes the idea as its *absolute truth*, as the truth that is in and for itself; the infinite idea in which cognizing and doing are equalized, and which is the *absolute knowledge of itself*" (SL 675/WL 6:468). In the *Encyclopedia*, he writes: "The notion of philosophy is the self-thinking idea, the truth aware of itself. . . . In this way, science has gone back to its beginning: its result is the logical system but as spiritual principle" (EG 574).

2. SL 824/WL 6:549.

3. For example, in his Introduction to his English translation of the *Philosophy of Nature* (London: Allen and Unwin, 1970), Michael Petry writes that Hegel's "treatment [of nature is] almost entirely free of epistemological quibbles, and consists of extremely detailed assessment of the whole range of the natural sciences" (p. 16).

4. SL 735/WL 6:549.

5. See especially the discussion in the *Vorbegriff* to the *Encyclopedia Logic*, and the *Lectures on Aesthetics*. Cf. Jean-Luc Nancy's *The Speculative Remark.*

6. Cf. Alison Stone, "Hegel's Philosophy of Nature: Overcoming the Division Between Matter and Thought," *Dialogue* 39, no. 4 and essays in *Nature and Spirit: A New Direction,* ed. Heikki Ikäheimo, *Critical Horizons* 13, no. 2 (2012).

7. In contrast to nature, Pippin writes, spirit can be understood as "*itself a kind of norm*" (*Hegel's Practical Philosophy*, p. 177, see also p. 62).

8. Ibid., p. 53.

9. Ibid.

10. That nature is 'mere existence' is itself a normative perspective. For Hegel, a mechanistic conception of nature does violence to nature; it treats nature as dead. See Hegel's critique of mechanism in SL, and the account of organic life in PN.

11. LA 1:36.

12. See LA 1:1–12.

13. See LA 1:102, 1:22, 10, and 1:11, 25. See Pippin, "What was Abstract Art from the Point of View of Hegel?" *Critical Inquiry* 29, no.1 (2002). See also Deligiorgi, "Modernity with Pictures: Hegel and Gericault," *Modernism/Modernity* 14, no. 4 (2007).

14. EG 575; see also 183.

15. EG 572ff.

16. Although my account diverges substantially from Markus Gabriel's, I am here indebted to his discussion of the syllogisms of philosophy in "The Dialectic of the Absolute," in *Dimensions of Hegel's Dialectics*. See also Catherine Malabou, *The Future of Hegel*, and Burbidge, *The Logic of Hegel's Logic*.

17. See EG 575.

18. EG 576.

19. EG 577.

INDEX